The Novel Inside You

Writing, Reading and Creativity

Paul Magrs

Proudly Published by Snowbooks in 2019

Snowbooks Ltd.
email: info@snowbooks.com
www.snowbooks.com

British Library Cataloguing in Publication Data
A catalogue record for this book is available from the
British Library.

Hardback |
Paperback |
Ebook |

The Novel Inside You

Writing, Reading and Creativity

Paul Magrs

Contents

PART ONE – THINKING

PART TWO – DOING

PART THREE – KEEPING ON

Pr.   20&2   The Professor's Hat.
       agosto
       2015

Introduction

'They say everyone's got a book inside them, don't they?'

It's a horrible old cliché, of course. But I think it's true that everyone has a story to tell. Most have more than one story. And when you really think about it, you've got loads of stories you could tell. But who wants to hear them? And how could you ever write them in a way that would make people want to read them?

I've been teaching Creative Writing for more than twenty-five years. I've taught just about every way you can: classes and workshops and courses, tutorials and seminars in universities and schools, at festivals and conventions; I've taught on residentials and retreats, by correspondence and even in cyberspace. I've taught beginners and professionals, kids and Phd students and people in their eighties.

I love teaching. I love telling people stories about the different ways to write, and about the many different books I've read and writers I've met and learned from. I've got loads of good stories.

I've learned a great deal about writing from other writers, both on the page and in person: all these things I try to share when I teach.

I've been a teacher for all that time and a writer for much longer. I've been a published novelist for twenty-four years and I've written in most genres and for every age group. I've been a serious diarist all my life and I believe that it's in our journals that our real writing actually begins. Our *Busy Books* as one of my first and most brilliant teachers called those books in which we are allowed to write, draw and create anything at all, and never have to show another person, unless we decide to do so.

Our journals are where we have complete freedom – and that is the place true writing begins.

So, in this book I want to tell the story of how it all fits together for me. The real writing practice of journals, the story-telling involved in teaching, and how putting stories together can seem like the most fantastic activity ever invented.

I don't want this to be a kind of A-to-Z How-To book. There are many books like that on the market. I want to this to be a Go-and-Do book.

I once co-edited a book that worked its way very carefully through the chronological stages of creating, drafting, finishing and publishing a piece of creative work. It's called The Creative Writing Coursebook and Julia Bell and I published it with Macmillan in 2001 and it's really pretty good. We drew upon the expertise of forty contributors and produced a book lots of people have found very useful over the years.

This present book isn't as programmatic or as logical as that one. It's much more personal, I think. It's about my life in stories and teaching, and how I've worked for all these years at ways of approaching the telling of stories. The only way I can present that learning is through further stories. So, reading this book won't be a case of following chapters to do with characterization, plotting, responding to feedback, etc. And it won't be a case of following instructions and doing carefully set-out exercises, either. There will, however, be lots of exercises and things to try out along the way. But the going will be more colourful and chaotic, perhaps, than it would be in an orderly text book. I'm afraid this isn't an orderly text book. It's a journey into my own writing practice and an attempt at explaining some of the things I've learned.

It's my story and it isn't perfect. I've made mistakes and taken wrong-turnings over the years, and I've learned from everything. I want to tell that story of my adventures, and not in some stripped-down impersonal way, organized into easily-digestible lessons. I'm not going to spoon-feed the reader. I never believed in spoon-feeding the students I was teaching, and I certainly don't intend to start spoon-feeding my readers. We teach best through stories, not bullet points.

In this book I'm plundering my past writing, reading and teaching experience and I'm zig-zagging through time. I'm presenting you with an array of epiphanies I've had about fiction and autobiography.

What I'm hoping is I've written a book that's about nourishing the whole creative self.

Maybe I should write – and maybe you even want to read – a book about how to write a commercial novel, and do it step by logical, cynical step. Maybe I could show you pie-charts and flip-charts and diagrammatical structures. But it would ring hollow, I think. It would taste like nothing. It would be boring as hell.

If you want to write the real stuff, then you have to know your real self. And you do that with your Busy Books, with your journals. You have to hold onto your hat and dig down deep. It might be a bumpy ride. If you want to write the real stuff you soon find out it's not for the wimpy. Short cuts and slick ideas and commercially-minded recipes aren't worth much in the end. Just look in charity shops (I do all the time!) and take heed of the multiple unwanted and unloved copies of hyped-up crap. Look at all those heaped-up paperbacks of 'Fifty Shades of Gray'.

You want to write books that someone will treasure, don't you? Not books that they'll just sling away, once the thrill has gone.

I'm not being snobby here about commercial fiction. I love popular fiction far more, as it happens, than self-consciously literary fiction. All I'm saying is that, in order to write anything at all of lasting value, you've got to reach deep into yourself and pay attention to the person you set free when you give yourself permission to write completely freely. I think you have to do that first, before you can write anything at all.

Like I say: no short cuts. No easy answers.

So, I should point out that 'The Novel Inside You' doesn't necessarily refer to the massive-selling blockbuster that's waiting inside of you to break out.

The novel inside of you is actually your endless journal. It's the ongoing story of *you*. That's what we're trying to liberate. And it's the thing you have to remember to go looking for. There'll be many distractions along the way. But you have to remember to keep looking for *you*.

And that's what this book is hoping to help you do.

PART ONE

—

THINKING

CHORLTON BOOKSHOP

BOOK SALE TODAY

GREETINGS CARDS

'Chorlton Bookshop 25th April 2015

Paul Magrs.

All the Answers

I don't have all the answers.

People often go on courses and I think they expect to be handed the magic goblet to drink from, just because they've paid their enrolment fees. Here you are – you may drink from the same golden cup as the blah-de-blah bestselling, prize-winning whoever.

But it doesn't work like that.

'OMG you teach on *that* course? Isn't that supposed to be the best in the country?' And whoever it was talking to me used to look as if I'd been handed the keys to some strange, ancient burial site or mystic barrow, where all the secrets to the Kingdom of Fiction were buried.

Well, they weren't. It was just a university, like any other one, with slightly shonky teaching rooms that smelled of crumbling plaster board and old lino.

The point is – any course is only as good as the students on it and the tutors teaching. There is nothing else.

On a good course, there isn't even a curriculum. There isn't a set, ordered, logical progression of *things* to be taught in the correct order.

This makes some people feel worried and insecure.

It's a good test of people's nerve!

I'd say that, in writing fiction, there isn't a curriculum – but there is a corpus of knowledge. That sounds a bit pretentious maybe – but it is quite exact for what I mean. There are skills and tricks and methods and just *stuff* that you need to learn about writing fiction. But there isn't an orderly way to learn it. And not everyone can or should learn it in the same way. Like all the best educative processes, you have to discover the answers for yourself. Only then will you actually learn something.

I can't tell you how many times people came to me looking piqued that they weren't being dictated to.

Everywhere I taught novel-writing at an advanced level, there were always a few who couldn't see why writing fiction couldn't be taught in the same way as medicine or accountancy. They'd come to me looking cross. Stuffed with knowledge from other subjects they'd mastered, and their daytime professions. 'Why can't you do a lecture a week? Telling us point-by-point how to create characters? Organise plots? Create settings?'

Hmm. I'd frown. I'd try to tell them that, yes, that would be perfectly possible. But it wouldn't help you really. That's pretty rudimentary, really. It's what we have on all the undergraduate courses, when we're keen to give students a picture of the basics that they have to get to grips with. Here are the constituent parts. Yes, for the sake of argument, you can break down fiction-writing into these kinds of topics – genre, form, pace, release-of-information, plotting, point of view, characterization, etc etc.

But that is just a grounding. And this is an advanced class.

In an advanced class it really isn't about the tutor being the font of all knowledge. Every tutor's knowledge is different anyway. They've usually had to figure it all out for themselves. Every tutor is their own unique product of their practice.

If they sit spouting off like the font of all knowledge, then what they'll produce is a classroom full of clones.

I've seen this happen many times. Sometimes people assume that's what Creative Writing teaching is about. The famous writer sits spouting off all about his or herself and all his favourites sit listening. They gasp and admire. And the rest of the class – the non-favourites, who soon come to feel that they're just there to make up the numbers - become disaffected and mutinous. I've seen this happen quite a lot with these ego-bound professors who come in to do some teaching. It isn't really teaching at all. It's just an extended public appearance.

The tutor should be there for everyone in the class, and they should be listening to everyone equally. Everyone should get their chance to participate.

The tutor is certainly there as themselves, and as a practicing writer. But it isn't all about *them*. This isn't their show.

Sometimes, as I taught these courses at universities in the late 1990s and early 2000s I thought that what some people really wanted was a kind of Simon Cowell X Factor thing. With the moneybags genius sitting there, giving the nod or the wink as the student writers auditioned like prancing ponies. And they were writing with their hearts set on fame and fortune.

I loathed this X Factor thinking that seemed to pervade some courses.

On TV talent shows like that people talk about putting in 'one hundred million per cent' worth of effort in order to reach 'stardom'. We know they don't really mean that at all. They just want recognizing for the brilliant star they already think they are. They don't want to put in the actual effort. They just want to be given the tap of approval by the millionaire judge.

Maybe the world of books is a bit like that world of pop music. People are puffed up and are the flavour of the season for a while. Fortunes are made, reputations are built overnight.

But if you're here to learn – to really learn – how to write on your own account and write well, then you've got to forget about all that X Factory talent show rubbish. Your tutor isn't Simon Cowell or Sharon Osborne…

He/ She should just be listening and, I've come to think, the less he/she says in your workshops, the better. When he/she does, he/she's just one more voice, with an opinion that weighs no more than any other writer on the course. He or she should be gently guiding the conversation through aspects of the work-in-progress under discussion. The teaching should be implicit, subtle. The students should hardly know that it's happening.

That's just my preference. That's how I believe teaching should work.

I can't stand the idea of these weekend-long master-classes where some lauded fogey stands up at the front and delivers the same old patter each time, telling everyone the rigid and incorrigible rules of successful, blockbuster story structure.

How can a course be the same each time when the students are always different? Every single course should be completely different. Every course should be about the students.

I want to know what it is that you want to do.

Who are your characters?

Where do they come from?

What kind of story are they in?

What kind of story do they think they're in, and how does that effect their behaviour?

What genre do you think you're writing in?

Who do you love to read?

Have you written a synopsis?

Have you constructed a wall-chart of the plot?

What does your novel's structure look like?

Can you draw it?

Can you explore it through knitting?

Can you tell the story of your story in words of one syllable?

Can you explain it aloud to the class right now?

Or do you want to explore the story in your first draft, letting it evolve and organically suggest itself as you bring your characters to life?

I want answers to all of the above.

From all of you.

I once – when I was first teaching – sat in on a very famous writer's novel workshop. Just to see how the practicalities worked. I'd be taking over the class the following term, and I needed to meet the students and see how they carried on in class. I needed to hear a little about their work, and to see how the conversation flowed.

It was a three hour class. I was auditing it on a dreary October afternoon. I remember that there were no tables in the room, just a circle of chairs for twenty people. Everyone was looking at the professor, who sat there, quite relaxed. It was an agonizing silence. You could feel the grinding of great thoughts going on inside the professor's head. It was as if no one wanted to interrupt his cogitations by actually venturing an opinion of their own.

The embarrassing pause went on so long it became something almost profound. The gap in the middle of the room where the tables should be came to feel like a pit opening up under our feet. I felt like flinging myself down it.

How could they sit there like this? Wasn't time precious? Weren't they all just pretending to be having deep thoughts?

Excruciating.

They were considering a monologue of five thousand words from somebody's novel. 'The character is of working class extraction...' said our professor at the start of this endless silence. And he asked, '...in this section to do with him going out to supper and choosing a dessert.... Err, umm.... Do we – as a class – believe that such a character would *actually* know what zbaglione really is? *That* is the question.'

And so they sat there for minutes on end. Probably thirty minutes turning this amazing thought over in their heads.

I, too, was speechless.

Six years before, when I did my own MA at Lancaster, our tutor there was often silent, too. But he was silent in a different way. He'd provoke us all into conversation – often loud, clashing, impassioned conversation – by tossing out some gnomic or provocative observation about the work in hand. We didn't sit hanging onto his silence, waiting for him to follow up his comments. We just went for it and argued the toss – one hour about each piece we were discussing. It was refreshing, rambunctious and we all learned a lot.

Back in Lancaster, when I was in my early twenties, a part of me wanted our tutor to be more definitive. A bit more X-Factory. I wanted him to say, 'this is good,' or 'this is bad.' I wanted the keys to the kingdom and the golden chalice. But I learned pretty quickly that all that was a fool's game. No one has the answers. You've got to figure that out for yourself.

Our tutor back then – David Craig – had two things he would ask of a piece of work. He wouldn't always ask them of every piece of work. Just sometimes. They were his catchphrases, though, and we'd hear them at least once a week.

We loved these questions and we'd dive in to answer them, even while we gently mocked their inevitability.

They are still excellent questions to ask about any chapter or story you are considering.

'Is every element of this sufficiently on camera?'
and:
'Does anyone get any meaning for this?'

Take a look at a piece you've been working on.
What do you think David Craig's two questions really mean?
Apply them to your piece of writing.
And - don't whatever you do - go waffling about how appropriate or otherwise the zbaglione is.

All the Lady Writers of the Grange-Over-Sands Hotel Workshop

The first writing class I ever taught was in Grange-over-Sands, near the Lake District.

I had been recommended by the professor who'd been in charge of the MA I'd just finished that summer. I was living in Lancaster, at the end of a terrace of doll-sized houses by the canal. The people who ran extra-mural classes in the area were short of a tutor for a ten week course in Creative Writing in a small coastal town, some thirty miles north of Lancaster, and my professor had suggested me.

That's how I found myself catching a train one Tuesday afternoon in October, and for all the following Tuesdays till Christmas 1992.

It was a stunning journey, through small grey towns and bright forests and steep valley floors. I saw the woods turn every colour from lush, verdant green to gold and scarlet and then stark black and silvered with snow. After the forests of Silverdale the train line emerged into the flat brown sands of Morecambe Bay and the train seemed to fly across the very water itself towards the headland and the distant, toy-like town of Grange-over-Sands.

The whole trip there and back each week had a touch of magic about it.

The classes were held in an Edwardian hotel, not far from the station. It took me about two hours getting there, door to door. There was an epic quality about my Tuesday afternoons – not least for the glimpse of Cumbrian mountains in the distance and the grey sash of the Irish sea.

I met my class in the public lounge, in front of a tall fireplace. We sat in a circle of high-backed armchairs. As the days drew in shorter, and colder, the fire would be lit for us and we'd sit together with the flames flapping and crackling and shadows dancing round the room as freezing rain blew against the hotel windows. It felt like we were there to tell grand, heroic stories aloud, sharing them round the campfire.

Halfway through our two hour session each week a waitress would bring in a golden hostess trolley, tinkling with china cups and saucers and weighed down by plates of chocolate biscuits and cream cakes. The ladies of the Grange-over-Sands writing class would put down their books and pens at once and fuss about over the trolley in their haste over who would be mother this week.

They were all, of course, ladies. And they were all over retirement age.

In the first week I gathered that their usual tutor – who had moved on to do something else, but who had worked with them for quite a few years – had been female and closer to their own average age. They looked at me indulgently, that first day I turned up. Twenty-two and male and, I think, probably quite shy-seeming.

The first thing I had to learn – and learn fast – was to talk more loudly. My twelve elderly ladies were all rather deaf.

'What? Speak louder, young man! What? What's he saying? Is he talking?'

This went on for the first half of my first afternoon, as I tried to outline who I was, and what I thought I'd be doing with them in this new class of ours. I had all sorts of ideas I'd like to share with them for how our time together was going to work. Ideas which…

'Is he still talking? I can't hear a word! Can you tell what he's saying?'

I was scalding red with shame. I sat there with my new cardboard folders and class lists and notebooks. I sat there clutching my notes about how I thought we might organize ourselves. And already I was dying on my feet. I dried up. I coughed a bit. Now they were all talking and rustling amongst themselves, turning to each other and complaining loudly about how they couldn't follow me. And I heard something about what a lovely, clear speaking voice 'Marion' had had. Marion had been my predecessor.

One of the younger women was sitting closest to me, and she took pity. 'You must raise your voice and speak more slowly,' she said, kindly. 'You must think about our poor, deaf old ears and slow wits.'

I nodded, smiling and looked down at my notes. I'd filled pages and pages of A4 with thoughtful scribbles, just the day before. I'd rattled through them all in my first ten minutes, and no one had followed a single word, it seemed. All this stuff about Magical Realism and the Postmodern Novel and vernacular story-telling. All this nonsense.

What had I been thinking of? It seemed so pretentious and silly. Completely unsuitable for this class. Useless! Stuff that had been in my head. Stuff that interested me. Stuff that fired me up. Franz Kafka, Gabriel Garcia Marquez, Angela Carter, Angus Wilson. But why was I so sure that these women wanted to hear about all of this? What had any of it got to do with their afternoon writing class?

I had been trying to introduce myself and what I was all about.

And I hadn't even been able to talk loudly enough for them to hear.

Such a fool. Why should they give a toss about my magical realism and my writing about the council estate I grew up on? Did I really think they'd be bothered about what I thought about the State of the Novel Today?

'I think,' said the nice lady to my left. 'You'd better speak up. Or pretty soon you may have a full-scale riot on your hands. These old dears can become rather fierce, you know.'

I nodded. I cleared my throat.

Speaking too softly and quietly had been the bane of my life up till now. I gabbled, too, running one word into the next, as if my thoughts were moving faster than my mouth could. I leapt from thought to thought and idea to idea. That might be okay in a student, but it was hopeless in someone trying to teach. I had to make myself plain.

This wasn't about me expressing my thoughts and ideas.

It was about *them*. The ladies of Grange-over-Sands.

In a flash I realized that I didn't have to do as much talking as I thought. I was just gabbling away to fill up the ominous silence, wasn't I? I was actually rather scared of them and the ornate public room and the very thought of my callow, over-complicated words echoing around it. I was talking quieter so I wouldn't feel such a fool.

But that was no good. I had to be bolder and braver than that.

I tucked my notes about myself and my own thoughts on fiction writing away, into my new cardboard folder. 'Well, that's enough about me,' I said in a voice almost completely new to me. It was definitely louder and bolder. 'What about you lot?'

They stopped muttering to each other and rustling and fiddling with hearing aid dials. They turned to me, some of them smiling.

'That's better,' someone said.

'Has he started talking now?' said another.

They were all dressed up for their afternoon out. I could see that now. Ruffly blouses and woolen two-pieces. Even a bit of jewellery in evidence. Some were more casually dressed. But they were all sitting there with notebooks and pens at the ready. They were keen. This was their afternoon out, having a class. This was where they came to express themselves. To write stories and bits of memories. To put things down in pen and ink. They knew how these classes ought to work. They'd been doing it for years.

And now they were relieved that I was talking properly and I was suggesting an exercise where they wrote and talked all about their lives, by way of introducing themselves to me.

I also saw that they were as nervous of me as I was of them. For all their bluster and moaning aloud about losing their beloved Marion, they were anxious about whether this was going to work out. But they wanted it to. We all wanted it to. We wanted to have a series of lovely autumn afternoons together, learning something.

Just then, with a bit of kerfuffle, in came the oldest lady of the lot, some forty minutes late. She was bent almost double with a dowager's hump, and wore a tweed cape rather raffishly. She came shuffling in with the aid of a stick, moving heavily between the high-backed chairs of the lounge until she reached us. A space was cleared deferentially. Evidently she had high status among the ladies of Grange-over-Sands. She stared at me beadily, and started messing on with her hearing aid. It whined and she frowned and fiddled with it. My next door neighbour glanced at me and smiled encouragingly. I must have looked very scared indeed.

Then the new arrival looked straight at me and beamed. 'Come along then, young fella. I hope you're going to impress us. We're in your expert hands. What do you want us to do?'

'Okay,' I said, very loudly. 'Shall we begin?'

My first exercise with any group is always one that just gets everyone writing and loosens them up. I knew that this was the thing to do, even back when I was starting out and I didn't even know how loud I had to speak.

Try this. Set yourself a theme, or a trigger word. Pick it at random or get someone to suggest a word to you.

Tongs. Spider. Wonderful. Saucer. Unnecessary.

Any kind of word will do.

Write it at the top of your page and underline it.

Now give yourself ten minutes to just brainstorm that word. Write down everything that it suggests to you. Don't think about it. Just write down everything that the word makes you think of. Forget about grammar or logical sense. Don't even write sentences. Be wild and impressionistic. Just to see what you get. Don't hesitate or stop for a second. Doesn't matter if you veer away from the original theme. Just carry on.

Carry on and write whatever the hell you want to.

No one is going to see this piece of writing. You don't ever have to show it to anyone at all.

It's so important to stress this. You aren't writing with an audience looking over your shoulder. No one's going to come peering over to see how your spelling is, or how original your ideas are, or how well-written this piece might be. None of that rubbish matters just at the moment.

Here, in your notebook, or on these scraps of paper, you are free to let rip.

Okay? That's what I'm telling you. You've got complete freedom.

So – ten minutes to write about slippers, opera, wherewithal, sunset, regretfulness, Cleopatra.

Be as vague, pretentious, mawkish, or as weird as you want to be. Just fill up a couple of those pages with the messiest, loopiest handwriting you can produce.

Then, at the end of the ten minutes, do this.

Stop. Don't read back.

At complete random, circle ten words in the pages you've just written. Don't think about it. Just do it. Don't go looking for the meatiest, most interesting, most fancy words. Just let your pen land on the page at random and circle ten.

Make a list of those ten.

Now, you've got twenty minutes to write another piece. You're going to write more thoughtfully this time, and that's why I'm giving you twice as long. You're going to write to this theme:

'Why do I want to do this writing thing anyway?'

Write that at the top of a new page.

Okay – twenty minutes.

Off you go.

Only, you have to include all ten of your randomly-picked words somewhere in your new piece.

Ok?

See what you get.

Don't ask questions. Just take a deep breath.

Go go go!

After twenty minutes – stop.

Did you include all ten random words?

Did you trust the exercise and just do it?

Read back. What does it read back like?

Does it say what you wanted it to?

Or did the random words knock you off your tracks?

Did you end up saying something you never meant to?

Or did you swerve round the obstacles and come back to the points you wanted to make?

Maybe the words suggested new ideas to you?

Did you say what you really think about why you want to do this writing thing anyway?

Don't worry if there were no blinding revelations. Don't worry if the whole thing went wrong. If you wrote gibberish and couldn't include all the words, or if you just wrote something that gets nowhere near the truth of things.

Don't worry about any of that. Remember: no one else will look at your notebook or your working notes or your early drafts. They can be as bad and as crazy as you like. Even if you don't think the exercise has worked, or you've not done it right – nothing is ever wasted.

Everything we write with concentration, intensity and our whole hearts takes us *somewhere*. It always moves us further along. We might not see what that direction actually is yet... but if we're doing it like we mean it, then we're always moving on.

Aspirational

Here's an epiphany I had on the twelfth of April, 2012. It's to do with being told I'm not the right sort of novelist and it happened when my then agent (or my then agent's junior, who my then agent had passed me onto in recent months) emailed me to say that my then publisher was about to sack me.

I called my then agent's junior with a whole lot of questions in my head. I even wrote them down, and I felt prepared. There were a couple of things – vague hopes – that I wanted to ask about. My editor had said she would look at my next project. Also, that she would give me some feedback on What Had Gone Wrong with the six books I had written for her, during the past six years. While the friendly contact was still there I wanted some details and specifics on these points. Would she really look at something new with a view to buying it? Could she fathom out why those books had failed so badly? And why did it even take six books and six years before anyone noticed that I was so badly off the rails..?

I needed to write my questions down because it was my unfortunate experience that literary agents tended to take the lead in phone conversations. They set the agenda. They often said 'Yeah, yeah, yeah, yeah, yeah, yeah, yeah, yeah, yeah,' loudly over what I was trying to say. I am hopeless in those situations. I go to pieces when there's no gap for me to think or to say my part. Thinking back, I suppose that's what that tactic is all about: the yeah-yeah-yeahing person doesn't actually want you cluttering up the conversation with your own thoughts and point of view. You're the one who'd better be listening. You're the one who's been doing it wrong.

So, with my questions close at hand, I approached the phone. In my study, with the door closed. This wasn't just so that Fester Cat wouldn't be tempted to come running in, jumping on my desk while shouting and sitting on my notebook. It was also because I didn't want Jeremy overhearing my end of the call and witnessing what a pussy *I* was undoubtedly about to be.

'Basically, Brenda and Effie are dead in the water,' my then agent's junior told me, very early in our talk. My two characters – whom I loved, and who were loved by a fervent, cult-like and apparently very small audience – were completely and utterly dead and gone. I must never write about them again. We must never talk about them again. They were now non-characters and their novels were non-novels. I had to get that through my head and forget about them entirely.

All through the conversation I was haunted by that image. Dead in the water. My two lovely ladies bobbing about in the choppy sea. Their eyes closed, their old lady clothes soaked through and dragging them into the freezing depths.

Now my agent was telling me that I would have to come up with something else. And not just any old something else. It couldn't be something in the same genre (which I'd always defined as Comic Mystery) or indeed any other genre I might have worked in before. In fact, it was advisable that I wrote something next that was utterly new to me. Something that read like it hadn't even been written by me, preferably. Actually, not to put to fine a point on it, what I needed to do now, if I wanted to be published by anyone else ever again, was to not be myself at all.

Not be myself?

You'll have to be someone completely different, I was told. The books you have written don't work. Your publisher couldn't make them break through and get them to the market.

I asked about the feedback from my editor. What had she said? Had she pinned down what was wrong with the series, that it had failed so badly in her company's eyes? In everyone's eyes? Any feedback would be good, I said, if now I've got to think about reinventing myself and my work and reorienting everything before I approach a mainstream publisher again.

I asked – is it the genre? But the Gothic is perennially popular. So are mysteries. Is it because they're comic? Is messing with the genre a mistake, then? Are editors and booksellers and readers happier when genre-rules are adhered to and there's no blending or genre-mixing? Is that it?

Or is it that they're too old womanish? My heroines are ladies of a certain age. One in her seventies, one over two-hundred years old. They aren't slinky or kick-ass or all those other things heroines in Paranormal Romances usually are. But I thought readers might appreciate a change. Shouldn't there be starring roles for older ladies in genre adventure novels?

Yes, my agent was agreeing. Yeah, yeah, yeah, yeah, yeah. You shouldn't have written about old women. You shouldn't have put jokes in the books. They need to be edgy and dark and kick-ass.

Also, he went on, why do I need to concern myself with the adventures of outsiders? Why was my writing always about underdogs? Why was I always celebrating the freakish and the outlandish?

My agent told me about a Chick-Lit author he was working with. She wrote about glamorous locations and sexy young people. What you need to do, he told me, is write aspirational fiction like that. Not about dark, dank coastal resorts and old women and monsters. Cosy and macabre isn't aspirational. If you ever want to sell another book you must think up aspirational characters and aspirational plots. They must live in aspirational locations and aspirational houses. They must do aspirational jobs, if they even have jobs at all. If they have so much money they don't have to work, then they must do other, fun, aspirational things instead. They must be glamorous and sexy and they must be both in aspirational ways. Even their dogs must be aspirational. And you've got to make your reader feel aspirational too.

Ah.

I don't say it, but I'm thinking – I hate things like that. They're hollow, materialistic. They're funny in spite of themselves. They're completely and utterly fake and crap.

And I see the conversation getting out of my control. He's told me what he needs to tell me. I've had my allotted time and my telling off. Now I have been told what I need to go away and aspire to.

Suddenly I see that all the questions I noted down I've asked already, and essentially they're pathetic. They all boil down to, basically, Why don't 'they' like me? And what can I change about myself and my books so that they will maybe like me?

That's my epiphany, and I have it in a rare gap of silence during a conversation with my then agent's then junior.

How can I change to make them like me?

I know at once – instinctively – that, as in life, this can never work. It's a foolish thing to even try. It's a betrayal of yourself and your talent.

So, we finish the call. I tell him I'll think up some new ideas. I'll write some outlines. I'll figure something new out.

He's encouraging.

But before I could get back to him with the 'knockout', all-new book proposals I'd put together to wow him he'd already left his job. He'd left his job in order to pursue another career entirely.

Barbapapa

That morning the headmaster put the sign outside the main entrance again. 'Welcome to our New Pupils'. It stood on a chair and we had to edge past it to get to the door, Mam, Dad and me. It was several months after the beginning of the school year, and I was starting late and alone, but the headmaster had put out the sign just for me.

Inside the foyer the floors shone with a deep russet glow. The reception area smelled of polish and trapped sunlight; rubber plimsols and the flowers on the table by the office. There was also that smell of plasticine and crayons, a chemical tang that would soon become as familiar as the smell of palm sweat.

I don't remember the headmaster and his secretary welcoming us in person to Springfield Infants School in Darlington that day. I remember the shuffle and squeak of sandshoes from the large hall next to the reception. While the headmaster talked to my parents, I was aware of the mass of kids in there. They were singing *'The big ship sails through the alley-alley-oh...'* and moving around in a stately dance. They were ducking under each other's arms and intoning the lines as someone bashed out the tune on an upright piano. The morning sun was slanting through the high windows and the air was bright with dust. I'd never seen so many kids in one place before. I was my parents' first child, my grandparents' first grandchild. I was used to being in places with grown-ups.

I don't remember my Mam and Dad leaving me there on that first day. I think my Mam would have found it extremely hard to turn her back and go. It was me and her against the world. We were very close and, in my first four years, we'd hardly ever been apart. She had fought so hard to keep me in the first place, she had kept me close ever since. Dad simply wandered out of the reception, back to the yard. It was my first day of school. It was something everyone had to do. No use making a fuss about it.

I was led to my classroom by the headmaster. He was youngish, I think, and he towered miles over me as we walked down a window-lined corridor. I had a tremendously exciting feeling of walking somewhere on my own. Heading towards somewhere I didn't know yet. The walls of these sunny corridors were lurid with sugar paper friezes. There was daubed artwork and stories written in best handwriting. I couldn't wait to get started on all that stuff.

At last we reached a door and the headmaster knocked and introduced me, quite formally, to my teacher. I was led into a dazzlingly large and airy classroom, the far wall of which was all glass, giving a view of playing fields and trees and the backs of the older houses in the village where we lived.

It was a beautiful part of Darlington we lived in then. It was a village called Little Houghton with a Norman Church that looked as if it was sinking into the green mossy grass of the graveyard. There were acres of reedy fields and winding streams and tall copses. Just thinking about the time we spent there brings back the smell of bonfires and sticky-backed plastic on library books. It was almost like being in the countryside – with the bluebells, horse chestnuts, helicopter seeds and hedgerows laced with Baby's Breath. It was the nicest place we'd ever lived. We hadn't been there long. We'd had a year or so immediately prior to our move to Darlington in the tiny New Town of Peterlee, a little further north. That was a town where everyone lived in little boxes on a hillside. Perfect cubes that still smelled of drying plaster and new carpets. But we had to move with my father's job, now we were on a 1950s estate and it was a bit like stepping back in time, living in what was called a Police House. We were living in a proper, old-fashioned street, with cars parked outside, front gardens with flowers and long back gardens that stood at the edge of school playing fields.

There seemed to be a lot of space around. Fields and wasteground and playparks. And all the neighbours' kids and I were allowed to wander around all of it, roaming pretty far away from home. Shortly after we had moved into the Police House on Bishop Close I wandered off with a gang of older kids, going much further away from our street than I was strictly allowed. We ended up on a wasteground miles away, where they built a bonfire out of rubbish and danced around it. They locked me in an old shed and taught me to swear, which amused them no end. Of course when it was apparent I was missing, my father – the keen young copper – whipped up a manhunt to find me, rousing the neighbours, panicking and shouting his mouth off. They found me at last, and I was walloped shortly after I was rescued from the teenagers' den. He carried me home, furious, and sat me down in our kitchen. He sat me on the draining board and leaned forward to give me a talking to. It was about how I was never to go astray again. I was never to go disappearing away from where he or my Mam could find me.

I listened to him going on and waited for the right moment, when he'd stopped his ranting. Then I rolled my eyes and told him to fuck off. And I got belted again, but I'd loved seeing the shock in his face.

When I went into that classroom – the source of that scent of crayons and chalk dust, pencil shavings and fresh paper – they were already doing the register. There were two teachers for this class, it seemed. One was holding up the huge green book and ticking the names as the children replied, and the other was ushering me along. Leading me quietly into the room was Mrs Johnston, who was kindly and motherly, and who seemed to know rather more about everything than her counterpart did – the somewhat feisty Mrs Moustache, who was calling out the register with great vigour. Mrs Moustache really was called that, as far as I can remember. My Mam and Big Nanna used to hoot with laughter when I mentioned her. They swore I must have got it wrong. Whether I had or not, she would always be Mrs Moustache to me, striding about with her jet black hair and her brightly-coloured nylon blouses and her funny, Spanish way of talking.

Mrs Johnston led me quietly to the back of the room and the small library. It was a kind of pen formed by wire bookcases and a few tiny chairs. All the storybooks were face-front, creating a bewildering display. Mrs Johnston told me that I must sit in a chair quietly and that I could choose any book I liked and I could look at it.

When she went I was happy to spend some moments selecting a book, and it was one of those moments I've come to recognize in later years as my very favourite thing. A whole library to choose from and no rush.

This time I chose a Barbapapa picture book. I'd seen the cartoon about these amorphous French characters on the telly, and I hadn't realized they were based on a series of picture books. I already knew that Barbapapa was the head of a family of similarly globular creatures. He was pink and the kindly and curvaceous Barbamama was black. Their children came in a pleasingly multi-cultural range of hues, which was a nice nod to world peace as well as great for colouring in.

In this particular story the Barbapapa family were concerned with creating their very own home for themselves. They tried out a number of possibilities, but found they couldn't settle anywhere. They were remarkably good-humoured, this family. They weren't prone to despair or noisy rows or twisting themselves up in anguish (which they could well have done, given their plasticity): they didn't get overly fretful that they couldn't find the right home. They simply mooched along and eventually came up with a marvelous plan.

The parents have the children pour concrete over them while they are adopting a more or less spherical shape. When the concrete has dried around them, mama et papa squeeze their jelloid selves out of a doorway or window made for the purpose. After a number of these operations – hey presto! – the Barbapapas fit the globes together into a pretty nifty organic homestead. It's all curves and natural forms, of course, and it fits them all beautifully.

For me, this tapped into a number of themes that were already spinning through my tiny mind. First of all, the Barbapapas were a big family, all living in the same house. This immediately appealed to me. It was just me and Mam and Dad at ours, wherever we lived. Dad was often away on police work or courses. My grandparents – my Big Nanna and Little Nanna lived many miles away up the A1, so time went by between visits to or visits from them. And we hardly ever saw the whole family in one place because, as Mam had told me, both Nanna's didn't get on. They hated each other's guts, and had done ever since their children had conceived their first grandchild at much too early an age. Perhaps both thought each other's offspring had led the other astray. Nevertheless, I was the result and both Nannas doted on me. I'd have loved all our family to be together all the time. Even living in a strangely futuristic house like the Barbapapas, each having their own little space, but that was never to be.

I've spent so much of my life trying to bring people together in the same place: in real life and on the page. Even when the characters involved aren't overly keen on the idea. I think I felt very keenly that sense of animosity between people I loved. I thought: if I loved them and they loved me, why couldn't they love each other? I've spent most of my life trying to shorten distances between the people I care about. They don't always thank you for the effort.

Something else I recognised in that book about the Barbapapas was the idea of a search for home. I knew what it was like to be concerned with finding the place where you can settle and make yourself comfortable. I had observed at first hand, as Mam and Dad made their new home in Darlington, not long before this first day at school. I'd watched the furniture being carried in, and both parents judging where everything should go. I'd watched my Dad fix up curtains – bright, swirling patterns in purple and blue. I was there when Mam got used to lighting an open fire again, first thing in the morning, just as she had as a schoolgirl. I watched as she rolled the newspaper and made the rolls into skinny triangles and formed a pyramid of coal on top.

Also, I'd been there when we'd helped my Big Nanna do a moonlight flit and leave her nasty second husband. That very year – 1974 – we'd loaded her stuff into a small van and got her away from that brute, Fred. My Big Nanna had moved to a flat in Jarrow, where she built up a new home for herself, doing it up just how she wanted, away from the tyranny of that awful man.

The other thing I picked up from the Barbapapa book – and this would have resonated a lot, I think – was the idea that everyone had their own thing. Everybody had their hobby and their obsession. Each of the Barba-babies did up their little spherical rooms in exactly the style that suited them. One loved painting and drawing; another loved books; someone else played every kind of musical instrument and another was given to scientific experiments in his bedroom. This kind of thing – the gathering of paraphernalia close to your heart - fascinated me, as I was only just discovering what it was that I liked to do.

I loved reading, I knew that. When I was reading it didn't even feel like that's what I was doing. I hardly saw the words on the page. It was like being inside the world of that book – whatever it was – and communing directly with the characters or the writer. Purnell Disney books, Enid Blyton's Noddy and Ladybird books' Well-Loved Tales: these are what had jump-started my reading and fired my imagination. Whenever we went to the newsagents, though she couldn't really afford it – Mam always ended up buying me a book, right from the start.

I read the Barbapapa's right through to the end, avid to see if they were happy with the home they had built. Of course they were, and I flicked through the slim volume again, to properly appreciate their choices and the twists in the story, and to see how they had come so far. And just as I closed it at last, I looked up and saw that Mrs Johnston had returned to the library at the back of the room. She was smiling down at me expectantly.

'Sorry to leave you waiting back here,' she said pleasantly. 'Would you like to come and sit down at your desk now, Paul?'

I stared at her.

'It's time you joined the rest of your new class.'

I stood up, and I was in shock. I picked up my brown satchel with orange piping – bought especially for my first day. I was dumbfounded. Sit at my desk? Join the rest of my class? I almost felt upset. I had to do what I was told, though. I was a good boy, who always did what the grown-ups told him. But somehow I hadn't expected this. I didn't know that there was a desk waiting for me, in the middle of all the other children.

I really thought I'd already been in my place. I thought they'd leave me in the library all day long. I'd actually thought that's what school was going to be.

Brilliant Days Writing

It's always a battle to get somewhere decent to sit in places like this. *Spirit* is one of those Canal Street bars on different levels and you can spy at each other on little perches like monkeys in the zoo. Just got a settee and this woman tried to get it at the same time. I'm better at these negotiations now: 'Well we can both share it, can't we?'

So she's sitting here, gabbing away with her mate, who's got a purple goatee and I do some writing.

This afternoon I'm quite content to watch and just sit staring into space quite a bit of the time. I'm not so driven today.

Sometimes I like other people coming out with me on afternoons like this. Even if it's just one other person, I can get us both writing and we can sustain each other with the proper, inspirational vibes. Which only means taking it seriously and having a laugh; actually thinking, we could write something great just now, sat here together. And we can get drunk together. And see who's about on the street.

Nell Dunn said to me, a couple of years ago: 'I like to be very close to the street ... and all the sounds I want, all the voices and language I want in my books ... it's all... from the street ...'

Richard was the one who got me out like that. In Edinburgh, starting in 1995, when I really first starting writing journals obsessively, minute by minute, letting them spiral out into experimental routines and then different bits of novels and stories... Richard was out drawing in these cafes and bars. Richard was always half-smiling as he concentrated and drew. He'd rub his head, which was shaved and dark. There was an ease and physical awkwardness to him, both at the same time. He'd go loping along enthusiastically from cafe to cafe ... We would sit at tables with papers, pens, pastels, felt tips, all spread out. We'd take turns at drawing and writing. It was him who started the drawing-with-your-wrong hand business, to see how it would turn out. To see if we could draw like kids again. Him left, me right. The idea was to switch off the internal censor. To make more direct that gap between hand and eye. To lose the learned technique. The tidying up.

And finding a way to do writing like that.

I'm reading a biography of Dylan, and what appeals to me about him is the way he has always apparently written: standing up in the kitchen with a glass of red wine, at music stands adding new verses, or in the back of a car on long dry hauls. Everything, it seems to me, every scheme, every form, every kind of art, begins in notebooks. Something you can carry around and always have with you. Richard used old hardbacked novels from fifty years ago. He'd buy them for 20p and cover pages of print with squares of brown wrapping paper. Glueing them in, carefully as he'd prime a canvas. He'd have to rip out reams of the original pages so the book wouldn't get so fat the spine would burst. And these excised pages of text he'd make into something else: pages of print to paste onto paintings. All of it a great recycling. Everything cheap and inventive. I loved all that.

I used - as I still do - exercise books. Or Daler and Rowney hardback sketchbooks. Something with some space.

I suppose that's what, recently, I've been trying to train my students in. To spend days like I did, once I got free of university after seven years and I'd sold my first novel and I had the time, space and gumption actually to call myself a writer. So I went to live in a city and sat in the cafes and bars. Sometimes winding up in conversations and adventures ... but more than anything: turning out many, many pages of writing. Vast amounts of writing. The kind where your hand rarely stops touching the paper.

What you should do is this:

Go in gangs of two or three to some place you're comfy and have never been. A padded corner in a pub. Maybe there's a fire burning. Talk with each other. Keep a running observant commentary going in your notebook. And when you sit somewhere like this the stories will come out of nowhere and straight onto the page if you let them. Think in terms of three categories: anecdotal, historical, mythological. You should include all three types of story and each one should take you further from yourself. From your place here and now. You should keep grounding us back in this moment, however; keeping it concrete and exact. Give us the exact flavour of this afternoon, this particular place ... and all the people you'll see coming through, who needn't be there - who aren't really there, historically-speaking, unless you notice them *now*. And try to explain to yourself why they snagged your attention away from your page and why they made you stop writing about yourself.

If left to your own devices, would you just carry on writing about yourself the whole time? What does it take to divert you from the great big tale of you?

Or is it the opposite? You would fill all the books of your life with other people and places - anything to keep the spotlight off you?

But you should be an agent in the world. At peace with it and watchful and busy. A recording angel. All of these things at once. All this going on in one so still. You should be someone who, when asked to join the dance, or when the mood suddenly takes you, can nod and say hello to a stranger. You should take the initiative and break the spell of your concentration ... let in some other life, for a while ...

Otherwise you're writing the scratchy handwriting only you can read. Covering miles across pages only you ever have to see. This is the stuff that keeps you going. Raw material. You interacting with real life. To an extent, anyway. These pages ... they're the stretched and fraying and gorgeous interface between the space in the world you fill and the books you've yet to write.

We're writing on the overlap between art and life.

It's a performance. Doing the splits. Walking the highwire.

And these can be brilliant days writing. The idea is to be left with the kinds of souvenirs money can't buy.

Character Building

When we went to Rome to visit our friend Yona in 2003, we had this game that we played almost every day. We kept going back to the same café and we sat outside under green umbrellas. There was an ancient priest and a very old woman sitting at the table across from us, just about every time we returned.

Wherever we were that week, we'd return to the subject of that old couple. We were trying to invent their backstory. What had brought them here? Why were they together now, and what were they talking about? In life they were intent and secretive-looking. We invented stories and honed them, the three of us wandering about the city. We were teasing out the tiny hints and nuances and trying to turn them into something.

That August I was reading Alice Munro's *Collected Stories*. She really helped my writing and making things up. She's a writer who teaches you to take your time. (I love the way that, as her career has gone on, her stories have become longer and more intricate: more Chinese boxy.) She is a writer who reminds you that you have to give yourself enough space to really *imply* everything you want to about your characters…

Jeremy surprised me, when we were having our coffee. He asked Yona: 'When you step outside of your writing… or look down on it from a height… is the voice in your work separate from you? Does it create a world on its own?'

I loved that question. Jeremy often gives the impression of not being at all bothered about literary stuff. He's surrounded by writers all the time, bless him – and I think it must get boring. He's a more visual person.

'I like writing that makes its own world,' he said, thoughtfully. 'And then you can get drawn into it.'

Yona was writing a huge novel based upon the lives of her grandparents and parents, set in Rome and Eritrea. It was a book seething with many voices and dialects and embedded tales. She told Jeremy she wasn't sure if her voice was creating a world of its own yet. She's very modest. We talked about writing in a way that was brave enough to let the characters' voices take over. We talked about how not to let a single voice dominate, explain things and flatten the drama.

Those last days of our holiday, everything had a sleepy look. The waiter slouched about, combing out his hair with his hands. The corners of his mouth lifted slowly into a smile when he saw the ancient couple turning up again, to claim their usual table.

That day, the priest and old lady were looking a lot fonder of each other than they had the previous afternoon. Some of the stiffness and formality was gone. It was as if they had made a breakthrough in their new friendship.

I was thinking that day, about these changes in relationships that tend to go on in novels. DH Lawrence would have his characters go through 'thresholds' as they developed and changed. His moments are always grand, crashing epiphanies: all stars and bells. Changes aren't always like that. You can pick out certain nights and see them as important afterwards. They can be highlit through detail and richness, and they gain importance through retelling: through being turned into narrative. Subsequent things start to depend on them.

The old priest and the old woman don't speak much today. After a while one of them will offer a small, almost silent comment and the other will incline their head and, with an equally quiet reply, agree. They both smile at the waiter as he bends to take away their coffee cups. They smile at him, but not at each other. He lays things out for them almost reverently.

They sit and drink in the early evenings and they take little sips. Not the big thirsty gulps of people parched for ages, just cautious sips. Then suddenly, the priest knocks back his hot espresso quickly, and crunches up the grounds. He spoons up the molten sugar and slurps at it.

Now you see them from a different angle today, you realise that he hasn't got a dog collar on. He's all in black again. Are you even sure he's a priest? Yesterday you were convinced he was, that he came from the Vatican. That twenty years ago he had a mad affair with this old woman and she had given birth to a son, and never told him. She gave the boy away for adoption and he grew up in Rome. Now she has orchestrated a get-together and is about to take revenge on the complacent old priest. When the waiter brings the bill she'll say to the priest: 'He is yours. This young man is your son.'

But now you think you've read the situation all wrong. He's not a priest. She hasn't got revenge in her heart. They might be some very ordinary couple, content and quiet in each other's presence. Maybe it's that kind of quiet, after all. And – as usual – you've been filling the quiet with all kinds of ideas.

I love lists. Make lists of character points about your people.

Find a person at large in the world and draw clues from their behaviour.

Given them a name that really suits. 'Madeleine' really suited the old woman in the Roman café, when I still thought she was planning revenge.

Then start a whole page of sentences where you try to sum up what your invented person is like…

Madeleine is the sort of person who…

Can't abide mimes, jugglers, fire-breathers, street performers. She wants to push them over in the street; push them into fountains. In the Palazzo Novona it's quite a temptation…

Madeleine is the sort of person who…

Reads the first third of every newspaper article, interview, editorial, and thinks that's all she needs to know. She knows how to get the gist. She knows how things end.

Madeleine is the sort of person who…

Dreams of playing the accordion outside of restaurants. A child-size one, and her father would still be alive, playing his own accordion.

Madeleine is the sort of person who…

Knows that her city is changing, but refuses to see anything different in it. The new people and buildings simply don't have the same substance as the old ones. Anything new is transparent and soft: laid over the background she lives in.

Madeleine is the sort of person who…

Never eats in public, if she can help it.

Madeleine is the sort of person who…

Colouring Book Epiphany

29th October 2015

Something that's struck me about creating this 'Lovely Levy Colouring Book' is that I just can't be stopped! That's not being immodest I hope. I mean that I'm slightly demented, as well as irrepressible, I think. I have agents who despair at my 'quirkiness', my 'originality'. I have publishers who dump me, pulp me, remainder me and drop me. I have backlists tied up in rights hell, rights tied up in option hell and tie-in editors who tell me that I am not always a 'good fit' for their niche market. But doing my drawings for the Colouring Book, and making plans about getting it printed, and announcing it on Facebook and getting such a rush of attention about it – all this business has made me realise that even if everyone in mainstream, professional publishing stopped dealing with me or talking to me or noticing me forever, I'd still be making books somehow. I would find a way.

Look at this – just a hitch – just a hiatus – just a funny little gap when I felt demoralized and worried about what the future held. What did I do then? I slowly, carefully taught myself to draw again, and to paint – and then came up with an idea, and made a book. I sent it to the printers and we picked it up ourselves, and I will hand-sell it in the pubs and the cafes and down the market or through the post. I will do all I can to put it into people's hands. I'm just a person who makes books of pictures and stories. That's what I do, and I can't stop myself coming up with new ideas for things to put on paper and sell to people. It's just the thing I do.

NARCISSUS

the Blue moon Ca

Happy August
nights at the
Blue Moon Café
Edinburgh

R.L.

Could it be Magic?

I sold my first novel and, together with a bunch of friends also in their mid-twenties, ran away to Edinburgh. In the summer of 1995 there was a lot going on. We arrived just as they were filming 'Trainspotting' on Princes Street. Remember Ewan McGregor running pell-mell down that long street of shops, past all the passersby? 'Lust for Life' by Iggy Pop pounding out of the speakers. That was the sound and feeling of that time. It was the time when Cyber-cafes were opening up everywhere. We moved in during festival season, and the annual books jamboree was taking place in leafy Charlotte Square just a few blocks from where we were living. We were at the top of a warehouse, reachable only by umpteen flights of steps up a fire escape, high above the canyons and the restaurants of the New Town. We ran up and down the city all day and night. It was bliss.

That summer was all about dancing at CC Blooms till dawn, and sitting late at night in the Blue Moon café having Mexican food, or drinking lager and eating Loveheart sweets at Over the Rainbow, where they had a life-sized mannequin of Glinda the Good Witch in their window. Once, when my editor was visiting, we were drinking in there and Glinda's head fell off spontaneously along with her tiara still attached and it bounced down the length of our table.

There are so many stories about Edinburgh in the mid-Nineties I could tell you. Some of them would make your hair curl.

The point is, I wrote a lot. Much of it was in the form of journals. I went to cafes and bars all across the city, writing and drawing all day long. I filled book after book in places like the City Café and Café Kudos. But mostly I was in the Blue Moon. It was the place that every evening began and ended: the magical Queer café that I fictionalised in my stories as The Scarlet Empress.

I started work on 'Could it be Magic?' and it was a kind of sequel to both 'Marked for Life' and 'Does it Show?' Those two novels were first drafted in 1992 and 1991 respectively and they were linked by being set in the same place and time. I wanted to write a third book to connect and unify them, further developing the ideas and the stories I'd been working on. And so 'Could it be Magic?' began with a party thrown for all the characters from those two previous books. It was a silly literary joke and a bookish knees-up, inviting all those characters to make cameos, updating us with what they'd all been up to. It set up the action for what was to come and it thrust into the spotlight the heroes of the current book.

I remember thinking a lot about magic and realism and how far magic can impinge upon a grittily realistic, sometimes hostile world. Could magic lead to salvation or just solipsistic madness? In this book I went on to push the surrealism as far as I could take it at that time. Some of the things I did still feel pretty audacious to me, and that's something I'm very glad about.

I'm not sure what readers knew what to make of it all. Perhaps the mix of elements was too rich and esoteric? Was I ahead of my time? Weren't people ready for 'One Hundred Years of Solitude' in a town just north of Darlington?

I was once accused of only writing Freakshow characters. Tattooed men, ancient lesbians, boys covered in leopard-skin spots, ballsy transvestites. Maybe twenty years on from that the world is more comfortable with a cast as mixed up as this? Maybe genre-mashing and all kinds of ambiguity are more welcome now than they were at the end of the last century? I'm not sure. I hope so.

Either way, Chatto and Windus and their paperback imprint, Vintage, had been publishing me since my first story came out in 1995. In quick succession they published 'Marked for Life,' 'Does it Show?', my short story collection, 'Playing Out' and then, in 1998, 'Could it be Magic?' Pretty soon after that they dropped me. My editor left for the US and the incoming editor made it plain she had no interest in Queer Working Class Magical Realism. I was dumped and it felt absolutely terrible.

By then I had met the man, Jeremy Hoad, who was going to be my partner. I'd had two years in Edinburgh, whizzing around, having adventures, and a great deal had happened. I was in my late twenties and I had published four books. By 1998 I was down South. I had taken up a full time post as a lecturer in English Literature and Creative Writing at the University of East Anglia. I'd moved to Norwich and Jeremy moved south to be with me pretty soon afterwards. At twenty-seven I was teaching the MA course in Novel Writing begun by Malcolm Bradbury and Angus Wilson: the course that had produced Ian McEwan and Kazuo Ishiguro and a whole host of bookish luminaries. I was teaching with Andrew Motion, who was just about to be crowned Poet Laureate. It was a heady, hectic, over-busy, exhilarating and bizarre period in my life.

There are stories I could tell you about UEA and Norwich that would make your hair stand on end.

Anyhow, 'Could it be Magic?' came out and I was teaching people who were older than me on a very prestigious postgraduate course. I had found my genre and completed a trilogy that had answered lots of the questions I had been formulating for myself during the 1990s: about Queerness and magic, storytelling and identity.

Big questions, it seemed to me. But at the time, despite some nice reviews, the world didn't give all that much of a fuck, really.

I was in a pushy, grabby, noisy, strange campus environment, working with all kinds of very creative people – some of them very nice, others horrible, and some of them completely crackers and a bit of both.

I was teaching full time and my writing became my secret nocturnal obsession all over again. Busy in the daytime with everyone else's books I had to find time to concentrate on my own. I had to pick myself up again in order to reinvent myself and write another book, even though I'd been dumped. I got to it and I wrote a novel that would take place chiefly in the city I had loved and recently left.

I used to think of my first books as a trilogy ending with 'Could it be Magic?' But all these years later I can see that this isn't quite true. The story went on, telling itself to me, unfolding in different towns and cities, following me both geographically and spiritually wherever I went.

I went from book to book, at more or less the rate of one a year. Some were published, some went by the wayside. I moved from publisher to publisher, trying to find a home that would last. I've been called a 'cult writer.' That's what they say when you have a smallish but fervent following. Well, I've been called worse.

I'm happy in the knowledge that mine aren't like anyone else's novels, ever.

Covering the Dead

When I first read James Joyce's 'The Dead' I couldn't understand why I hadn't read it before. What a fool. There, at the end of that story, is the perfect example of how the lyrical moment must arise out of the very particular, specific, minute-by-minute drama of small rooms and ordinary people.

This is one of my recurring themes and ideas: that the quite mundane and quotidian can be as lyrical as anything else.

Vic Sage at UEA always called Joyce's novels the great 'tool box' novels. Anything you could ever want or need for writing fiction is to be found there, stowed away in readiness.

So, in coming to 'The Dead' relatively late, I feel foolish, because I'd had to make up some tools for myself. I'd grasped after the words and the images to suit the shapes of things, moods and scenes, and all the things I wanted to get at.

I think I'd avoided Joyce. Put him off like he was too hard. Too much to deal with. People feel like that about other revered novelists, too, I know.

But these writers covered this stuff before us. They figured some of these difficulties out, and sometimes added to them, compounded them. But this material is left here for you, as a writer of fiction, as a reader of fiction. Who else were they doing this for? Only you. You should never be put off it. It's a great gift.

I've always thought it would be interesting, to take a great, old story like Joyce's 'The Dead' and to let a workshop group rewrite it.

In this exercise everyone has to tell the tale again, after one reading, or listening, and try not to deviate from the details and events.

The idea is to play it – to *recite* it – in their own way. (Perhaps the musical subject of the story put me in mind of this musician metaphor.)

Wouldn't that be interesting, though? To see how we reconstruct someone else's story on the page? What do we take away with us? What do we value or foreground? What do we forget, or let slip away?

You could try it with Katherine Mansfield, Virginia Woolf, DH Lawrence. I think it would be even more interesting, somehow, to utilise stories in which very little actually happens.

In teaching and thinking and learning about writing, I think we get much too hung up on the idea of being completely original. We stress the importance of making up new stories; of inventing and flexing our imaginations. Surely, in order to develop a style, or a voice, we'd be better off colouring within somebody else's outlines? At least at first?

I'm not sure. I'm just saying: try this out.

Like bands cover songs by other artists they love.

Or, like in scientific experiments, where they put a control in place: they make one element stay the same. Then they see what variations can be played out in the experiment, and what that does to the results.

I'm using great Modernist fiction here, but you can use anything you like, to rewrite, to vandalize, to turn inside out.

It's useful to choose something quite old, and then you could perhaps update it. What would the story be like if it was set *now*?

I think, personally, I'm attracted to great Modernist fiction because of the way the characters *fret* all the time. It's not something that gets said very often about the characters in great Modernist fiction but, really! What a bunch of mitherers!

Daily Memory Exercise

It's early in December, 2014. I'm in a café in Darlington and waiting for my friends. We're meeting here and then driving up to Northumberland for a weekend writing retreat.

I'm looking out a plate glass window at the market hall and High Row. I'm deluged by memories, sitting here. For some reason I'm flashing back to my birthday in 1978, when we came here after school to have tea at the Great British Burger, at the end of High Row. That's when they used to bring burgers and buns to you on actual plates, and you ate them with knives and forks. That birthday I was nine and in love with Battlestar Galactica. I read the novel and my step-grandmother Rini borrowed it afterwards.

Now I'm reading Nina Sankovitch's wonderful book 'Tolstoy and the Purple Chair' in which she describes a year spent reading a book every single day. It's a book about grief and mourning, and healing yourself through reading. I'm so tempted to try something similar. Though reading a book a day might not suit you. You love to spend two, three, four days reading a book. Living and breathing the same book. Letting it stew. You love to sleep happily squashed between chapters.

What's just occurred to you is that, rather than a reading project, you should set about a writing project: a daily discipline.

A warm-up exercise every day. A single clear memory. One moment every day. It can come from any time in the past. A huge moment or a trivial one. It should be a memory that you can capture and contain in one or two pages.

Do this every morning for a month.

Then, at the end of the month, what will you have?

A whole set of fragments and shards of memories.

Maybe you could shuffle them round and put them in order?

I love the idea of this exercise.

And sitting here, in Darlington, I'm beset by little moments.

Here's a nice idea for this exercise: you could stock-pile and bank up a series of strips of paper. Each has one line that triggers a particular memory. You could choose one at random at the start of each day's writing.

Examples…

Burgers on plates and Battlestar Galactica on my ninth birthday.

Chris has a recipe for Chinese Cabbage Leaf and offers to cook a romantic dinner – it's sometime in autumn 1994. He never cooks, so this is really something.

My finger gets crushed in the car door outside Gladys's flat in 1974.

Pigeons in Huddersfield.

Beryl Bainbridge's two bits of advice to you – sitting in that King's Lynn café in 1996 – don't fall in love before you're thirty. And never drink when you're writing.

Some memories will come in the form of images only. No narrative at all. Just free-floating moments.

The idea of a daily, disciplined, creative act also comes from reading a fantastic art book called 'One Drawing a Day' by Veronica Lawlor. It's about getting into a routine and a productive mindset, and making sure you draw something – anything! – every single day of the year. It's got me thinking that I'd love to start drawing again, and keeping a proper sketchbook by my side, like I haven't in years. And, of course, it's got me thinking about how to adopt her advice and her practice for use in writing.

I did a full month of memory exercises. Every morning I sat down with an open mind, and let myself pluck a memory out of the air. I wrote at least two pages each time.

I began during that weekend retreat, and through December and Christmas into the start of the new year. (In the New Year I also made a resolution to create a drawing or a painting each day, but that's another story!) I was buzzing with creativity, all at once. I think the discipline of having regular exercises really helped.

I wrote memory-pieces about:

Our study in Onley Street in Norwich in the late 1990s, where we'd have these brilliant dinner parties.

The morning in 1980 when we were having breakfast and the news came over about John Lennon being shot.

Saturday shopping trips to Newcastle in the 1980s and the amazing 'Timeslip' comics shop.

The Christmas when we tried to make table decorations like they did on Blue Peter and it all went wrong…

And on and on, for over a month. Stuff I was sure I'd forgotten about!

Back it all came!

You get into the habit of remembering.

Doing these exercises through December meant that I was remembering a lot of Christmases past…

'The most Christmassy flavours in the world round our house were always – pickled onions, cheddar cheese, hot dogs and hot, homemade ginger wine. Party flavours.'

I filled two whole notebooks with all these December memories…

What will you remember?

Does it Show?

I began writing 'Does it Show?' in the summer of 1991, when I was preparing to return to college to start my MA in Creative Writing. It's quite common for people to do those courses now, but not so much back then. I could hardly believe that such a thing was allowed: that I could get a bursary to spend a further year at university, writing my novel.

That summer I was back at our family's house in Newton Aycliffe, on an estate where everything was built of black brick and which I call, in those early books, Phoenix Court. I hadn't been back for a while and that summer it was good to absorb the sights and sounds of the place again.

There was hardly any room in that house. Certainly not to work and write. I ended up more often than not perching on the back doorstep, reading library books and watching the world go by.

Our house in Guthrum Place was by the main road connecting all the estates. You could watch the minibuses running up down, doing circuits of all the streets and ferrying everyone to the town precinct and back. The precinct looked like 'Logan's Run' or 'Conquest of the Planet of the Apes', but with pensioners in anoraks, pulling shopping trolleys.

I watched all our neighbours and the way they went from one house to another. The women would drink tea in each other's kitchens and when the sun came out they would drag their chairs into their front yards and sit smoking and gossiping, their voices drifting over the dark, creosoted fences.

All the kids in our street were little that year. My sister was four and playing out with a whole gang of small kids who would go haring around, holding hands, in the wind and rain and some gloriously hot days.

There was so much going on to keep up with. There was the mother and daughter who were dragged out of their house by the police in the middle of the night, and everyone hurried outside to watch. It was well-known they were running a kind of brothel in their two-up two-down. Then there was talk of someone being held hostage. And there was the gang of rough lads across the main road in the Yellow Houses, who set their pit bull terrier onto the old man who lived next door to them. It was supposed to be a joke, but he fell down dead of shock on the hottest day in August. Everyone was out watching this happen: I remember the dog barking and the appalled silence.

I kept taking notes all summer. I kept writing down the dialogue. I was keeping tabs on everything, just as I always had, since I was a kid.

Gradually I formed a story to do with a woman who once lived in these streets in the Seventies and who was moving back in the Nineties, having reinvented herself out of all recognition. She had a daughter who was starting at the local Comprehensive School. Both women find themselves drawn into new friendships and relationships and the book would be all about huge human emotions and life-changing moments being played out on a seemingly tiny scale. It was going to be a Magical Realist epic on a council estate in the North-East. A phantasmagorical opera set in the midst of concrete brutalism.

Lancaster University was similarly concretized and minimalist. Soon I was back among its dreaming spires of poured cement. I had intended to use my MA year writing a gay bildungsroman, telling the tale of my childhood, my parents' divorce, my artistic and sexual awakening and all that jazz. Then the course began and I found I was writing about Phoenix Court.

The workshop group was composed mostly of well-to-do lady poets in their forties, returning to education. Some were friendly, some were not. It was all very middle class and polite, with the snarkiness dialed down for the few hours we spent in class each week, then unleashed full force in the vegetarian cafes and coffee bars where we wasted our afternoons. Again, I was agog – watching how all these characters behaved.

For my first submission to this class in the autumn of 1991 I found myself handing in a chapter about Fran and Frank on a hot summer's day in their yard. I loved the dialogue, that's why I chose to show it to the workshop, rather than writing a chapter of that Queer Autobiography I'd been planning. It made me laugh. It made some of them laugh, too. Others, though, were mystified.

One of the poets said, 'Forgive me, but can we really call this literary fiction? And isn't literary fiction what this course is about? I don't know what you would call this, actually. These are hardly the kind of characters one would expect to find in a literary novel.'

Someone shot back with an example or two of working class characters in literary fiction. They mentioned Faulkner. 'But that's in America. That's different.'

'And besides… this is much too like a… soap opera, isn't it? People talking like this in the North?'

'It's just fiction,' I kept saying, all that term. 'I don't believe in genres. There are two types of fiction. There's the good type, that you want to read and there's the bad type, that you don't want to read. There are books that are crap and sound bogus. And there are books that ring true. Books that are *about* something. Books where the voices are alive.'

Maybe I didn't put it as concisely as that at the time. But that's the position I was trying to articulate, all that year, as I wrote my way into the story. Mostly I just kept quiet and smiled at their comments and wrote my weekly chapter.

As later submissions went in and were photocopied and disseminated I gave them episodes of gay sex and tales of Goths and taxidermists and pensioners finding love late in life. I delighted in mixing and stirring up my characters and having their stories overlap as the weeks went by. I loved revealing the secret of the novel's 'star', Liz. The class was shocked by the big reveal. They were disgusted. Some of them refused to believe it.

I tossed in surreal moments of Magical Realism. I let my narrator wander between points of view, moving stealthily from house to house, all over Phoenix Court.

'It's a kind of Magical Realist Queer Working Class Heterotopia,' I told them. 'Not a Soap Opera.'

For me, it was about how people can live on a grand scale, even in reduced circumstances. A woman can be a queen in her own council house and in the midst of her own community. And so can a man.

Anyone in the books I write is capable of finding love, and sometimes they find that the things they're really looking for are quite surprising.

I was working all this out when I was twenty-two and doing my MA. And twenty-four years later I look back and see that I was learning to be my own kind of novelist. I was discovering that dark comedy was my thing. Also, that ensemble casts were my thing. I was finding that I love lots of dialogue and for description to be pared back, and I love flicking swiftly from scene to scene, moving as swiftly as TV movies do. I enjoy swimming from mind to mind and getting my readers to eavesdrop on fascinating characters as we witness them at their very best and their very worst moments.

My basic thesis was – and still is – that everyone has a fascinating life, whoever they are. It just depends on how much of it we are allowed to see, and how much they are willing to let it show.

Don't Stop

My one-time friend said, 'You're a long time dead, you know.'

I laughed because I knew she meant it, and because she'd said it to me many times before. I also laughed because it was so pathetically true. It made us both sick to think of wasting time in the house at night when you didn't want to be in, or doing stuff in the daytime they could pay a monkey to do. Wasting our time - that was one of the worst dreads we could have - even worse than the dread before a stiff day at work. Worse, really, than the dread of tricky decisions.

You're dead a long time. You might as well make the most of it while you can. You shouldn't compromise too much. The world's full of people looking back on wasted years. It's full of people holding you back.

At that point in our friendship we'd known each other for ten years. That was a long time. That was a lot of mucky water down the canal. It was a lot of cups of tea in Betty's tea room in Ilkley, a lot of bottles of thick red wine and precious home-brewed sloe gin. It's a lot of post cards sent back and forth across the country with cryptic updates in fine black marker. A lot of curlews under the eaves, signalling spring and desire, or lambs jumping in through the study window, trekking mud through the new carpets. A lot of starlings trapped in the chimney piece. A great many midnight drives over the moors, on perilous roads hemmed with drystone walls - ribbonlike roads across the moors, blurred with snow pale as pasta.

A lot of compilation tapes with Scott Walker, David Bowie, Melanie, Mary Black, Joni Mitchell. It's a lot of poems and a lot of stories. It's a lot of shrieking phone calls and laughter in cafes and jokes that no one will ever understand, even when they ask and it all turns to ashes in your mouth as you try to explain.

Lots of tramping round bookshops. Lots of hissing; enthusing in high pitched voices; choking on other people's dust. Lots of cackling and shared history, haircuts and shoes. Getting the giggles at readings, recitals.

Lots of swapped novels, till we hardly know which ones on whose shelves really belong to us - but never mind, we remember them anyway – if not line by line - we know the colours and the characters - the bits that made both of us laugh.

I suppose because we first knew each other in a workshop, in a place where writing was being read and being scoured over, we learned to catch each other's eye and egg each other on to giggle. Same as reading now - wanting the book that will tear the flesh off our bones, but the comforting book as well. The one that will be close enough to home so you can take it to bed. It'll still pull you close enough to life and its being so hard. And it *is* hard - even when you're cushioned by a talent that makes you so impervious you can go anywhere.

I remember us being able to turn any scene into something fabulous. With accoutrements - with stuff like chocolate serpents in silver, ribboned boxes; with coffee percolating; cocktail cigarettes; anemones and gin and hardbacks bought on the never-never and all our old records.

And people in common. Introducing our respective friends – expecting them to fall in love with each other and recognise each other. As grand as we said they really were. Aren't they great?

Never mind those who tell us we laugh too much, swear too much, read and write too many things down.

We've spent this long - this long - training ourselves and daring each other - to be just this way.

Jeremy made me do one of his self-perception inventory tests. I came out as 'low' on 'balance and security and pushiness and success for the sake of it'. Guess what? I'm great at knowing the precise, illogical thing that I want - not the best, not the most sensible - but I'm apt to go hell-for-leather on my own peculiar course.

Imagine my surprise. And there it was in numbers, as if proved and true.

He'd just been on his course and he'd come back, true as an evangelical and full of this stuff. He'd stayed in a chalet in Northumbria, been forced to shin up trees in the dark and be part of a team.

Who needs anyone but their best pals to tell them what they're like?

And who would see it as something you need a course for?

It's like when Joan from the MA class tried to make us relax before writing. She thought we should lie on the floor of her dance studio and straighten our spines. She thought we should make peace with ourselves and our childhoods and breathe easier before we wrote anything down. Of course we ran away to buy chocolates in Marks and Spencers and we wolfed them in the car park.

We know what we're like.

It's like Lorna Sage said to me – and she should have known – 'Yeah, of course we can all be too fucking clever for our own good. But that's their fucking problem - not ours.'

So I'm fetching out your poems from the shelves tonight and upstairs Jeremy's flicking through designs for doing up the bathroom. I hug him as he sits there - we're about to go out to dinner. He asks, 'Have you been drinking?'

And I'm, like: 'It's tea time - I'm writing, I'm listening to David Bowie full blast, all the windows are open on the October night - I'm reading poems that tempt me to be worse, better, worse, better than I already am. Of course there's a bottle of wine open on the dining room table. There's a ciggy burning in the ashtray and books open. These are the things I do and call it research. I'm thinking about my friends. To me it's like pouring chemicals in tubes, it's reading nineteenth century novels at a desk in the British library.'

The difficult lovely stuff to do with my friends *is* my research. That's what I think about, and what I write about.

We're being hazardous and grand every day, just doing what we do. Really, us - every day, all day. I mean, Jesus, God, and Dusty Springfield - we never stop, do we?

Dusty Verb Colour

I'm interested in people, and that's why I write.

Now, of course I know that novels and stories don't really have to be about people.

Theoretically, they don't even have to have any characters in them at all.

I'm pretty well read. I've got three literature degrees and I've spent my whole life reading. I've read all kinds of experimental and non-naturalistic fiction.

But the books I respond to and get involved with, and the books I wind up staying in love with – they all have characters in them. They're about people and the way they behave and the things they get up to.

Even those way-out novels about amoebas or rocks or shopping trolleys – most of those are still, really, about people. They're just rock-shaped characters or amoeba-like personalities. We're human beings and, when someone tells us a story, we're looking straight away for human experiences. We're looking for the points in the story that touch upon our own lives. We're looking – we can't even help ourselves – to have our sympathies stirred.

We want to identify with the people we read about. Whoever and whatever they are.

I think that's what it's like, anyway.

Maybe one day I'll read a completely abstract novel and change my mind utterly. Maybe it'll be about colours or dust or words themselves and describe the carryings on of these things so ravishingly that I'll forsake the more traditional forms of fiction forever.

I doubt it, though. Even if I'm swept away by 'Dusty Verb Colour: A Novel', I don't think it'll convert me absolutely. I don't think I'll give up reading stories about people. I'm addicted, I think, to books in which people do the washing up, talk about things in cars as they drive through the night, have knockout sex and cause family arguments at Christmas gatherings.

I'm nosey, in the end. I can't feel nosey and avid and gossipy about amoebas or verbs unless they're amoebas and verbs with terrific personalities. That's just not me, otherwise.

But I can feel very nosey about any kind of person, living in any time or place. I want to know who their friends are, and their enemies. I want to know their most exciting secrets and their most shameful ones. I want to know about the best day they've ever experienced. I want to know what they feel about the government and the home they live in. Have they ever had a pet they loved? Do they also love to read novels? How much of their own past have they forgotten or repressed? How far have they travelled? And how much have they stayed at home? What do they feel guilty about? Do they still love their parents?

See? Endless questions. I could go on like that all day.

For me, stories and novels are great big repositories of all kinds of knowledge about people. People who might or might not have lived. The actual characters on the page might not be literally real, but the experiences are real in a very definite sense. In a well-observed, well-written novel, the experiences are real because they have been drawn from life. The emotions are real because someone, somewhere has actually felt them. They have just been transplanted from real life by a skilled observer. They have been rendered vividly on the page by an expert in messing about with language: by someone who can bend the written word around and turn it inside out – simply in order to make it seem natural, living, and breathing.

I think the language of fiction is best when it seems like language in flight. Like it's coming straight out of living people. When it gives us that wonderful illusion that, in reading these words, we're living in real time with these people.

The people can be as realistic as you like. As fully-rounded as you want. With all kinds of psychological tics and warm, glowing flesh, and skin and hair you feel you could actually touch. Or they could be those amoebas spinning about in microcosmic space, pushing shopping trolleys about and buying up abstract verbs. So long as the language they think in and speak in is vivid and rich – and somehow buoyantly in flight – I as a reader will be right there with them.

But I think I've got to feel like I'm in company. That I'm surrounded by people and everything's buzzing with wordy, complicated life.

I know that this isn't for everyone. But it's how I like to feel about fiction.

I want to be entering into a world of new and intriguing people, every time I start reading.

Here's an exercise I've developed over the years. I've done it with workshops, but it's something really easily done by one writer alone.

It's about creating a new character and getting inside their heads.

First you find a picture of someone quite unlike yourself.

I like getting people to write about characters quite unlike themselves. The first temptation for any writer is to create someone a bit like themselves. I guess it's natural. But writing about yourself is really hard. You don't always see yourself in the round. You try to be honest – but you can't *see* yourself completely.

Better try your best to get out of your head right at the outset and pretend to be someone else.

A pirate, a wrestler, a magician. A tapir or a rock monster from Verbatim 6.

Remember the joy of doing that in the playground? Those terrific kids' games we all used to play, so unselfconciously? Tearing around outside, inhabiting different identities so easily. Without any seeming effort I was Batman, Doctor Who, Alexis off Dynasty.

It was the same when we wrote stories for ourselves when we were kids. We didn't always worry about how convincing it was or whether it was 'right' or not. We just did it. We were those characters. We were inside those stories.

We need to get that feeling back.

So.

Find a picture.

Could be a photo. Could be a painting.

Hunt through newspapers. Scour through reference books. History books. Art books. Anything you can lay your hands on. Have a look through the billions of pictures that float past us every day. Faces of people we'll never actually know.

For the purposes of this exercise, it's probably best not to choose anyone famous or well-known. Or someone we actually know anything concrete about.

The picture is a trigger for your imagination. Best keep your imagination as free as you can for this.

Let it fly.

So – choose someone who intrigues you.

A different age to you. Another gender. A foreign nationality. A different species, even.

For your first go at writing about this person, I just want you to describe them.

In the first person. Using all five senses. From their point of view.

What do I look like? What am I wearing today? What do I smell like? How do I feel inside my skin? What can I hear right now? What does my voice sound like? Do I sound different to how others hear me? What's that taste in my mouth right now? I chew my fingernails – what's that taste like? What colours do I love to wear? How's my complexion? Am I wearing make-up? What could I change about myself?

Five minutes. Go on.

Ok. Got that?

Now I want you to give yourself five minutes answering each of these next questions – in that same voice.

Where are you sitting?

Where in the world do you feel safest?

What's you're happiest memory?

Who is the most important person to you in the world?

What's the biggest secret you know?

How was that? Did you do five minutes exactly on each question?

It's good to stick to the rules. Keep a stopwatch. Set an alarm on your phone. When time is up, stop what you're doing, even mid-sentence. Yes, really!

Remember, it's about language in flight. Language as lived. Words tumbling through the mind of your character, or spilling out of their mouth. And words like that don't always get polished into tidy sentences, do they?

The harsh conditions of these exercises – Stop! Start! Do this! Do that! – are important. If I simply said – yeah, write about just whatever you like for an hour – you might flounder. You need parameters and prompts. Within the boundaries of the exercises you'll find complete freedom. (I promise you!)

Okay.

Now read back everything you've written. Look at the picture now and then as you read. Can you imagine these words coming from this character? Do they ring true?

Now, you're going to answer each of the next five questions – but very quickly. In a matter of seconds. Quickly.

Go with your first thought. You might surprise yourself.

Give your character a name.

Where do they live? What's the name of the town, the city, the boat, or the mountain they live at the top of?

How do they spend their days?

What is the date? They're speaking and thinking – but when? And how old are they then?

On this particular day, someone comes to visit them. Who is it?

Got all that?

You're building up little fragments of knowledge about this person.

It's a jigsaw with as many pieces as you like, and one that can fit together in any way you decide. It isn't a rigid jigsaw made out of wood that only goes together in one specific way. You're not trying to make the same picture that's on the front of the jigsaw's box. These are soft-sided pieces. They're organic fragments. It's up to you how you push them together and it's all down to you what picture that might create.

Remember, none of this is set in stone. Anything can be changed at a later date. But I want to see what you come up with when you trust your impulses and instincts. I want you to see what you invent when the exercises jump you into action and you have no time to tidy things up.

Okay. Now, remember what I said about being nosey?

I want you to think of two really good, meaty questions that you want to ask this new character of yours. Already you have some inkling about who they are and what their preferences and secrets and desires might be. You have a sense of the circumstances of their lives.

Now, think like a nosey person and come up with two sharp questions that your character must answer.

This visitor who's come by to see them? Perhaps they are asking the questions. They've been building up inside them for ages. The questions have been nagging at the visitor. And now they can't contain themselves any longer. They've decided that today's the day to pay a visit on your character and ask these two important questions.

So – write down the two questions, as your visitor would ask them.

Remember – two questions that are probing and tricky. Questions that seek to get to the heart of something important.

Five minutes. Now.

How does your character react to being asked these things? Affronted? Shocked? Pleased? Relieved?

Take three minutes to write down exactly how you think your character reacts. Again – no neatly polished sentences. Just fragments of thoughts and phrases. What goes through your character's head just now?

And for the final part of this exercise, I'm going to give you a bit longer. You're going to answer both questions.

Answer both questions in the voice of your character.

Answer both questions twice.

What do I mean, twice?

I mean – I want the outward answer and then the private answer.

So, you're giving four answers and I'll give you ten minutes to write each one. Set that alarm clock again!

Ok. Question one.

Answer it first in the way that your character would answer it aloud. What do they actually say to their visitor? What gets said out loud?

Now – answer it again. But this time I want to how they'd answer it to themselves, inside their heads. What is their private response? Is it the same? I bet it's quite different. Which is truer? Neither? Do they lie to their visitor? What's going on?

Now do the second question, in just the same way.

This exercise should get you working pretty hard, I think.

It's a very concentrated way to get you to focus on character. But you should get a great deal out of it, in terms of getting to know your made-up person. By the end of this you'll have learned a lot.

And, in the gaps between the inner and outer selves, and the glimmers of the things they might be concealing, I think you might also have the beginnings of a story becoming apparent…

Do you?

Early 2005's Thoughts About Writing Novels

Every year – for as long as I can remember – I have run novel-writing workshops. Usually I'm in the middle of writing some novel of my own while I'm teaching other people. It keeps me on my toes. I learn so much from the students, every year. By the end of a course your head ends up swirling with all these thoughts and ideas about novels and how to write them. All the answers are there, somewhere… in amongst all your notes about novels written by eighteen other people and more… if you could just assemble the notes into some order… that's the thing.

Here are some thoughts that came out of novel-writing workshops I led early in 2005.

*Beware of too much going on in one sentence.

*When you break a scene and leave a very dramatic, white pause between sections, be consistent in what the gap represents. Is it a shift in time, place or point of view?

*Is 'engulfed' too fancy a verb? Verbs are so important to get right. They have to be muscular. They keep the prose and the story going, and the tension up… and that's (one of the things) keeping the reader reading.

*What?? What does this mean? Is it wilfully obscure and knotty? Are we supposed to be *puzzled* by this? There's an art to being mystifying; to learning to intrigue your reader. It's about stringing them along – but also about learning how not to piss them off. Don't lose them.

*Cluttered sentences. Nasty show-off sentences. Trying to sound too *novelly*. By 'novelly' I mean someone's idea of what a novel should sound like. IE, someone's rubbishy, middlebrow idea of a novel. Don't try to sound like someone else. Especially someone rubbishy and middlebrow.

*Keep your action sequences simple. Tell them clearly. We have to picture this stuff. We have to be able to see it.

*Too many characters coming in at once? You'll make the reader want to scream. Assume that readers are lazy. If they get too much info all at once, they'll stop trying and chuck your book away. Let each character register, and make their impact. Underline and underscore their presences with physical, concrete detail, with tics and traits. Repeat them *just enough* on each reappearance.

*Don't – as writer – assume that the reader knows about and can see the characters as well as you can. Don't assume we know how old they are, for example, or what the relationships between them are. You have to smuggle and shoehorn that kind of information in, very subtly, very carefully. Don't deluge us with info.

*Don't explain too much.

*Why's your writing getting overly formal and ornate? Why's it become show-offy and novelly? Usually because you've run out of story.

*If things have gone a bit rococo, ask yourself: Who is narrating this story? Whose voice is this? From what point in time? Does this voice betray an attitude towards the characters and their milieu? Should it?

*Adverbs can be great. Mostly, they're shit. Mostly, they're used *shitly*. They soften the impact of a verb. They betray hesitations on the writer's part. Especially when they are words like 'fairly', 'actually', 'seemingly.' Just think about the redundancies in current cliches of speech; those dreadful adverbial doings: 'literally,' 'basically', 'at the end of the day…' These are phrases that mean nothing. They're good in dialogue, though.

*People talk such shit. Let's hear it.

*Time has to *move*. Begin with events and keep them going. This sounds obvious, but it doesn't always occur to people. They think they can hold back time – and explain everything to us at great length – like Rod Serling used to in *The Twilight Zone*.

*Time has to *move*. Keep it moving and fold all the info we need into the mix – but don't stop to explain too much. Don't get mired down.

*Be aware of how much it's possible for a reader to remember. Discover more about how your own memory works when it comes to novels. Ask other people how their memories work. Can they reconstruct the four dimensions of a story in their heads? Do they reconstruct it backwards or forward, or from a point in the middle? Do they remember characters or plot beats? Ideas or sensations?

*Don't neglect to include crucial plot beats. The reader will know if you've left out an important step in the unfolding of the plot. These are what the French critic Roland Barthes used to call 'cardinal functions' – ie, important stuff happening, that will lead to other, important stuff. Different to 'indiceal functions' – which is all the atmosphere and detail and richness. Make them work together. You need both: pushing forward, as well as depth and richness. They're in constant tension, but don't neglect either. One impulse wants to push onwards; the other wants to dwell in the moment. A balance is necessary.

*Learn how to feed necessary exposition to your reader. If it's unsubtle the reader will feel preached at. They'll realise this is 'important' plot beat stuff they'll need to remember, and they'll probably skip it. Avoid having a character feed us exposition by letting them dwell on recent events inside their heads. This holds up the action. It freezes time. You've got to think: can this exposition possibly be done in dialogue, in real time? And then you can let your reader eavesdrop. The reader feels flattered by that, rather than patronised. If they earwig on a conversation filled with clues, they feel that they're being given something meaty to work out. They don't want to be given all the answers on a plate. Also, the reader likes the clandestine feeling of eavesdropping. There's a frisson of pleasure to that.

*Mention delicious smells. Gorgeous colours. Music. Art. Food. Sexy goings-on at any opportunity. Epiphanies of all kinds. Don't forget to appeal to all our senses. Make the bodily and the intellectual and the emotional try to meet up in sensations we can imagine. Seduce the reader with these moments.

*Give the reader pleasure whenever you can…

*The first time novelist always gets meta-discursive. Every single novelist seems to do this! They adopt a godlike narrator's voice that starts to question its authority, that starts to play literary games with the reader, and clever-clever tricks on the reader. Or the protagonist is a novelist who tells us all about novels and the nature of truth and illusion. Aaaaagggggghhhhh! This is your first novel! Nothing's happening! Get on with it! Stop playing with narrative form and ideas of intentionality and trying to shift the bleeding paradigm! You got into this stuff in the first place because you liked making up stories! What's your problem? Why have you stopped?

*How come it's only page one and you're already up your own arse?

*All this stuff is a symptom of the writer dealing with their own authority. These are metaphors and strategies to delay the writing process; the actual business of making things up; the embarrassing business of having characters actually *do* things and saying 'he said, she said'. It's about avoiding the task in hand. Do I dare invent?? JUST DO IT!

*If you're doing some kind of literary pastiche (Oh, Jesus – on university courses it's always Nabokov, Rushdie, Pynchon,

Eco) you REALLY have to know what it is you're meant to be pastiching. If you're going to play all the literary games and flag up the literariness and all that jazz – if you're going to mess about with the textiness of the text – its *writtenness* – then you really have got to get it right. (There's nothing worse than a half-cocked attempt at flagging up your materiality.)

*Usually, in your first draft – your first five page splurge of writing – there is a fabulous detail or image or event or idea on about page two, or three. Most often, two thirds of the way down page two. This is where the whole thing should start. This is when you warmed up. Be brutal. Cut out everything up until that point. Start there, at the good bit. That's your hook.

*Don't let it get messy. Correct small typos all the time. Vigilance. Use that time as thinking time, when you're still inside the text, tinkering about. It's like musicians, tuning up between songs.

*You can learn an awful lot about stories-within-stories, framing devices, flashbacks and points of view from old movies. All the tools are there. Movies are good for novelists because they are stripped down: you can hold the whole shape of one in your head – more easily, sometimes, perhaps, than you can a novel. Movies keep time moving and demonstrate how time works because all movies are, necessarily, all about time.

*Make us laugh. What would be the point of a novel with no jokes?

*Fancy syntax turns to crap in some people's mouths. Calm it down.

*Archaic language. 'Akin,' 'Beholden.' What?? I blame the Bible. Listen to how people speak now. 'At the end of the day, like, it's literally the time you're, like, living in, yeah?'

*Learn to have a lighter touch. In a dramatic scene, give us the words, events and gestures. If necessary, let your character reflect on it later. While the scene's happening, let the reader do the reacting. Don't tell the reader what to think or feel. Don't muffle the impact of a scene by having everyone *thinking* all the time. When every single response and reaction is nailed down and spelled out, all the fun goes out of things. It stops being dramatic and edgy. Leave some gaps. Fiction needs to have everyday chaos in it. Fiction needs mystery in it. It needs gaps in it, for us to mull over…

*First person narrators. Everyone loves writing these – because they think they're easy to do. They aren't.

*How does a first person narrator manage to give a strong enough sense of themselves to the reader? Without it seeming like they're telling you too much and banging on?

*We have to see them in action; living through time. We have to see them perform *live*, as it were. Then we can make up our own minds. We're very close to them, when they speak to us in their own voices. Are we close to someone we like, or someone we despise?

*A first person narrator can (or think that they can) stack the deck, in terms of what the reader finds out. They think they can have it all their own way. For the reader, it's like having a very bossy friend, or someone standing extremely close to you – chatting on and on and on. They try to dominate your view of this world.

*The skilled writer will make the first person narrator say things they don't mean to. They will slip, and give themselves away. The reader will glimpse their world – and unspoken truths about it – over their shoulder…

*JD Salinger 'For Esme, with Love and Squalor'; F Scott Fitzgerald 'The Great Gatsby'; Christopher Isherwood 'Goodbye to Berlin'. By Spring 1990, when you were twenty, you had read these three again and again. You've read thousands of books since, but I don't think you've learned nearly as much from anything since those three.

*Remember: *Clever* is good. *Clever-clever* is shit. *Clever-clever-clever* is good again.

I don't know why.

Eavesdropping on Roofers

It's the first sunny day in ages, right at the end of August. For days the skies over Manchester have been Tupperware-coloured, but not today. I'm at the bottom of the garden in the Beach House trying to write, despite all the noise of the builders up on the scaffolding. I find I can't help myself eavesdropping on the older guy with the Brummie accent and his Emo apprentice – a boy with the face of a scowling girl and a ridiculous fringe. His trackies and pants are slipping down as he traipses up ladders at the back of our house. He really doesn't want to be here at all.

'But I can't climb all the way up there!' he said on the first day. 'That's the roof!'

'We're roofers,' said the Brummie. 'And when you're in this trade you work anywhere and everywhere the bosses tell you.'

Over the past few days I've overheard various highlights from the scaffolding. The scene in which the older man coached his apprentice on the correct way to saw into a plank – 'getting your shoulder in line with your wrist and the wood and pushing harder on the stroke and taking it more softly when you pull back…' I found it rather tender, that coaching.

Then there was a tetchy exchange at the end of a day, when the apprentice asked him not to talk to him like he was an idiot. He didn't want telling off all the time.

'But I'm teaching you, ain't I? And you've got a lot to learn. That's the point!'

'But you shout at me!'

'Only when you need telling. And if you do something badly or awkwardly it takes us extra time, doesn't it? And time is money, you see, and so you have to be told. You need all my learning and experience. When I shout at you because you don't know the difference between a screwdriver and a drill bit, like the other day, I'm only doing it so that you know next time. And I'm not really taking the piss when I laugh, you know. And I'm not really angry when I shout. You just have to learn, and this is the way it's done.'

The apprentice mumbled something – I couldn't hear what.

Later I learned that he wasn't just an apprentice, he was the roofer's son.

All this drama going on up the scaffolding round our house! While I work in the garden and Bernard Socks dozes all day on his adirondack chair. The new covers are the exact green of his narrowed eyes as he watches me writing. When I'm not scribbling I'm reading Cosy Mysteries and a dumb mermaid novel I wish I hadn't started but can't quite give up on.

I've had a few days of attempting to pull my thoughts together, as I consider my writing options and decide on what my autumn project ought to be.

It should be something I *have* to write.

That I *really want* to do.

It doesn't have to be an adventure story. I had an epiphany about that. Why was I ever trying to write adventure stories? It always ended up with me wishing I could write like someone else: someone who was good at writing action scenes and did them with great panache. Writing only ever works when I'm doing my *own* thing.

My other recent epiphany was that I should *only ever write one thing at a time.*

Over the summer months I've got myself twenty thousand words into two separate stories – one of them a mystery about Sherlock Holmes' housekeeper Mrs Hudson, and the other a kind of modern day comedy set in our part of south Manchester. Both books are on pause. Both are at the point (a quarter of the way into a full book) where I need to review their first chunks anyway and start marking out their parameters: where do these stories need to go next? What kind of shape should these novels be? Those kind of hard, searching questions. Do these beginnings really deserve to have middles and endings..?

At the same time I reread my manuscript about Fester Cat and I found myself thinking that I ought to write memoirs and stories and essays about real life all the time. When I write about my own life there's a greater urgency to it, I think. That's how it seems today. Do I want to spend an autumn raveling up my own life story and dragging out the tittle-tattle?

I also listened to an early edit of my play for Radio 4, which I'd just been sent by the director, Scott. After two years of imagining it, actually hearing it was odd. It came across as more dramatic, touching and sweet than I was expecting: it took me by surprise. It was less smart-arsey than I had dreaded it being. The scenes with the mam and dad surprised me. They sounded very *me*. Listening to this very slick BBC radio production, and yet it felt like eavesdropping on my own life. Some of the more tender, and more embarrassing moments of my younger life. That felt like a moment of success to me. I was writing about something real.

So – real life. You visited quite a lot of it when you wrote your memoir through the voice of Fester Cat. You told flashbacks in his voice, looking at episodes in your life he was never there for. You worried they'd seem intrusive or too bolted-onto the text, but they didn't, when you reread them. You made it seem like Fester the narrator was interested in your life, and Jeremy's. And it made you realise that living together in the same home is about going into the future, but it's also about settling down into your past as well. The book tells the tale of going forward as well as settling down.

It's a good feeling, realizing that Fester's book does exactly what I want it to do. It makes his voice permanent. It means he's there forever. His years with us are a bubble of time and now anyone can visit them, any time in the future.

I hated to admit it, but my mystery novel about Mrs Hudson wasn't convincing me any more. The characters and their story just weren't real. As a book it wasn't alive or focused any more. By twenty-five thousand words into the book it had even drifted away from its prime location and the narrative was revisiting characters from an earlier story. It was as if the writing itself was trying to tell me something...

You let it turn into mush. You let your characters forget their motivations. They all forgot what it was they had come for.

And now what you must do is think about where your heart truly is.

Even in your contemporary-set romance you're having trouble. You really don't want to write this chapter about a wedding. It feels like a bottle-neck in the plot: an obstruction before the story can move on. Maybe you need to put more conflict in? Perhaps one character wants the wedding and the other doesn't? It's true, sometimes you forget that you need to have conflict in a story. Hating it so much in real life and you do everything to avoid it – but fiction is the last place you need to excise it from.

I think you're having trouble with both stories because they lack tension and conflict and so they're boring you.

And so you're going to stop writing both stories right now.
There.
Quiet.

This is what I've learned. I've learned it before, but I've learned it again, this summer. The hard way.

Only write it if you really want to.

Only write it if it *sings*.

Wait until the very moment that you simply *have* to write it.

Are you able to wait until then? Can you afford to?

Because that would be best.

It has to be the *right* thing, and at the *very* moment.

That's all I know.

Maybe novels aren't even my thing..?

That would be something. To learn that now!

In Edinburgh at the weekend with my pals. On the bus on Saturday, crawling down Princes Street. It was so busy and the half-dug tramlines were in disarray and the sun was red hot coming through the windows. George was asking about when and if I'd get my backlist back into print. Those novels from the late 1990s – would I get someone to bring them back out?

I surprised myself in that moment by saying that I didn't care anymore. The world didn't seem to want those books the first time around, when they were fresh and pertinent – then who the hell would want them now, nearly twenty years later?

Maybe I sounded bitter and cross. But really, what I'm really interested in is where I'm at now and trying to find stories to express that, somehow. Right now, everything I've already written doesn't seem good enough. All of it makes me cringe. I feel like

I've never succeeded in anything I've ever set out to do. It's like I've given myself a monstrously long apprenticeship. It's kind of grotesque, actually.

This is the kind of negative epiphany you can have when you're sitting on a too-crowded bus on a too-hot day when the traffic's moving too slowly.

I decided I needed some radical re-thinking going on.

Be honest about your gifts and limitations.

I love characters.

I don't like densely-woven plots. I give up following them when I'm reading, and I can't write them at all. Unless by accident. And then they go wrong.

I know when I finish something, or pause halfway through, and it rings hollow, then something has gone wrong. I'm not afraid to abandon it if it's gone wrong.

I can't bully myself into doing it right. I know myself well enough by now. Sometimes I can even see what needs to be done to fix a story or to tighten the plot. But I can't force myself to do it, because I know it will ring with that hollow noise afterwards.

But I still feel like I ought to be bullying myself to do things right. To make them watertight and conventional. I feel obliged to bully myself.

I bully and cudgel and force myself to write something and keep going until I've got a hundred thousand words of it.

What I love more than anything – in reading and writing – is fragmentary episodes of memoir.

I love short stories that are malformed: tantalizing, wispy, broken off.

I love stories that aren't even tempted to come to a finish. I love it when it feels like they break off with a shrug, and then take a drag of a cigarette and that's it. The reader fills in the rest. Lovely.

Is it short stories I need to be writing now? I was wondering as we went around Edinburgh that weekend.

I was supposed to be on holiday. Visiting friends, having a laugh, hanging out in bars. Revisiting the place I spent my mid-twenties. Instead I was giving myself a hard time: wanting to write stories, but wondering if that was just a kind of failure, too? Was I finking out and failing at the long form? Had I messed up every attempt I'd made at the novel?

I was right at the point where I needed to write something I could sell.

You're ridiculous. You've got a nice, brand new journal and you're filling it up with self-doubt and drivel.

But a year ago you were having such a great time with your writing. You set off on writing a novel about Mars for kids. You were conscientious and wrote a set number of words a day and stuck to your plot and created a coherent adventure story. You were, in many ways, on best behaviour. And so far – everyone has rejected it. You got to Edinburgh and got an email and it was the last rejection.

So – all through your weekend away, you're thinking: what now? Where now? What do I try to do next..?

Perhaps the thing to do, from today, is don't even call them stories or novels.

Don't even label them as fiction or memoir.

Just write them.

They could be two thousand, five thousand or just five hundred words long.

Just do them and let them stand and let them contradict each other, or complement each other. Or let one piece suggest the next. Let it evolve. Let it be organic, rather than trying to force it..?

Never let it get so that it's like pulling teeth.

Something else you said to George this weekend in Edinburgh – while you still in the same self-doubting, grumpy mood – was that your utter lack of success at writing has meant that you've never rested on your laurels. You've never had the opportunity! It's meant you've never taken anything for granted. Mostly, you've had to pick yourself up and start from scratch with each project. You've had to reinvent the wheel every time. No one has ever been tempted to say: hey, this works. Keep doing exactly this thing. Never deviate from that. For gawd's sake, don't change.

I think what you need to do, as a writer, is find out what makes readers want to read you.

This doesn't mean you follow the market or try to work out what's commercial, or what the next big thing might be… It's different to that.

It's about discovering the thing that is unique to you that a readership of some kind will be drawn to.

That's one of the secrets, I think.

It's to do with finding out exactly what's unique about your own writing and doing it the best way you can. But whether that will appeal to anyone else at all is anyone's guess and, I think, a matter a sheer luck. But I don't think there's any other way of doing it. Not for me, anyway. All I can do is be myself, as well as I can.

Later on that Saturday in Edinburgh, a small party of us were sitting outside Iguana bar, by the university. There was me and

Stuart and George and we were joined by Roy, and then Ellie, the bookseller from Blackwells, down the road.

This whole area was my backyard, once, at the end of the 1990s. Somewhere I've written about sitting in this very bar on sunny afternoons, drinking endless frothy, frozen coffee and writing pages of trippy psychedelic Doctor Who adventures.

Ellie has just come from a long, long book-signing at which she was looking after Neil Gaiman, and she's buzzing. I think about Neil's massive, global success and how there's something compelling about what he does that makes such a huge audience take him to their hearts. They're not just on his bandwagon because of hype. Sure, hype is there and there always is when big business comes in, but Neil is giving his audience something very specific and real, that only he can give them. They feel like they're in his club.

I'm listening to Ellie telling us how she had him signing 450 books for her shop and it's mind-boggling, really.

I think the issue to really think about is how you make yourself – your writing, your books, your style – indispensable to the reader.

How to make them really want this story. That's the key.

Is it to do with plot? Character? Momentum?

Is it to do with a conceit or a concept that hooks them right away?

Or is it an invite to a very special world?

At the same time as mulling over all of this in Edinburgh, and scribbling all this despondent stuff about your failures and stories you've abandoned... your mood might actually just be the result of what you're reading right now.

Right now I'm reading a How-To book.

I know. Shoot me.

I'm reading a How-To-Write-Mysteries book.

And it's making me think I've never written anything properly at all, let alone a mystery.

It's made me feel like I'm not even qualified to *read* a mystery, let alone *write* one of the bloody things.

But really… did I ever set out to write anything in the proper way?

Proper..?!

What kind of a word is that? It sounds so dismal.

When you're questioning and self-doubting, don't read how-to books.

Some days you put yourself through hell, feeling particularly sensitive. You put on your cardigan of shame and sit at the bottom of the garden.

I read horrible online reviews of things I've written and feel just dreadful. I end up thinking I've never done anything of any value at all.

I suppose the answer is not to read how-to books, or to read reviews.

I want to read go-and-do books, rather than how-to.

Truman Capote once wrote about the panic he felt – he got into a state a bit like this one – when he wrote the preface to 'Music for Chameleons.' He described how he looked back at all his previous work and saw that he wasn't happy with any of it. It didn't do what he thought it had done. All of it was lacking in his eyes.

Today I can't even hold a thought. I can't even hold a pen straight. My handwriting's all over the page.

Maybe the self-doubting days are best expressed in the medium of terrible handwriting? Maybe then you can't read them back?

But they're a useful thing to keep preserved. Your older self can learn from these fearful days, I think.

In the midst of all this worrying, Bernard Socks makes me lie down on the bed settee in the Beach House, just so he can curl up on me for a few minutes, before taking a stroll around the garden and returning to his chair. It doesn't matter to him if my writing is unreadable and illegible and if my books don't appeal to the kind of readers who want novels to adhere to prearranged genre rules. He couldn't care less whether I've broken through or sold out, or what my agent is saying. Bernard Socks thinks that most of what I do is great. Though I think, on the whole, he's less interested in writing and books than Fester Cat was.

Fester was quite literary, in his own way.

The next day.

Yesterday was awful..!

Reading how-to books is a bit like when people pore over home-doctor medical books and decide they've got every disease under the sun.

By the end of the day I'd decided I'd never written anything of any value and I couldn't see a way forward at all. I couldn't see what I could possibly do next.

At least today I can laugh about it.

It does seem a bit of an over-reaction.

What I need to find again is that feeling that I can write absolutely anything. I need that feeling that I can take everyone with me, wherever the story leads – and I can make everyone care.

That's the feeling I have to work on getting back.

Later that morning.

Agent Charlotte forwards an email from Penny and Janet at Firefly, confirming that they're both very interested in the whole trilogy set on Mars. They're going to talk next week when everyone's back in their offices. They will discuss it all.

Someone wants my science fiction novel!

I've felt despondent about it since last Friday, when I arrived in Edinburgh and met Stu and when we went to the pub the first thing I did (so stupidly) was check my email on my phone – and there was another rejection. Just as my holiday weekend was starting. No wonder I went into the doldrums. Everyone I knew in Edinburgh was doing events at the Book Festival. Steve, Roy. And Neil Gaiman was signing 450 books! I'd had that rejection on Friday afternoon and I was ready to chuck it in. Okay, so science fiction maybe isn't my genre. I'm no good with sf, fantasy, or any kind of adventure. I was a fool for even trying. Middle-grade isn't my age range, either. I've failed.

Though deep down, of course, I never believed any of that. And I always absolutely believed in the characters in my Martian novel: Lora and her Da and Toaster and Peter and his cat-dog and the City Inside. And I really wanted to be able to write the next two books in the trilogy. I was nowhere near ready to give up. Imagine having that kind of schedule and that kind of goal. I'm in the midst of writing a trilogy set on the planet Mars and a publisher is waiting for it. Heaven!

Hold onto your hat.

You're happy because you've heard that someone wants something from you. You're happy because now you have something to do.

Part of the despondency of the past few days has been the idea of going on and not knowing if anyone will want what you write next.

You're happier when you know there's an audience waiting.

I rush to tell Jeremy and he's in the bedroom, laughing because Bernard Socks is sitting on top of the tallest bookcase. He's as high as the ceiling, then jumping off, onto the bed. SSPRROIINGG! He keeps running and jumping back up on top of the bookcase to do it again and again. Each time he wears this incredibly surprised expression. He's got bags of energy this morning. He's zooming all around the place.

It's the start of September. It's a year exactly since I immersed myself completely in writing the world of this book.

Sometimes you finish something and you have to rest and wait, and listen for news before throwing yourself into the next thing. Sometimes you have to let yourself get a bit down. But don't worry too much, and never chuck the towel in just because things aren't turning out right. I'm not saying they definitely will. But you'll never find out unless you keep trying.

Keep jumping off that bookcase like Bernard Socks. There are worse ways of spending your days.

Saturday
afternoon
22nd
august
2015.

Escaping the Dust Clouds

Monday and the decorators are pulling down the bathroom ceiling. Dust sheets are half-covering furniture and our belongings. There are black clouds everywhere. One hundred and fifty years' worth of soot and ash is dropping through the house. They've got their Radio playing loudly as they bash away at the wattle and daub and the lath and plaster and Bernard Socks is locked in the bedroom.

I think I need to get out into town, and away from this. I might stand a chance of doing some work that way. Yesterday I began something new and spent all day long hammering away at the idea. I'm still full of the excitement of it.

I catch the train into town. We live right by the railway tracks and Levenshulme station. It's a five minute ride into the heart of the city. It's never stopped being a novelty to me, the fact that the city is so close, even after almost ten years of living here.

It's freezing, drizzly and grey. Under the vast canopy of Piccadilly Station it's dry and busy. By the departures board, in the middle of the crowd, I spot Jeanette Winterson. She looks small, dark and harassed. As I breeze through the crowd my first instinct is to smile and say hello and maybe to gabble at her. I want to tell her I've been reading her since 1990. I can remember borrowing Steve's copy of 'Sexing the Cherry' – having woken up with him after a complicated night out and furtive, glorious sex. I can remember reading each novel as they came out through the 1990s, and where I was living, and what stage I was at in my own dramas. She's one of those writers who has formed the backdrop to my life. But I resist the urge to say hello and to thank her for those years of 'The Passion' and 'Oranges' and all the others. She looks pretty cross, waiting for her train to come up on the board.

All my books, all my signed first editions, all my tacky paperbacks and my folders and notes and everything: they're all falling under layers of oily black soot and dust. As I walk into the rainy town I know what's happening at home.

I walk up to the Northern Quarter and the cosy basement of Art Nexus Café. I order chai and a roast garlic and chickpea soup. I'm still a hippy at heart. I'm still a student with my notebooks and pens and sitting in a café like this in a rainy city where most people are dashing about doing actual jobs in the real world. I'll never grow up. That's something my stepfather wrote on my facebook timeline recently: that I'll never grow up. He also wrote that I was a self-deluding shit. There's a lesson there: don't accept friend requests on Facebook from dodgy family members.

Adult life sometimes seems disastrous. A friend texts to say their partner has just lost their new job. He didn't fit the private company's ethos. I just got a rejection email from someone who says they don't think my submission was 'proper, dark and edgy' enough for what they're looking for.

I remind myself: you'll never fit in. Don't try to make yourself dark and edgy or 'contemporary.' You could chase those chimeras forever. Just write what you want to. Write what you can. Write the things that only you can. This should be your only mantra.

Always, always remind yourself of that. Write what only you can. Write what you most want. Only you can write it. Only you can do this. Give yourself permission.

One of Jeanette Winterson's characters used to have a refrain: 'Trust me. I'm telling you stories.'

Your refrain needs to be: 'Trust yourself to tell your stories.'

Yesterday you wrote almost five thousand words in a blur of luminous activity. You sat at the dining room table at ten a.m and didn't move until six thirty in the evening. It's unusual for you to sit rooted like that, chasing one idea. But it was a very particular thing. You wanted to write about a series of books – the Doctor Who Annuals – which were published between 1964 and 1984, by World Distributors – a publisher based here in Manchester, just two streets away from where you're sitting right now, in Art Nexus Café. These Annuals with their strange artwork and stories even weirder than Doctor Who on TV have always fascinated you. Yesterday you sat down with a bunch of them and started to write about exactly why they still exerted such a pull on your imagination. You wanted to analyse and encapsulate your love for these books. You were caught up in the writing. It's exactly the kind of eccentric project you love. No one reads these books anymore. Even Doctor Who fans only collect them in order to hoard them for their value. But to you they have a secret at their heart. They tell a secret story and you can only crack it by rereading them this autumn: reading the whole lot all over again and writing thousands of words exploring them. It's a crazy kind of project and in the freezing October days with soot dropping down through your house, it seems irresistible. To bury yourself in brightly-coloured books from vintage Christmas days.

I'm escaping them pulling down our ancient ceilings and the setting free of sooty clouds. Poor Bernard Socks has the sniffles already from running about in the rain all night. He comes running back indoors and lies on my legs and then Jeremy's and dozes for a while, then he's off again outside via the catflap. The weather doesn't bother him at all.

I keep getting these blank emails and facebook messages from my mother. It's like she's inviting me to fill in the blanks with my own abusive text.

This café is adorable, with its mismatched tables and chairs, tiny teapots and cups, its skinny artistic boys with heavy bags and laptops, sitting beside giant teddy bears and crocheted cushions, carnival masks and placards from demos. I'm eavesdropping on a young woman who's telling a young guy about the medical research she's involved in carrying out. She's combing the whole country for babies with hearing problems. She asks the young man if he's in a relationship? They're eating lunch. It's clearly a while since they last saw each other. 'I don't do the long term thing,' he replies. 'I haven't for years.'

'Who was the last?' she asks. 'Wasn't it..' Samantha..?'

'That's amazing you remember her name!' he gasps.

She smiles and looks down at her salad. 'My memory's good.'

And I'm thinking: She remembers your ex-girlfriend's name because she actually cares about you, you idiot. She remembers because she's bothered about your life and who you're seeing.

When he goes he doesn't kiss her goodbye. There's an awkward kind of hug across the table and she hovers there when he moves off. Then she goes off, too, to research her deaf babies.

Wednesday and I'm in Costa café near Piccadilly, just after ten in the morning. It's my third day of getting out of the house and letting the ceiling men just get on with it. Jeremy is pinning sheets over the doors, ready for them to smash the top landing ceiling down. Bernard Socks is confined to the living room, but he's on the alert, as if he knows something big is happening. I opened the living room window for him so he can skip out.

I'm tired from gadding about with my bag and all my work things in it, looking for somewhere to settle with my books. Coming into town after the commuters and spending the whole day in the city centre – it's exhausting, but it feels a bit pathetic complaining. People travel to and from work, proper work, and they do long hours. I guess I'm used to having things much easier, working from home. Or is it that I'm used to living too much in my mind? Aside from anything else, the discomfort, mess and the yawning, knee-cracking ache of living in a building site is getting on your nerves and keeping you awake. You're hoping it'll impact on your work and make for interesting writing. I'm getting on with projects as best I can, host-desking round the coffee shops of Manchester.

Your sinuses are black with soot and maybe you're getting a cold. All this coffee is making you want to pee all the time. And it's a mistake to go looking in bookshops as a respite from working. Looking at new books in shops can be fatally off-putting.

Maybe I should get on a train and go into the countryside?

It's October. The countryside is cold and damp.

I wish – when I saw Jeanette Winterson the other day under the station clock and the departures board – I'd asked her: what's the secret, Jeanette? Where do I go from here? How do I reinvent my life with magical realism right now, like I thought I could in my twenties? Your books made me think life was going to be fabulous, if I dedicated my life to art and storytelling. Back then I was obsessed with your stories and I thought they were a kind of manual for having an amazing life.

But as I say, she looked cross and wet and fed up with waiting for her train. So all I did was smile, and she scowled back at me.

One of the things I've learned: writers don't have all the answers. They don't have many answers at all. Mostly we're muddling along, with soot and dust on our clothes and braving the chilly rain and looking for somewhere to sit and get our books and pens out.

Fancy Man

I moved to a new publisher in 1998. After three novels and a collection of stories I was moving on and writing a new book. I wanted to write something grand, set over a larger span of time – maybe twenty years or more. The novel was to be the story of a young orphaned girl who falls into the hands of her slightly unscrupulous aunty and who makes good and bad choices and good and bad friends as she moves into her twenties, discovering new places and relationships as she goes.

In many ways (I now see) it was the story of myself in my twenties in the 1990s. But it was also the story of Isabel Archer in Henry James' 'The Portrait of a Lady', a novel I'd read with great attention and enjoyment during my last summer in Edinburgh.

In essays I read about Henry James there was talk of architecture and the structure of his novels: these faultless erections of his. I thought: I'll have a bit of that, then. So I decided that my Wendy would follow a similar path to James' Isabel. In a kind of cover version of the old book she would begin in one city and move to others, resisting temptation and the lure of wicked people wanting to exploit her. It would be all about money and finding love and trying to find a place to live and who to trust and what to feel. It would be about sex and self-delusion…

And I wrote all of this in the gaps I could find in my life during my first year lecturing at UEA in Norwich. I was teaching the

MA course in Novel-writing, long-established as the oldest, most successful course of its kind in the UK. Most of my students were older than me and some looked askance at someone they clearly felt was callow and not famous enough to be teaching them. Here was this self-effacing northerner with a daft sense of humour telling them all what to do and sharing teaching duties with the Poet Laureate. I often had quite a fight on my hands when it came to showing people at UEA I knew exactly what I was talking about.

In the midst of this I was struggling with my 'Fancy Man.' At some point along the line my new editor – who had apparently loved my earlier books, even sent me fan mail about the first – decided he hated this new one. He couldn't stand what I was doing with it.

'Why are all your characters freaks?' he burst out during a phone call. At first I thought he was joking. My position was that all characters are freaks because, essentially, everyone in real life is a freak, in their own particular way. This had been a constant in my thinking and my fiction from the start. It was precisely what I wrote about: everyone is as fascinating and as fucked up as everyone else. If you look hard enough and sympathetically enough at anyone, you will see that they are freakish and unique and wonderful. If I had a constant theme, this might be it.

Anyway, the editor wasn't happy about that.

'Everyone you write about is a transvestite or grossly overweight or they have no legs or something else horribly wrong with them, or they believe in aliens...'

Yes, all of this was fair comment.

Then he said, 'Don't you know any normal people in real life? What's the matter with you?'

Up till then he had seemed such a kindly soul. Really, a gentleman, with interesting stories of his own to tell. But he had seemingly gone off my writing overnight. I remember a parcel of manuscript coming back in the post and when I unwrapped it I found that he had crossed through almost every single page with thick, greasy pencil. (It reminded me of the pencil with which my grandfather the butcher used to work out sums on bloody parcels of meat.)

He'd left hardly any words at all still standing on those four hundred pages of 'Fancy Man.' It was the weirdest thing. I was in a panic. What was I to do with a book where all the words had been crossed out and were somehow wrong?

He told me that I kept going off and getting too interested in secondary characters. He thought I must keep my main character the focus in every single scene. I didn't agree with that idea at all. Surely one of the great pleasures of novels is all the detours you can take? A novel is a forest we are invited to lose ourselves in.

My then-agent didn't help much.

My work was developing, as it should, changing from book to book and yes… perhaps this one was even wilder than its predecessors. But why would anyone set out to write a book tamer and less demanding than their last one?

This one had a suicide cult, alien replicants, nasty old witches and a cameo by Marlene Dietrich. All these things were delightful to me. If I made them delightful on the page, I was sure my audience would follow me.

My then-agent said: 'You should develop and mature more sensibly. You should mature by writing less about northern working class people. Write about more middle class people. Write about the south.'

For some reason it wasn't until 2003 that I sacked her.

As it happened, 'Fancy Man' was all about moving away from home and finding a whole range of different kinds of people coming into your life. But I guess the message from that daft agent and that daft editor was: only write novels just like other people do. If you want us to sell them and other people to buy them, you've got to make it all a bit more… conventional.

I just couldn't. I couldn't see what they were talking about when they said make it more normal. Looking back, I can catch a glimpse of the kind of thing they might have wanted me to do. Make the romance more orthodox. If it had to be gay, keep it light and vanilla. Put in fewer unicorns and alien replicants. Keep the sex fluffy rather than quite so in your face. Less melodrama, fewer cocks, fewer flights of ludicrous fancy. And maybe don't make every single character a writer..? (In 'Fancy Man' almost every single character is busy writing novels, memoirs or letters, or they are bursting into some kind of ragged verse to express their feelings. But this was just a joke of mine. In any other literary novel (Iris Murdoch, say) no one would turn a hair if all the characters were writers, philosophers or critics. Why shouldn't that also be true in novels written by me? In novels about hairdressers, shop girls, lottery winners..?

Because it isn't very realistic or true to life, comes the answer...

But I never started off writing novels in order to be true to life. I wanted to be true to my characters and a fully-imagined world of my own. I wanted to interrogate the myths and lies of realism and break it apart from within. When you come from a working class background the literary world expects you to write gritty realism, so you can look back on squalor and make everyone shudder. Well, fuck that for a game of soldiers, I thought.

The other route you can escape into as a non-posho literary author is horror, sf or fantasy. But they were kind of a boys' gang then, and mostly still are. What I really wanted to do was to take the outrageous tropes of those bastard genres and put them into literary novels. I wanted to create a wonderfully spicy stew of fictive elements...

Anyhow, somewhere between teaching all those courses that year, fighting to convince people I knew what I was on about, and editorial difficulties and ultimately the cancellation of my fourth novel (did I fall or was I pushed? The book was cancelled either way…) I lost my confidence. Somewhere between the devil and the deep blue sea. I found myself alone with my manuscript and all my confidence suddenly gone. My great new editor had said my book was nonsense and my agent couldn't help.

The book, as far as I could tell, was ruined.

This felt just like being a tightrope walker, jolted out of his delicate spell of concentration. He looks down, sees the ground, and wobbles. He needs to get his balance back right away or he's going to plummet to his doom.

So I put 'Fancy Man' away. Up in the attic in the house I'd bought in Norwich. Every copy of the manuscript. The one where I chopped it down to half its length. The one where I excised all the Magical Realist elements. The one where I chopped out all the aliens and cocks. The version where I edited out the long section set in the brothel above the gay sauna on Leith Walk, run by the woman with no legs. The version where I'd hacked each scene into exquisitely arty, poetic fragments… Every single copy I put away out of my sight.

Then I went and did my best to forget all about it. My year with Wendy and Timon, Aunty Anne, Colin, Belinda, Captain Simon, Uncle Pat. I abandoned the freakish lot of them, people who'd been as real to me as anyone I knew in 1998.

I got on with life. I started a whole new novel in 1999 – 'Modern Love', which was a very dark domestic thriller with no fantasy at all and lots of murders. It came out with a different publisher – my third – in the year 2000, when I was thirty.

Time moved on. Eventually we moved cities and jobs and houses. I chucked out boxes, folders, files, papers, letters and manuscripts. I chucked out, I thought, every remaining version of the doomed 'Fancy Man.' My partner Jeremy despairs at me throwing stuff out. I prefer to clear the decks, but he won't hear of it.

Anyhow – fast forward to 2016.

There's the marvelous news that Lethe want to republish my

first three novels, with new covers, introductions, added extras and contemporaneous short stories. I'm cockahoop. Writing these introductions for them, I still can't resist grinning at the very thought of these books being made available again.

Then, when I'm racketing about in old boxes in the Beach House at the bottom of our garden (we live in Manchester now, in a leafy enclave down by the railway lines) I find something interesting amongst my old files. Amid the letters and old stories and notes and ideas I find 'Fancy Man' again.

I assume at first it's the tidied-up version. The truncated version. The bowdlerized or bastardized version. But it's none of these. It turns out to be the four hundred page version. It turns out I hadn't binned it after all. Not even in a fit of pre-millennial self-loathing and pique.

It spent six years in the Norwich attic, then ten years in the Manchester cellar and then a year or two mouldering in the Beach House. It's damp and blotchy and warped.

I read it all again, very slowly.

And I love it, all over again.

It seems very me. Me as I was at twenty-nine. Not as hampered and crushed down and worried and care-worn as I became a little later on.

It's like finding a little clone of yourself, or a recording of your voice with your friends, or a set of photographs of a happy time you didn't even know had been printed.

So.

I feel confident all over again about the 'Fancy Man' phase of my writing career. The novel reads like a missing link in my books and it should rightly slot into 1999 – right between 'Could it be Magic?' and 'Modern Love.' Now the whole story can be told. It's been restored and polished up and put with the others.

It's there to be enjoyed. Even though it's full of freaks, oddities, aliens and cocks. Welcome back to the end of the twentieth century.

Gateshead

On Friday I took the train north from Levenshulme and Manchester. I returned to the North East. Through County Durham the fields and forests were so green. Miles and miles of green, and then those deep gullies in the woods and the winding rivers.

At Newcastle Central Station I took a cab driven by an old man – a Geordie Sikh in a natty turban. 'It's been so warm and blue all day. Was it like that in Manchester? I think someone is smiling down at us for the start of the weekend.'

A kind audience at Gateshead library. Not a huge number, fewer than twenty in this purpose-built lecture hall. There were twelve year old Doctor Who fans ('I regenerated every night of the half-term break and wore a different Doctor's outfit every day!'), older readers, polite young men, a shy girl with her mum, and three Gothed-up ladies who'd tried to attend one of my readings a couple of years ago, in Whitby. ('We had to stand outside the bookshop on the cobbled street in the dark! It was so busy inside they wouldn't let us in. And we'd driven all the way down from Newcastle, just to see you! We were absolutely furious!'

Oh yes -! The one time I'd sold out completely! I felt so guilty. Sixty hardbacks were sold that night, I was told. It was amazing, but I still didn't understand why these three (with their kohl make-up, their basques and their batwings) hadn't been allowed inside. But I'm more than happy to sign their books this evening.

There's a nice, enthusiastic poet from the university – tall, gangling and stooping down to talk. He's got electrified hair. 'I just love what you do. I have done for years. You see the heart of a story, or whatever you're doing. And you go straight to it and grab it, and everything follows on from that. It seems so simple and plain, but it's not. It's completely different to most people, most writers… I tell my writing students this. Don't go covering everything in fancy writing and deflection – that's what they do! They cover it all up and obscure it on purpose – because they're hiding the fact that they don't know what it's even about. Or where or what the heart actually is.'

Later, I was getting a taxi to my hotel, which was in a field in Low Fell, right underneath that grand, metal statue of the Angel of the North. I thought – yeah, that is what I try to do, isn't it? I think about it – and I try to get the story to break open for me. Or the memoir piece, or non-fiction piece, or the review, or blog, or workshop idea or whatever it is that I'm working on.

No, not even thinking about it too hard. Not letting myself worry at it. I just let it all wrangle around inside there, deep underground. I let the thinking about it get on with itself. After all these years I have learned to trust my own processes. I don't have to lean too hard on my conscious mind. I can let the old unconscious work its mysterious magic, and gradually let go of the image, thought, sound, idea – the very thing that forms the heart of the story.

And it will come – or it won't.

Or it might manifest itself obligingly – and I might forget it. I hope not. I hope I'll catch it. I keep umpteen notebooks going all the time – in different rooms and bags and on piles of books, everywhere to hand as I move through my days. I do this in order to capture these things that pop out of my subconscious. These hearts of stories. These floating seeds.

I always have a notebook very close by.
Do you?

That is the first, easiest bit of Creative Writing teaching.

When people ask that perennially favourite question: 'Ah, but can Creative Writing actually be taught?'

I always ask back, 'Do you carry a notebook?'

Did someone one tell you to?

That was the first, very necessary bit of Creative Writing teaching you received.

That's the first lesson. It was my first one.

The second lesson is:

Write whatever the hell you want to, and it's okay.

Has anyone ever taught you that, yet?

No? Then you need to be taught it.

Yes? Then you've been lucky.

You've been well taught.

So, I always have confidence that I can find the heart of the story.

By sleeping on it. That's one way. By letting my sleeping self dissolve away all the unnecessary stuff and pick out the clean, bare bones.

What you have to find is a way to fight off all the other distractions. Then you can see what the heart of the story is. You have to find the way that works for you. For me it's about sitting quite still and focusing on what it is I most want to write in the whole world. Right here and now.

What is it?

Here's your exercise.

What's at the heart of your story?

How can you tell?

Staring too hard at the same old thing won't always help you find out.

Tinkering with the same old thing – revising, rehashing, mucking it about – well, that might help. But not always.

Putting it away and letting it rest can be good. Put some distance between you and this particular piece of writing. Don't be so caught up in it.

I love to remember that bit in the Orton Diaries when Joe is becoming successful and in demand. He's going from one commissioned piece of work to the next, and learning to be businesslike and focused about it. When he completes his first draft of the stage play 'Loot' he tells us that he puts it away for six months in order to 'let it mature.'

It sounds like this is something happening to the manuscript of its own accord. Like it's fermenting and bubbling away like homemade wine.

But Orton is of course talking about heady changes going on inside himself. He's talking about letting his mind forget about all the particulars and all the ephemeral stuff in his script. And we must do the same. All the bits of our writing that we've become over-fond of, the neat turns of phrase, the surface cleverness… all the stuff and fluff we clog it up with. We have to wonder if it's all best-placed. Haven't we just put it there to disguise the fact that we don't know what the story's about yet? We're hiding the gap at the heart of the tale with a bit of spit and polish and hoping for the best…

Let it mature.

Let your memory of the particulars fade.

After a month, say, take the manuscript out again, or open the file – and then reread. And aren't there bits that you want to trim away, straight away? Jokes that seemed funny at the time.

Over-explanatory bits that seemed so necessary back then. Fancy, fiddly things that you thought were just dandy... they kind of make you cringe now. And doesn't that bit read like a bad pastiche of whoever it was you were reading just then?

You were gilding the lily a bit, weren't you?

Taking your writing out and holding it up in the light can be quite liberating. You can be frank, even brutal with yourself. It doesn't hurt as much as an instant self-critique. After a month – you're a different person!

So give the pages a bit of a shake and see what dust and glitter falls off. See what's left behind.

Read the piece aloud. Which bits turn to ashes in your mouth? Which parts are still excitingly alive? Which bits surprise you?

Another way of doing this is by refusing to read your original draft. Learn to trust that the essence is already in your head. Redo the whole thing from memory (I seem to remember reading this is how DH Lawrence did some of his second drafts! Word processors make things too easy. They glibly preserve everything we hammer out.)

What's essential? Does it all come back to you?

Don't worry. The original draft is still there on your hard drive, in cold storage. You could still hoik it back out if you want to rescue all or part of it.

Remember, though – I'm telling you – it's good for your writing soul to chuck stuff out. To abandon things and crumple them up and move on.

I think we can get too precious about these things.

If you labour over them and tinker with them too much, all the energy can start to leak out. Your stories will turn into zombies, still shambling around, but with bits hanging off, and held together only by sticking plaster, crusty scabs and hellish will power.

Sometimes you've just got to stake those suckers through the heart, chop off their heads and move onto something new.

Don't get precious!

Here's something else. A way to put some distance between you and your current story. A way of breaking it open to find the heart.

Put it down. Go and do something else.

Do this. Have a very deep, hot bubble bath in the middle of the day. Lie back. Close your eyes.

Let the quandary of your story sink through the deeper levels of your mind. Let your mind tick over anything it wishes to.

Nine times out of ten – for me – before the bathwater's even lukewarm, the answer comes to me. The story wakes up again and suddenly I'm jumping out of the bath, drying and dressing all in a rush. I can't get to my pages quick enough to write down the few, crucial thoughts that have surfaced.

It might only be one word.

But it's enough.

As I said earlier, sleeping on it is good, too.

You need a special notebook placed permanently on your bedside table, along with a collection of pens. Try going to sleep with the thought of your story in your head. Again, let it sink down and down as you relax towards sleep.

When you wake up – be it 3 a.m, 7 a.m, or midday – before you even sit up – ravel up the threads of the dreams you've been having. Grab that notebook and write down the first thoughts in your head. Capture the images in the most straightforward, vivid phrases.

Most often you'll find an answer there.

Maybe it won't be obvious straight away. And maybe it won't work every single time. But there will be at least something intriguing there. Something worth considering once you're back in the land of the living.

Do this.

Consider a piece you wrote a few weeks ago and put away unfinished.

There must be something. What was it? A story? A blog piece? A first chapter that ran out of steam? A fragment of a memory? Or maybe a letter, even, to a member of your family, about something important?

Something that you abandoned, anyway. For whatever reason.

Have a think back, and bring it back to mind.

Is it your ongoing novel? How long have you been at it now? How far through your first, third, seventh draft are you? When did you last sit down seriously with it?

Okay. Now, you have ten minutes.

Every piece of writing – whatever it is – implicitly asks big questions of the world.

Tell me now – what are the two big questions your piece of writing is asking of the world?

And give me these two questions in words of one syllable only.

Getting into Heads

I'm speaking here as someone who might be described as a 'gay writer.' Often, if a bookseller or a newspaper wants to refer to you, they want a pigeonhole, and that's the one I can get. Great.

Immediately, a limitation is set upon you, once you are labelled like this.

But we are here to use our imaginations, and to get into heads that are not our own, nor anything like our own.

Whoever we are, it's always difficult to get into another head. Whatever makes us want to be fiction writers leads us to want to know what it's like to be inside somebody else's head.

But the 'gay' tag is a tricky one. It's useful for political visibility, solidarity and all the rest of it – much as 'feminist' was a useful strategic label for a host of women writers of the Seventies generation... but it does make me wonder what people might expect of a 'gay' writer.

Can he get into the heads of his straight characters?

Gay men are known for writing well about women. See, for good examples, the work of E.M Forster, Angus Wilson, Patrick Gale. But what about straight men?

Can you write with any authenticity about the inner lives of people diametrically the opposite of you? Men whose dreams and desires are quite different to your own.

How 'authentic' does it have to be? Isn't it all just made up, anyway?

Can we fake it on the page?

Is writing just one big drag act? A series of impersonations and postures?

Getting into a character's head is a very intimate, strange thing. You really know when it's working, and when it isn't. The character really does speak to you.

There is a sense in which, when you're really writing a character, and are really imaginatively close to them... it is as if you are both slumped together in stupid, drunken complicity. For the two of you it is as if it's perpetually last thing at night in the pub. Closing time, and the staff are sweeping up the fag butts and sawdust and mopping up the spills. The two of you are murmuring, protesting: 'You're my best mate, you are. You know that, don't you? You're my best, best mate.' Whoever, whatever they are. That's how you feel about your characters. And I think it *has* to be like that.

Here's a relatively straightforward exercise, that will allow you to start to create a character, and to think from their point of view.

Choose a photograph or a painting of a stranger, in a magazine, newspaper or book.

Describe them physically, from your own point of view.

Describe them physically, from their own point of view, in their own voice.

Write for five minutes, in their voice, letting them describe their favourite room.

Write for ten minutes, letting them talk about the best year in their life.

Write for ten minutes, letting them describe the worst day of their life.

Think of three really tricky, personal questions to ask your character. You know their secrets. Think up a way of winkling those secrets out of them.

In the voice of your character, reply to the three questions...

First, giving the public response, to your interviewer.

Secondly, giving the – perhaps truer – private response, as if inside your own head.

Think about the ways you can get your character to give themselves away... without them even knowing it.

PART TWO

—

DOING

Getting Into It

I'm sitting in Blackshaws café in Stockport market place on Sunday afternoon. Jeremy's been rummaging through a thousand vinyl albums on the record stalls.

Walking along, I was thinking about reading Haruki Murakami. I'm in the middle of his most recent, massive novel. I find it all a bit wanky in places – especially the way he goes on about women and making them into fantasy creatures more than actual people. But there is still something that draws you into his books. He holds you in his world. I would find it hard to disengage and stop reading this novel, unlike a couple of other books I've nipped in the bud recently. (The fifty page rule is very liberating! If you put it down after fifty pages, are you tempted to pick it back up again? Would you rather read something else..?)

Back in the early eighties, when I was about eleven my stepfather's widowed mother, Rini, moved into our home for a few months. She was my reading Guru for a while. She sat up very late at night, way into the early hours, reading paperbacks in the narrow spare bedroom. Her reading light would spill through the transom window and keep us all awake. I'd be envious of her being allowed to stay up all night reading. I'd imagine an adulthood where I never slept and read deep into the darkness every night.

She read almost anything. She loved great big thick romances. She had us searching all the bookshops of Darlington for a copy of 'Gone with the Wind,' which proved surprisingly elusive at that time. We eventually found it in a magical shop on the North Road that was called 'The Great Big Book Exchange.' When that door opened it was like stepping into Wonderland for all of us. Those were very happy Saturday afternoons, with the whole family building up a small pile of books each, and bringing in old, no-longer wanted books to trade.

When Rini lived with us, it was the first time I remember this phrase being used: 'I just couldn't get into it,' or 'that was so easy to get into.'

I loved that whole idea of 'getting into' a book. It conjured up the image – the very sensation – of stepping over a threshold into another world.

'Getting into' also connotes, I think, that idea of getting 'into' something – ie, becoming a fan. Often, the phrase was used about music. At that time we were all getting into 'New Wave' music – all the post-punk bands such as Blondie and the Police. We had all those albums. 'Scary Monsters' by David Bowie. Having good taste in music was important, and so was good taste in what you read.

'Getting into' could also mean literally getting into a space. A three-dimensional space. Or perhaps we could say that fictional space has four dimensions? Clearly a novel takes place in time itself: there is duration for the characters, and there is the subjective time of how long you, as a reader, actually spend inside the book. Reading is a curious interplay of time-schemes. I like to think of fiction as solidified time (in the way that ice is solidified water, perhaps. It is real life with the atoms crushed tighter together.)

Perhaps a book is simply a box filled with time. And you can enter it, play inside it, run with it, dawdle through it, or feel it passing through your fingers. You can wish it away, savour every moment, or skip the more tedious sections. You can take it at your own rate.

I think, as a child, I had problems with my reading stamina.

I was easily bored. I was even resistant. I had a boyish restlessness with books. I always got fidgety when it came to overly long descriptive passages…

But in more recent years I have seen these resistances as an early expression of taste. This is booorrrinnnggg! Get it moving! Make something happen!

It's very interesting – as writers – to listen to our own reactions, and to remember our early reactions – to the process of reading.

And remember that, if the reader's bored… it's not necessarily the fault of the reader's attention span…

We did exams in my secondary school and I revised like crazy. I made a revision timetable chart for the two weeks of the Easter Break in 1982. Most of the stuff I was rote-learning was just the usual hoop-jumping nonsense – algebra and snippets about Roman Britain and verb declensions. But one of the exams we were going to be sitting was in English and it was on the subject of Roald Dahl's 'Danny the Champion of the World', which we had read as a class that term.

I read that book once a day for ten days that Easter break.

When the class test came it was all about facts. Dull stuff. Questions about the events of the book, so that we could prove we had understood it all.

I was so familiar with the atmosphere of that novel. With every single detail of the lives of that boy and his father, and their caravan and the woods, and the details of their plan involving the raisins and the pheasants. I was familiar with the fabric of the novel and the sentences it was built out of. I had ravelled them up and taken them apart and read them again and again. I felt like I had spent two whole weeks inside that book.

All the factual details they tested us on soon vanished by the wayside. But I think a lot that I learned by getting so thoroughly inside that novel has stayed with me in all the years since.

Haruki Murakami himself writes a little about this business of 'getting into' a book. Early on in IQ84 two male editors are talking about the work of a young female writer. Though they find her writing clumsy and naïve, the story is still very gripping: it has about it that element of mystery that makes a piece of writing (that wonderful word) 'unputdownable.'

This is the quality, surely, that any editor is looking for, and any writer wants to evince? If your book is unputdownable then you have your reader captive. They have followed you into your world.

It's a quality that everyone – reader, writer, editor, reviewer, critic, teacher – finds impossible, in the end, to account for or explain.

If you could explain it away exactly, that might even ruin the magic.

I can list a whole bunch of books I've read this summer that have it. That Seventies shock-horror novel about the giant snake eating people in Central Park. That had it. That Chick Lit novel about the evening class: that had it. That very strange children's novel from the 1940s – with its off-kilter sense of humour and creepy atmosphere – that, weirdly, had it. On the other hand – the rambunctious comedy of manners about those ladies on holiday? It might be in the top ten paperbacks this week, but it really didn't have it. Neither did the first volume of that gazillions-selling sword and sorcery series. That didn't have the undefinable quality of perfect readability, either.

For me, anyway.

It's a very personal thing. Some things work for some people, others don't.

For me it has to be like butter melting on hot toast. That's the sensation of sinking into what I know is going to be a good book.

What shakes me out of a book?

The feeling like I've read this before, better, elsewhere. The feeling that this is a less bright, less engaging take on a theme or genre.

I also get shaken out of a book when I feel like it's taking itself too seriously.

Also, when it's forcing the comedy. Forced jollity makes me cringe.

I get shaken out of a book when it's all too earnest. When it's earnestly going about its stated aims and doing exactly what it says on the tin. I like stories to veer about and surprise me. (I know that's not how marketing works. That's what's frustrating about how books are marketed, of course: the fact that they want to mitigate against surprises, and that they suppose readers are buying tins of beans, rather than books. A good novel might *look* like a tin of beans, but actually contain swordfish, or sunflowers, or the rings of Saturn. Too many writers are happily filling those tins with beans because they've been told that readers just like beans…)

And yet… Murukami isn't funny. He's actually humourless. Even earnest. And sometimes he's a bit of a sexist old fart who goes on at length, explaining fairly mundane things to the reader.

So why do I get into him? And what is it about the world of Murakami that keeps me in?

Precisely because it *is* Murakami-world. His is a fictional realm unlike anyone else's. We know who we belong to when we are there. We know who controls the weather. It becomes a happy destination, even if it's pouring down and events take a frightening turn.

He has a definable, palpable world. If you've been there and its magic has worked on you, that space is carved into your head forever. It becomes locatable again, and you return there, the next time you pick up a book of his. This is true of many writers who have their own distinct styles and worlds: at random, I'd include Philippa Gregory, Rachel Joyce, Anne Tyler. I can find their world again, in my head, just by thinking about them. Each new book, or return to an old one, is an expansion of that world.

The worlds in our heads are infinite, of course.

It's all about the presence of a strong, unique story-telling voice on the page. It is the most essential thing there is in writing. That goes in the centre and the rest is either mystery or technique.

I actually had an agent tell me, in recent years: 'There's such a thing as being too unique.'

But there isn't.

There is far too much blandness in the world. Too many tins of beans containing... beans.

Blandness has got to be fought and countered.

A bland book can't hold me when I'm reading. There are bland books in the 'popular' line and in the 'literary' line. There's one particular prize-winning literary author of historical novels whose books I find so bland it's like licking margarine. Her books are completely non-stick. I can't believe anyone, anywhere, actually enjoys what she writes. But they must do. It's a failure of my own imagination – I accept this – that I think anyone must be crazy to get anything out of her crap.

But, you know. People still buy beige carpets. Some people hate food with too much spice. Some folk like a more neutral kind of life. Estate agents, maybe – who live their whole lives anticipating the bland needs and tastes of the lowest common factor.

Fiction painted in neutral tones is never going to hold me. Writing that precludes anything surprising, upsetting, dangerous or wildly funny is never going to get my vote.

In reading we vote with out feet. We get into it and we stay there. We go back to those worlds. We spend the money and we spend the time.

If you want to write you have to think a lot about this business of 'getting into' books. It's our bread and butter, innit?

Park avenue   November 3rd 2015

Haunted

You have to wait for the right moment to bring characters back to life.

I really believe this.

Sometimes they haunt your subconscious and flicker about at the edge of your vision. Other times they're jumping up and down trying to catch your attention.

But you can't fully do justice to them until the moment is right.

I guess this sounds a bit crazy, doesn't it?

Like the old clichéd idea of a writer's head being filled with all his or her characters dashing about inside. As a child I used to love that portrait of Charles Dickens in his study – have you seen the one? – and there are little puffs of smoke all around him, and characters from his novels can be seen floating around in each cloud. I thought it was a beautiful image of how writers carry all these people around with them, all the time.

Readers, too. We absorb characters, I think. When they've made a big impact upon us characters get incorporated by their readers and we never forget them. Readers are haunted just as palpably as writers are.

Anyhow, I was going to tell you about being haunted by Brenda and Effie.

These two characters are the mysterious sleuths in my series of six novels set in Whitby, beginning with 'Never the Bride', which I published in 2006 and wrote during the previous year.

But those characters and their town and the things they got up to had been in my head for quite a few years before that.

They'd been there since at least 1998.

Back then I was working at the University of East Anglia, and I was commissioned by Radio 4 to contribute an afternoon Short Story for their famous weekday slot. That week's collection of stories was to be themed around the idea of writers bringing new life to a nineteenth century novel by focusing on a lesser-known background character. I was told that, for example, the marvelous Shena Mackay was writing a tale from the view-point of Long John Silver's parrot.

For this, my first radio commission I was a last minute replacement, and I had less than twenty four hours to produce my 2,200 word story (precisely fifteen minutes when performed aloud.) I'll always be grateful to the legendary feminist writer Alison Fell for passing that commission over to me. She was our Writer-in-Residence that year and my pal in the next door office. When she found she didn't have time to do the story, she suggested me to the producer, in an act of collegiality that, effectively, changed my imaginative and creative life.

So, after a long day on campus I raced home on the bus and practically skipped all the way back to my rented house. I was so excited by the idea. Not least because I knew exactly who I was going to write about.

The Bride of Frankenstein.

Who'd ever done justice to her afterlife before? I meant, the version we read about in the original Mary Shelley novel. She gets constructed in a makeshift lab on a remote Scottish island. The great surgeon Frankenstein is bullied by his first-born monster to make him a mate but, upon seeing what he has done and, horrified at the thought of possible offspring, Herr

Doctor Frankenstein destroys his handiwork at once. He flees into the night, pursued by his monster, and the two leave the poor discombobulated lady behind.

I wanted to tell the tale – in my fifteen minute monologue – of what life had been like for the Bride in the ensuing two hundred years. Like many badly-treated women, she tells us, she had to pick herself up, put herself back together, and simply carry on.

Rushing home that Friday night, on the bus, down the street, letting myself through the front door, I could hear that voice. Homely, pungent, mysterious. I could actually hear her! I knew what Brenda the Bride of Frankenstein actually sounded like.

Actually, at that stage, she wasn't called Brenda. Her name in that first story was Bessie.

Her monologue was written in bursts of text throughout that night, on different bits of paper. I scratched away in pen and ink at the dining room table, sitting up all night with pots of tea turning darker and murkier as the hours passed.

I experimented. I free-associated. I sent myself into a trance. I took all the bits of writing so far and cut them all up into pieces and rearranged the order of paragraphs, sentences and each and every word. I tried to think how Brenda thought – this perplexing, scrambled, stitched-together woman. This creature of shreds and patches. What was her mind like? How did her thought processes flow? How did she reveal her secrets to her audience? How would she yield herself up? Would she tell all? Would she tease us? Would she hold everything back and just drop hints about her incredible, long ago past?

Dawn came up and the story was done.

And she was alive..!

I was very happy with the result, and I think my producer and the BBC were, too.

I remember listening with my partner Jeremy, in our new house, several months later. We had bought our house on

Onley Street and were filling it with all our stuff. We had men in doing plastering in the living room on the very day my story was broadcast. They took a break while 'Never the Bride' came on and we all listened – hearing the wonderful tones of actress Joanna Tope reverberating off the empty walls and the bare boards.

So that was Brenda in 1998.

Of course at the time I wondered whether I would tell more stories about Brenda. I'd brought her to life, and her snooty friend, Effie, and plopped them into the spooky town of Whitby. Were they really living in quiet retirement, though? Was this glimpse of Brenda really the first and last we'd see of her – right at the end of all the excitement of her life?

But other stories and other characters came my way instead.

Years went by. I wrote other stuff. I left one job, and left the city. Moved to another and started another job.

Still no Brenda.

Had I forgotten her?

Then in 2005 all of a sudden… I don't know what it was that provoked it.

It was the summer vacation starting. It was our first summer in this house in South Manchester. The lawn at the back was overgrown. I had a deckchair under the magnolia tree. I was sitting out there with a great thick pad of paper and I was writing in chunky black felt tip.

What was I meant to be writing?

My agent at the time had given me a very earnest talk about how I had to think very seriously about what I wrote next. I had to approach it very carefully and check out every stage with her. I had to do something we could all be confident about. Something that would 'break through' this time. Nothing too daft. Nothing 'cultish'. Something more mainstream.

Oh dear.

She was clear that I had to ratify my next fictional project with her first. We had to check and double check that it had *legs*. That it was viable. And that it was right for me.

Right. Okay.

I would do that.

Too often in the past, I thought, I had made the silly mistake of writing just what I wanted to. I had followed my own stupid, idiosyncratic nose. I had blundered into writing some of the least commercial or successful novels the world had ever known. Yes, I needed saving from myself and my ridiculous instincts.

Ok.

So what did I do?

I went out into the sun – it was late in May, 2005, and it was the beginning of a lovely long summer in Manchester. I flung myself down into the deck chair under the shade of that tree and I wrote and wrote like a demon. I wrote an entire book synopsis that afternoon in black felt tip. I wrote something like eight thousand words of outline for a novel called 'Never the Bride.'

Somehow, as soon as I was installed in that deck chair, my old ladies of Whitby came back to me. My spooky investigators were going into business!

And it felt supremely naughty, too. I was suddenly writing exactly what I wanted. And it was a very wayward, silly, eccentric novel I had in mind.

I just couldn't stop myself.

Not from writing that one, or the sequels that followed every year afterwards.

My then-agent despaired, I think.

But at least I was sure. At least I knew what I was doing.

But really, there was no choice in the matter.

I mean it. Even though it sounds crazy.

If you've got the knack of creating great characters – beware.

They will ambush you. Any time, any place. If you ignore them they won't go away. They'll wait years. Even when your agent wants you to write about something sensible… that could well be the moment that your characters decide to… POUNCE!

Do this.

Choose a character you have invented before.

Someone you have created – but you don't know the end of their story yet.

Someone who still intrigues you, but there has been no chance to revisit them yet.

Is there a character you've invented who you've even forgotten?

Or one you've never written a single word about? You've just been carrying them about in your head..?

Write them now. Summon them up.

Draw them out like a genie from the lamp.

Write their name at the top of a page.

Now spend twenty minutes writing down everything you know about them.

Have they got *legs*?

Hindsight

At some point you'll want to write about your childhood. Most people end up doing it. Often it's the first novel or story that people publish. It's as if we need to sort it out, somehow, before we can move on, into making up other lives. We need to tidy childhood up, or scrutinize it through making it into a story. We need to know who we've been and where we have come from. Some people go in for analysis. Writers tend to rove over all the bits of childhood they thought they had forgotten. They are always shaping tales out of formative memories and adventures. And all of it is interesting to them. Every little bit.

Jeremy said to me – only recently: 'Why do you have to go over things from the past again and again? Things that just make you miserable?'

I was flabbergasted. 'But… but that's what I *do!*'

Sometimes people write that stuff and it's best hidden out of the way. It's one long, lonely, first person rant: adolescent poetry writ large. 'Screaming out of the window,' as Margaret Atwood once memorably put it.

You can, however, learn to craft your autobiographical fiction into something more rounded and fully fledged. You can develop it so that it can be pushed out into the world, and start to mean something to other people, as well as yourself.

There was a poet – I forget who it was! Sorry! – talking on Radio 4 recently, about the business of writing autobiographically, and learning to push the work into the world as a piece of writing, rather than a scream. The wonderful image this poet came up with was the balloon. It's filled with your breath – and you've puffed and puffed and puffed. But you've also learned the knack of tying the knot, and pushing the balloon away, to float up, away from you.

Fantastic image!

You just need to learn the knack – of when to stop puffing, how to tie the knot… and how to set it free.

I'm a firm believer in empathy. I think, no matter who you are or where you're from, if you write these stories well enough, people will find correspondences in them, and echoes of their own lives. You can be from vastly different generations and cultures, but if you're writing well, your story will still strike chords.

(BTW That's why I can't be doing with fiction that is aimed at a particular set of readers in a very gender-specific, or culture-specific way: the awful assumption being that you only want to read books by and about people who are like you. That's just weird, isn't it? I thought we read fiction to get into other people's heads, and to experience massively different things to what we are used to.)

I wrote my own semi-autobiographical novel, *Strange Boy* when I was 31. I'd already written and published a whole lot of utterly made-up novels before then. I waited and waited till I felt like I could properly tackle and fictionalise the story of the summer when I was ten. And I wrote it as a kids' book because I wanted people from that age and upwards to read it.

By the age of 31 I had learned enough about crafting novels, I felt, to do justice to the material. I'd learned that balloon-tying knack.

Here are some random pointers about looking back and putting together a fictionalised account of your past…

You have to think in terms of scenes. You can't just talk at us and explain everything. You have to put us right back there, in the past. You have to conjure the rooms and the people and the dynamics and the scenes. You have to rescue all four dimensions from the past. Your memory will supply bits and pieces – perhaps the bulk of it – but you will still have to invent other parts.

Give yourself licence to invent things. If you don't know a detail or a date or a fact, it's just going to have to be okay to make it up. This isn't gospel truth. You aren't in the dock. This is a story, a novel. Stories will have their own way.

Get ready to offend people. Be prepared for kick off! It's worth looking into libel law, actually. Seriously. Don't go out of your way to character-assassinate people. They can sue, if they are still alive, and if you're saying stuff that will make them look terrible, or if it interferes with their public or professional life. If you're basing things on real life: be careful.

But, even if you're being quite nice about people, it can still be dodgy. They can still get the pip. Check out with them, if need be. Give them pages to read.

Don't write as revenge. It isn't worth it. Get some therapy.

Or wait till they are all dead. Then you can write as revenge.

Back to the practical pointers:

Think of your child-self as the *focalizer* of your story. Chances are, if you are a writer now, you were a listener then. Put your child-self in the centre of the story, whether they are the first person narrator, or not.

That means they must appear in every scene, and filter and comment on all the info we receive about the world around them.

The child-self hero in a novel is a kind of spy. They go shuttling between the adult world and the kid world. Remember that? Both sides suspicious of each other, with their own separate languages and rituals.

Remember how it was to look out through those eyes. To be at that height. Remember the things that made you laugh then, and the things that drew your attention. Are they the same things as now?

You are reconstructing a view-point, and the preparations can be as complex as they are for forming a whole new, fictional view-point. Are you still the same character as you were then? Can you truly say that you are? (See? It can get philosophical, this business…)

Don't let your all-wise, all-knowing adult voice intrude. 'Ah yes, I didn't know it then, but what was in fact, actually happening…' This can ruin all drama and suspense. It sounds terrible, and makes the whole thing tend towards sentimentality. Keep your adult-self out of it! Out! That grown-up voice stands in the way of the reader's access to the past.

Stay in the moment. Be brave enough to stay in the moment as it was.

Don't let the voice (first person confessional? Second person insinuating? Third person with-slight-ironic-distance?) intrude too much. Let characters, events and dialogue speak for themselves. And don't let that narrating voice comment judgementally: 'Oh, the sad, sad people! Oh, they were so poor!' Just show how things *seemed* to the focalizing character back then. Record only those impressions.

Don't have huge swathes of text theorizing on the subject of memory! Nope! Useless! Delete them! They make everything fuzzy and misty and indistinct. People have been theorizing that stuff for longer than we can remember. The human race doesn't need any more of it: especially not right in the middle of the tale of how, when you were five, Mr Flopsy the bunny had to be put down.

Make things clear and immediate. Do everything you can to make us feel involved.

Open these experiences out to us. Who surrounds the child at the centre of the story? Who is in their lives at this point? What are the limits of the child's world? What rooms? What visits? What's the wallpaper like back then? What does the child obsess about?

In this – and any other kind of fiction, come to that – the focus needs to be narrowed and carefully controlled in order to draw the reader in. When it gets too diffuse and anarchic – the narrating voice zipping here! There! Everywhere! – you run the very real risk of losing your reader's attention. Funnel all the details and impressions through one single body.

Just because you can remember it, it doesn't have to be there. Remember: detail is good. Off the wall, quirky detail is good. But indiscriminate detail – everything-but-the-kitchen-sink detail is boring. Don't cram it in for the sake of it. The rules of fiction still apply – the harsh, ruthless rules of editing – even if the material is something very close to you. Keep it moving! Don't dally for the sake of it!

Make sure the kids' friends are brought properly to life. They are what we compare your child-self to. How is the hero of this story differrent to his/her peers? What marks them out? What makes their POV special? Why are they the hero of their own story…? You've got to answer those questions – implicitly.

As with detail, same with secondary characters. Only include relevant ones, who pay into the story. It's not like sending Christmas cards: it doesn't matter if so-and-so will be cross to be left out. Sometimes you have to double characters up, in order to make the piece work dramatically.

Compare fiction with non-fiction. Compare DH Lawrence's *Sons and Lovers* with biographies written about him. Or Collette's fiction with Judith Thurman's wonderful biography. Anthony Burgess's two memoirs and his autofictional novels with Andrew Biswell's biography. *What have they done to their own lives?*

Do you lie? How much? Do you make yourself better, stronger, braver, nastier, worse? Do you make your mother the heroine and your father the villain, like Lawrence did? Do you distort things deliberately? Anything you do will distort things, from somebody's point of view. This isn't about writing an objective history of your past. How can it be? It's a piece of fiction.

BEWARE: if you write the story really well, you will find that, eventually, it will supplant your original memories. Seriously. The human brain likes well-constructed tales. It will abandon messy memory in favour of a well-crafted story. It's as if we only have a certain amount of room on the hard-drive: or maybe it doesn't like files that bear the same title. But be prepared for a weird sensation of replacing your own memories with something you've buffed up and honed and reconstructed.

What does *that* say about who we are? And how we create ourselves, and recreate our own identities every day..?

You need to time travel first. You need to get in amongst all those seething, tangled childhood memories. Put yourself back there. Recover the sights and sounds and smells and textures.

Go back to old houses. Pore over photos. Get all the old diaries and school books out.

I go crazy on Ebay. I've been buying up the records and TV shows and comics and books from my childhood. We moved around a lot, from one council estate to the next, and we couldn't keep all our stuff. We always had so much stuff! And now I'm collecting it all back up... David Bowie bootleg tapes, *Planet of the Apes and Dracula Lives!* comics... Target *Doctor Who* novlisations... These are the things that put me right back there.

So... *stuff.* Tactile, nostalgic stuff.

Now you need to brainstorm.

Do some writing routines – start short – ten minutes – and build up to an hour – teasing out strands of memory. 'That was the day when...' and 'That first morning at seconday school...'

Natalie Goldberg suggests a great memory exercise in her

book, *Writing Down the Bones*. She gets you to write for twenty minutes or so, without thinking or editing, or taking your hand off the page. You begin with 'I remember…' and you see where it goes. As soon as you start to run out of steam with one particular memory, you write down 'I remember' again, and hurtle into another, separate memory. And again and again. You can get some brilliant stuff out of this.

I would add to that some prompts, in order to narrow your focus: things like, My first field trip away from home; the fairground; the Top Twenty on the radio on Sunday nights; darts night at my paternal grandparents' house, etc.

In doing these exercises you will find yourself remembering things you had thought gone forever.

It can be uplifting and moving – and it can also upset you. Be careful with yourself.

＊

From the writing routines in exercise two, pluck out the best unearthed moment. You're going to reconstruct it as a fictional scene. Remember: Editing! Pace! Staying in the moment! Focus! Drama! Characterisation! Dialogue! Use all the fictionalising techniques you know.

Keep to this one scene and write it as fully and richly as possible.

Learn that knack of tying the knot.

And letting it float free.

I Like to Sit in Cafes...

...and bars, and watch what's going by on the street.

I like to watch what's happening at the other tables.

Here's a flashback to a Cologne gay bar, in November 1999. We were there doing workshops with UEA students, and students from the University of Cologne's English Seminar. We had a few hours off from British Council stuff, and I was in a bar, writing.

This is how I keep my journal. Of course, it's not the only way.

I think the waiter here has told the woman in the glittery shawl and leopard print jumper that I've been drawing her. She just laughed.

Jeremy's left for a final spin around the shops and Christmas markets. Those shops filled with silver Christmas decorations and golden tableware have lured him back.

The woman in the shawl and the leopardskin jumper comes in here every night, I reckon. She sits at the slate tables at teatime and the only other people here are gay men, meeting after work. Cher, then Randy Newman playing: *I'm Wishing on a Star.*

She's all in silver and gold and she's drinking her Tequila Sunrise slowly. She knows how to pace herself, letting the orange and yellow stripes settle in the long glass. Her hair is a perfect grey meringue.

She reminds me of that woman in the Italian bar in Soho – the one we sent Arwen over to quiz. We sent Arwen over with a flute of champagne, and the woman told her story, of course – about her brother who went missing some time in the 1950's – he vanished somewhere in the alleys of Soho – and he'd left her a scrawled address on a piece of paper. Arwen said the piece of paper was black with forty years' dirt. The old woman uncrumpled it on the wet glass bar. A place, a time and a date in 1960. A Friday night when they were supposed to meet again. And the woman had been back every Friday night since, hoping that he'd turn up to surprise her.

She wore a vast black astrakhan coat. All from real lambs, she assured Arwen. It was crusted with grease.

The people at the bar and at the other tables in cafes are the people you have met or imagined before. Some you have clean forgotten and others you are yet to meet. Maybe later you can match and judge dates and times and realise that you must have been in the same place and time, and then you'll both laugh. Not many people are strangers to you.

The bars and clubs of Soho remind you now of Dr Fu Manchu: and how he lured Dr Petrie and Nayland Smith into opium dens with a deftly dropped series of clues. He got them scrabbling onto a skylight: looking down at a haremful of girls and government ministers. The room below teemed with smoke and vice… and then he set fire to the building, and watched with satisfaction from the corner of Greek Street.

How addicted you've become to the novels of Sax Rohmer. And really, you don't usually like detective fiction. But… oh – when the badly-maimed Fu Manchu – the scourge of the civilised west – has a silver bullet lodged inside his wonderfully wicked brain… and when he kidnaps Dr Petrie, snaring him with the beautiful slave girl Karameneh – and when he forces him to perform brain surgery on his worst enemy in a makeshift operating theatre in a Soho sewer ...! How could you not become addicted to fiction like that..?

I'm getting drunk in a bar at teatime. The students have been sent off to do the writing exercise I devised, about exploring and recording the city.

(See the end of this chapter for instructions.)

Some of the results we've had already have been amazing. They're writing really well: loosely and crazily, and getting the good stuff. Richard, who's running the German end of the show, asked me how it is I get them to write *fluently* like that.

Good word for it. I like that: fluent. Because, really, you often see writers stymied and cross, cudgelling their brains: timidly unable to get on with it.

What I try to tell him is: I set *loose* parameters for them. My instructions are specific, but loose enough for fun. I get them to enjoy themselves, each other and where they are. I try to remind them that once upon a time, they started out writing because they liked to do it. It was important to them. It made them feel brave and grand.

I try to make them realise that what they think up is valid. Nothing they note down in their writers' diaries is too silly or trivial. You might not see the sense in it yet, but you will do eventually, I tell them.

I tell them to get it all down and cram it with colour and life and noise. I'm trying to teach them to write journals in the freewheeling and loopy way that I do. I taught myself how to do that when I lived in Edinburgh in the mid-nineties. It was my first time away from education. I'd published my first novel. I was teaching myself to write all over again (as I think you have to – again and again: reinventing the wheel.) And my journals were – and are – the best place to do that.

At that point, I'd been at the same university for seven years: I had three degrees under my belt. But I learned more about writing sitting at café tables in Edinburgh than I ever had done before.

Your notebook for company: like the thick, spiral bound book you've bought here in Cologne. There's even a black and white photo of a nice café on the cover. You're obsessed!

But how happy it makes you. Your book open and ready, soft and cool like a just turned pillow. A glass of wine and a coffee and you're alone with a barful of people you are starting to make into characters...

She's still there – the woman in the silver-threaded shawl and the leopard-print jumper. Sipping her Tequila Sunrise and staring ahead, with a ghost of a smile on her face, as if she knows you're drawing her, or writing about her. It's as if she's saying: Go on then, guess! Guess why I'm here! Guess who I am and what secrets I've got up my batwing sleeves...

The basis of this is the assumption that stories are everywhere. Anecdotal, personal, historical, gossippy, legendary, mythological. In a city, the stories are palimpsested even more thickly.

This exercise is about going out into a city that you know very well.

You find a favourite spot – indoors or out. It could be a graveyard or a pub. A department store or under a bridge.

You have to write a piece in your own diary voice. Let it wander and stray and observe your setting. Pluck some of those stories about the place out of the air, and set them down. Weave them together with all the associations this place has for you.

It's great to do this with a group: and everyone sets off separately, off to different parts of the city. You can draw maps of how to get there. I'm interested when people draw maps and do some observational sketches, as well as produce writing, in order to fix their place on paper.

Then, when everyone has returned to the centre – or the workshop – work is swapped around. And you get someone else's writing and drawing. You find their place in the city using their hand-drawn map, and you pick up the threads of story they have left behind. Do something with the stories and impressions that they have drawn out of the air. Continue them, subvert them, add to them.

This is a good exercise for trying out collaborative writing – which is useful for preventing you getting too precious about your work. You have to hand your work over and let someone else change it and complete it. And you have to do justice to somebody else's work.

I've led this workshop in Cologne and Norwich and Manchester, and the results are always fascinating. You end up with a weird, verbal, anecdotal map of a city. You can add to that drawings, photos, video clips – as we once did in Great Yarmouth on the *Fear and Loathing in Great Yarmouth* tour that set out in a charabanc from UEA. That was a great day out. Making our days memorable is how we bring writing to life, I think.

I like those trips, and traipsing around cities with other writers. As writers we spend so much time in the house, sitting at tables and computers.

I'm keen to get out and about, on outings.

I Wrote About our Dying Cat...

I wrote about Fester in his last few days, in the spring of 2013. I had a feeling I was going to want to tell the story of his life with us. He'd wandered into our lives and our house at the age of twelve, in 2006, and he never left.

We'd never had a pet of our own like that, for whom we were solely responsible, and who had chosen *us*.

When he died I knew there would be writing involved.

29th March.

'...And they turned off at the next path and, although they left this particular story, they carried on having adventures of their own.

'And maybe one day we'll get to hear about them.'

For me this has to be one of the most important sentiments in all kinds of fiction. In any kind of writing.

The people, characters, friends, family... everyone who leaves you and your story – who choose to leave, or who find they have to – they go on having adventures elsewhere.

Right now I'm rereading Michael Ende's 'The Neverending Story' and every character peels off from the main narrative, and goes away.

Everyone is the star of their own spin-off story.

How important this idea is to you.

Let them leave. Three dots… an ellipsis… and it's their footsteps leaving the page. Wave them off happily. Eventually there'll be word from them. A message. Perhaps even a reunion in the future. Another shared tale.

It's a very quiet Good Friday morning here. Just a clean, cool breeze at last. Jeremy is still asleep. So is Fester.

In the six-and-a-half years he has lived with us Fester Cat has taught us how to become a family. He has shown us how to live in one house together, and how to learn to be happy.

He made us be in one room. He would shepherd us until we were both sitting together. He was content when we were where he was, and both in his sightline. He would never let us split apart.

He taught us how to sit nicely, like he did.

He always sat so daintily and tidily, with his paws placed just so, underneath his chin. He was a very neat, very small black and white cat. He had the most perfect black eyeliner under both eyes, and a top lip that rode up like Elvis's, because of his teeth.

He taught us all about relaxing. His whole live with us was a history of different perches: of safe havens and special spots. He enjoyed long spells of curling up and working slowly towards that most contented of sighs – which he taught me to share. Sit here and relax and then do a really big, happy sigh.

He brought all this wisdom to our house, up the back garden, up the back steps and into the kitchen.

He was a stray who taught us how to live in our house.

Sunday 31st.

He's been gone just over twenty-four hours.

I've realized that his whole accomplishment was to make being happy seem so easy.

He taught me the truth of that.

Sunday afternoon I set myself a vital writing exercise. I need to get everything down before I forget it all.

What I need is a huge long list. Don't even try to write sentences about him or our lives of the past six years. Just list anything you remember. The tiny specifics.

Before they melt away.

The blue satin blanky

A kiss at the top of the stairs

Boop on his nose

Cat disco at lunchtime

Sniffing the morning and evening news at the open front door...

Dangerous animals – biting a frog.

My Smorgasbord...

Checking for monsters (last thing at night)...

The list goes on for three whole pages. It finishes with:

Feeling unwell and what to do?

The time I came home in triumph and got better.

And the time that I didn't.

The feeling that I'll always be in Fester's garden.

By the end of the list I realized that I was writing in his voice. I had adopted the first person. In my writing I had become my own dead cat.

When he was still an outdoors cat – when he was younger and there were fewer bullies living on the street - I'd call him in at night from the front doorstep, jangling my house keys and calling his name.

He'd appear in the street, under one of the lamps, or hop out from under a hedge. 'Ungow?'

It's amazing to think now that we'd let him stray and wander like that. Before Ralph came on the scene, ambushing and scrapping.

There was nothing like Fester Cat running towards you – and he really could run like the clappers when he wanted to. It was a joyful scamper. He did bunny hops. He flung himself straight at you.

2nd April.

I had to keep writing. I was so upset I just had to bury myself in writing.

I had started writing in a voice I had invented for him. It didn't seem invented at the time. It was slangy and Mancunian and a bit of a tough little wise-guy voice (but really very soft underneath): and it matched him. It was Fester's voice.

So I hid myself away as only a writer can. I started writing his story, in his own voice. And I started it sometime prior to his first moving in. I gave him stray cat friends – Bessy and Korky. They were real. Bessy was a large and powerful stray and Korky had a home, but liked to knock about with the street cats. I started extrapolating a life for them in these Manchester streets and gardens…

It quickly took on a life of its own.

I sat all day long on those bright days of the Easter weekend and the week that followed… I started writing more words per day than I ever had before. Six thousand, eight thousand, ten thousand. His voice never wavered. I wrote chapter after chapter. It was like he was bursting to tell his own story and I was just the medium…

9th April.

A week later and I've got all these pages. What is it I'm writing? Is it a book? Do I dare to call it that? Isn't that a bit naff? Even exploitative?

Or is it just for me? And for a few select friends of Fester Cat? Something to share with them, when it's finished. Something to memorialize that special little, gentle stray.

One morning, about a week after his death, I woke up and wrote my journal (in my own voice. Luckily, I hadn't lost track of that, in all my obsession.)

'I grew up thinking that all the best times had already happened. I had parents who were full of regrets. They were filled with bitterness and anger. Also, they were people who had been teenagers in the 1960s, and they would always tell you that there'll never be a better time in which to be young. So, I grew up in the 1980s and it felt like a let-down. I grew up with the idea of disappointment as a way of life.

'Now, a cat doesn't see it like that. They never think in decades or eras and they don't have this legacy of familial stuff on their shoulders. Cats don't have dogma.

'Cats are all about living the best life that they can right here and right now.'

I wrote this in my journal that morning, and it seemed so true to me.

The voice I'd created for Fester was telling me to stop hankering back with misplaced nostalgia. I had to enjoy life in the now. The sunlight is just as good as it always was. That's all a cat cares about. The days are just as long and as busy and as good as they ever were.

Let's learn to like our lives as they are.

I was being taken over by his voice every day, and thinking about all the events of his tiny life, and he was still teaching me about the way to live. That's what it felt like.

Do your very best to be happy. Write joyfully about the things you love. Do justice and tell those stories right.

My journal is filled with pages I wrote in longhand first, and then laboriously transcribed. Long, long hours sitting at my desk in the tiny study at the front of the house. Looking at the blossoming horse chestnut trees on our street. Missing that tiny cat body sitting on the table beside my laptop. He always thought he was helping me work by sitting there. He'd paw at the keys. He'd even sit on the keyboard. He'd nudge and nuzzle against the screen. All of it was pushing me on in my endeavours.

In my book about him I decided that he knew that I was writing books, and realized that he'd never be able to read them. But he knew that books were all just about talking anyway. They were just stories, like the ones you tell. What I did was all about speaking. And he was used to that. We would talk all day long to one another. 'Ungow!'

Writing about him was making me consider all kinds of issues.

Sometimes you write about a subject and you find yourself walking backwards into writing about something else entirely. It sneaks up on you...

Fester was my first cat. I had never had a cat of my own. I didn't even know the way to be around a cat. I didn't know how to carry on.

I'd never really had anyone to look after. No one of my own. I've spent my whole life being and feeling responsible and adult, but I've had no one who depended upon me absolutely. Not really.

Fester had never had anyone to look after, either. He was always either a pet or a stray. He had never been an equal before. A colleague.

He jumped onto my desk…

He began every working day by jumping on my desk and, sitting at the laptop, we'd have our photo taken together. Ready to brave the day. With his squinched-up mouth he'd look like he was smiling. Other times he'd be gazing heroically out of the window…

20th April.

My journals are filled with lists and plans and sums to do with word-counts and how many chapters I need to write. By now I think I've decided this is a book. There are notes-to-self in scrawled handwriting that say things like: 'Cats don't give a damn about the ordered consistency of time…'

My handwriting is just dreadful. It really looks like it's the product of someone without opposable thumbs…

I write – in his voice – these monologues and sometimes they seem just right… and they come out of me when I'm in that kind of trance… It reads like a poem down the pages. I've left lots of gaps and white space, as if I'm transcribing something straight out of the air…

'I want you to remember things.

These days of ours

Because I'll only be part of the story

I know your human lives are generally longer. And you had all that life beforehand and

I was twelve when we met up…

And you'll have more afterwards, I hope and maybe even…

Other cats..!

There might be others

I don't know
I can't imagine the future
But I want you to remember this –
These long days together.
And don't ever forget me?
Keep me separate
And special.
The human mind is bigger – with
More room
The cat mind seems smaller – but I wouldn't forget
I would never forget any of this.
And one day, if you see me
Through the leaves,
On the fence,
Up the magnolia tree
I can't promise to properly be there
I probably can't come running anymore
But I did, didn't I?
I came running for you
Like no one else ever did.
All your life has been goodbyes
I really didn't want to be another.
I tried my very hardest to stay.
I weighed myself down with all I could eat
I was digging my claws in as hard as I could
But I got lighter
And lighter
Thanks for keeping me going
Thanks for keeping all my stuff
Going along…

1st May.

Patisserie Florentin in Stockbridge. I'm reminding Jeremy of when we sat in cafes here – including this one – and we didn't have to be anywhere in particular. No deadlines or expectations.

Compared with most people, we still don't have any.

Rainy afternoon in Edinburgh with café-au-lait: we share a mille-feuille and a pear tart. French pop music and a very restful atmosphere. I feel like I'm back in my own life again. Anxieties pushed back a little.

Wondering if my agent is reading 'The Story of Fester Cat.'

Am I crazy? I wrote a whole book in a month. I put it away for a day or two. I reread it. I cleaned up some grammar and some sentences. I tightened it a little. But I thought: it's finished.

After a month!

And I sent it straight to my agent.

Perhaps she'll think I've gone crackers. When she opens the file and realizes I've written a memoir… all in the voice of my dead cat…

It's good to be away from home for a while. I won't expect to see him, padding about.

For the past six years I always felt so settled there, and safe with him jumping onto my lap.

Even in these recent years, with so much uncertainty, and Jeremy not working, and awful family rows - having Fester with us made everything ok. We danced for him at lunchtime – Cat Disco! – to encourage him to eat, to build up his strength. He watched all our foolishness with patient interest. He studied everything so carefully. He was fascinated by the objets d'art and tat and the cluttered accumulation of our life together. He loved it because he was a part of it all. He had a place with us there and he knew it. His settledness and confidence in his place and his role in our home was a joy to see.

Before coming away on this week in Scotland – as we gradually packed our belongings – there was a pause as Jeremy made tea for his friend, Penny. I went upstairs and I had a strange turn. I had to sit on the end of our bed with Fester's blue satin blanket and I was sobbing. It was five weeks since he'd gone, but I was realizing – maybe properly for the first time – that I was never going to see him, ever again.

For a full month his voice had been in my head. I've lived out being him, for the purposes of my book. Then, on the last Wednesday, suddenly I wrote to the end of his last chapter. And all at once Fester's voice stopped.

Did it vanish? Forever? I don't know. But all of a sudden, this tireless, anecdotal, chatty, catty voice was quiet and still. And I burst into tears then, too.

I've heard of that happening to people, at the end of a draft of a book. When the characters go away: it's like experiencing a loss. I've never had that exactly. But I did right then. I really did.

21st May.

I'm taking my own advice and I've come into town, and I'm at the Molly House in Richmond Street. I've had a walk around and it's sunny. I've let myself buy a dvd and a book. My agent Charlotte was emailing me with acknowledgements from editors. One was printing the book out straight away. Saying it sounds very commercial. She was going to read it at once. Another saying her family has a black and white cat.

I'm nervous. Fester is out in the world. But have I ever been more confident about something I've written? Have I ever felt more strongly?

I know they will love him.

Jeremy spent much of the day reading Fester's book. Sitting in the garden.

He came inside, heading for a bath. He needed a hug. He was just about crying.

Something I'd written had actually touched him!

He had notes and comments and corrections, of course. But he was actually moved.

*

Probably I'm spending too much time working. If I sold something, and was sure that something was going to be published, then I could pause. I'd take a break.

But I am in love with writing again. A thousand words a day. I've been writing bits of my how-to book again. Or rather, my 'go-and-do' book about writing. I'm going to call it 'The Novel Inside You', eventually, when it's finished.

All these pages and all this activity feel like flexing muscles and exercising and doing something real in the world.

*

I have a feeling – just a feeling – that Fester Cat is going to change our lives again. All over again.

*

Oh, didn't he just?

Before we were just too random. We could have flown apart at any moment. He made us stay at home and build a life together.

His tiny coercive actions. If you moved and he didn't want you to, he'd very firmly but gently place his paw on your hand, or your leg. He would squeeze, with his claws popping out only slightly. Don't move. Stay here.

5th July.

This week at least one editor at one publishing house made an enthusiastic offer – a small one, I guess, but it does mean the book will be published. This book about Fester – this book about *everything* (because that's how you felt it, writing it all through April) will come out in hardcover in time for Christmas this year.

You wrote a book about love, because you really felt you had to. It has no one's shape or genre but your own.

In the midst of so many disasters – and really, 2013 has been a stinker so far for so many family members and friends – it seemed a pure thing, this book. It was a perfect tune in your head. It was something to have utmost faith in.

This has been the sunniest of days in our back garden. You've been out since 8am at the Beach House. You've been working and picturing Fester Cat sitting in the garden chair opposite, checking on your progress occasionally, but mostly dozing.

24th July.

Yesterday was all about working at the bottom of the garden and it took till teatime to get your daily words done. This was because of the exciting distraction of talking to Agent Charlotte and learning that Penguin in the US has made an offer for Fester's book. It's the Penguin people who work in Greenwich Village, who publish all those wonderful Cosy Mystery novels. One of those mystery authors is a Facebook friend and you took his advice and went straight to the editor at Penguin who loves cat books.

She read it and made her offer in a flash.

Very different to the majority of UK publishers who wondered why I'd chosen to write the book from Fester's point of view and not my own.

Chosen?!

They felt – many of them – that my book was an uneasy mix of fiction and non-fiction.

What?!

Anyhow, my New York editor, didn't care about any of those qualms. It seems she loves Fester just how he is.

I couldn't be happier. I love the idea of a book written in such a Manchestery voice coming out in New York and in the whole US. After twenty years of being told that my work is too Northern and too English ever to travel abroad…

But I mustn't get carried away.

I love being *chosen* again. Someone who doesn't know me from Adam wants to buy my book. When you've no 'success' as it's generally measured (money, sales, awards, fame, blah) it means you have to start all over again with each new project. Often your older work stands against you, because most publishers would prefer someone new and untried.

Anyhow, all that's just about me and rubbish career stuff and the sheer joy of selling a book I put my heart and soul into. I never lost faith in myself and my own abilities. I can stop panicking and beating myself up for a while, anyhow, if this works out.

But, more than any of the stuff about me… this is about Fester Cat going to New York City! His photograph will be on the front cover of what my new editor calls a 'charming, moving memoir.' He'll be starring in a 'handsome trade paperback, possibly with French flaps.' And he'll be on display in one of those swanky American bookshops you loved spending all your time in when you visited.

Our little Fester Cat. Talking in his loud voice to people all over the world and telling his story, and the story of our lives round here on our terrace in Levenshulme, South Manchester.

It'll be the first time I'll have published a memoir, and something that comes close to my life and my current home.

But don't get carried away with dreaming. There's work to do on your current stuff. There's the daily words and dinner to cook.

But – you know – all the same…

Ungow..!!!

*

20th August.

I did a full, light edit on Fester's book before I sent it to my new editor. I tempered some things and adjusted other bits.

I didn't feel like I needed to put in a higher climax or more jeopardy. I think it all works okay. You don't want to overdo things. Sometimes you just can't improve upon life.

His voice is still very clear to you. This time – three months since you last read his book – you cried twice. When he flies back from the vets at the start, and when he imparts his final lesson at the end. It's stirred you all up again. It's a book where you want people to cry at the start and the finish, and to laugh through the middle.

It feels clear and smooth. The writing has a momentum and a determination to it. People must react to it. I hope that they will take it to their hearts.

I wanted to make something permanent out of something that was disappearing. A book that I could return to – and Jeremy could return to. And then it became a book for everyone, once it was underway.

*

I also see now that I've more to do on the memoir front. There's all this other stuff I want to say about my life and love and time and being happy, and I want to say it through memoir. Fiction isn't a reunion with the lost, and I think I want to it be. By that I mean that I want my writing to be a rescue mission. I want it to have that fierce need and urgency that Fester's book has.

This is the best go I've ever had at writing about love – and that's what gives me hope. I know I've got a lot more to say about that.

It's Tuesday the twentieth of August and this rereading of Fester's book has been a big deal for you. With it, you come to the end of this notebook, which you only opened back in March in order to start writing about him, in the days before he died.

This is the end of summer. September is coming up and that when you sit down with new, back-to-school stationery supplies and sharpened pencils and start writing something brand new. It's one of the artificial turning points you've built into every year.

What will you write this autumn?

You can spend the rest of this week mulling and mooching over that question. Scribble in your journal while you figure it out.

What do you want to write?

It's a big question.

Don't – whatever you do – rush it.

In other words, maybe take a break and stop fretting so much? That's what Fester would say.

Your best and happiest days spent writing are when you are working on exactly what you want. Don't try to impose an artificial idea of structure on the material. Let it be organic and grow.

I think you should stop trying to write book-shaped books. You need to find a way of always writing life-shaped books.

Like the story of Fester Cat: when somehow you listened to what the book was telling you, and nobody else. No one else apart from Fester, that is. That's the only way it can work.

Info

When my sister started college several years ago I told her: Watch out. They'll give you a million bits of paper. There'll be forms to fill in and sheets with details and bumph all over the place. Wherever you go, it'll feel like too much information. Too much to take in. Don't make the mistake I did - and that's attempt to take it all in at once. That's like swimming against the tide, and you'll go under in the end.

The best thing, I told her, is to take a large carrier bag with you, and just wander along happily, at your own pace, taking in all the sights and sounds and new stuff. Stop and chat with people. Learn to be more carefree.

Don't be a demon info-seeker.

The thing is, to stuff all those forms, flyers, papers, lists and leaflets into your shopping bag. There's always time to go over them later, at your own pace. Then you can find out what's relevant. You don't need to do it all now.

Don't succumb to the tidal wave; the blizzard of spurious info! There's no need to get panicky.

Anyway, my sister texted me later that week and said, Yeah, it was intense. They were chucking that stuff at them all Fresher's week. After a parched summer of no book lists, no details, no specific future - suddenly, all this. Too much!

I think she took my advice.

I know all about it because I still find it hard: getting caught up in flurries of info and keeping abreast. At work, in meetings, an agenda goes round, and then heaps of add-on pages in different colours... And don't even get me started on spreadsheets. I'm useless - because I start doodling on these, as soon as I get given them. The mostly blank, blocky shapes look like the frames of a comic strip and during deadly long committee meetings those pages are just crying out to be surreptitiously filled. These days, when I get given grown-up, vital pages of info I tend to vandalise them.

And yet, at school I was never like that. I listened to everything! I studied everything! I assimilated things! I absorbed things! I knew everything! I knew what was what and what was going on! I learned all my lessons and could regurgitate them in bullet points, all logically, all sensibly... What happened to me? When did I stop being a good boy?

I think it was when - at the end of the educational process - I realised that all of the school and university qualifications I'd taken were only about demonstrating my ability to respond well to these flurries of info. They were about sorting them into relevant pigeonholes and in the correct order.

So I suppose I stopped being 'good' in that orderly, decorous way when I started to take my reading and writing seriously. I had always written and read quite selfishly, idiosyncratically, rebelliously. I read and wrote fiction that felt right to me; according to my own wayward system and not anyone else's. I think I turned 'bad' at about sixteen - when I realised that that sort of education was far more important than my 'offical' one, where I towed the line...

Fiction became - and still is - a refuge from the world where spurious info streams at us all day long. We are supposed to do the breast stroke through this blethering, viscous nonsense and endless detail. We're supposed to keep our heads up and keep breathing. From early on in my life, reading and writing seemed to happen suspended in all that morass. They gave me breathing space.

This is all a long way round of saying that, just as I don't like a life afloat on too much info, I don't much like novels, either, that fling too much indiscriminate stuff at the reader. It turns me off - a writer's voice if it's going: Come on, come on, keep up! There's still so much to see! There's so much for me to tell you! - like a fussy, hectic tour guide.

The release of info is a very important idea to get a hang of when you're writing fiction. How and when should a reader be told what they need to know about the world of this story? If we don't want a blizzard of detail, or a deluge of facts - neither do we want to be told nothing at all. We want bringing in to a story surely and confidently. We want letting into the secrets of the story gradually. Not all at once. BANG - and all is disclosed. All suspense is gone. As readers we want to be seduced into entering the story. It's like a striptease in reverse. That's what the release of information is: a slow and tender accretion of detail; the building up of a world of tension, complication, drama.

What the writer has to do is drop delicious hints, and invite us to eavesdrop. It is vital that the reader gets intrigued. As writer you want them to go plodging into the shallows… and then to wander into deeper waters… and all of their own, fascinated accord. You don't want to be dragging them in by their hair, shouting: Look at this! It's interesting! Be interested! Look!

Snag them with overheard snippets. Snare them with oblique nuggets of detail.

You have to let the reader feel responsible for their own process of gathering info and building up a picture of the world you are creating. Then, they feel invested in it - and they feel a part of your world.

Don't batter them. Draw them in. Make them feel welcome, responsible, invested. Make them feel intrigued and enticed, rather than puzzled and cross. (That's how I feel about education and work, actually: as well as fiction.)

Look at openings of novels. First sentences, first paragraphs. What info is being released? What are you having to take in? Too much, enough, too little?

Can you figure out who is who, where we are, who's related to who, who's doing what to who and why?

Is too much being asked of the reader?

Can you get into this world? Do you want to?

Will you even stick with it and read on?

Ask these tough questions of the books you've chosen. Then think about the first lines of the stories you've already written.

Are you off-putting? Are you enticing?

Three intriguing lines of dialogue.

A good practise to get into is keeping a note - in your writer's diary - of the three best overheard lines of dialogue you hear each week. They can be funny, silly, oblique, nonsensical, sinister. You might hear them on a bus or at work, anywhere. Just keep a note of them. Three a week. You might forget who said them, or what they were even about.

One of my personal favourites is from Manchester central library, where the woman behind the counter was stamping my books and she was cross about the giggles and guffaws coming from the store room behind her. She sighed and looked at me. 'They call it multi-tasking,' she said. 'But I just call it carrying on.'

That's the sort of line I like to get down in my book. Or, another one... when I was in a comics shop in London this last Monday. A big fella with unwashed hair was at the counter, moaning away to the beleaguered staff about how his favourite comic had been ruined by a new creative team. He said, 'They have absolutely betrayed the spirit of the Man-Thing.'

How great is that?

Anyway: the exercise is to collect up three of these every week in your diary. Then you have to construct a short fictional scene, including dialogue that opens with that line first. You have to use the details and hints in that line of dialogue as a starting point to flesh out a full situation. What methods do you use to draw the reader in? How do you entice them? Pay close attention to the info you need to release.

Central avenue   November 2nd 2015

Marked For Life

I was building this place called Phoenix Court in my head.

When I started writing novels I invented a town in the North East of England, an industrial New Town, some miles south of the magical, Medieval city of Durham. It was a town rather like the one I was brought up in, full of promise and intricately-arranged estates of council-owned houses. Like the estate where I grew up, Phoenix Court was composed of blocky houses, terraces and maisonettes that looked like Toy Town. It was a minimalist, postmodern Utopia where a cast of thousands lived cheek by jowl in intermittent harmony.

Into this setting I plonked the characters of my early stories and novels. Some were based on real life gossip and hearsay, others were drawn from urban legend and scandalous news stories. Others came imported from nineteenth century novels or folk tales from faraway countries. All of these elements were transposed onto 1990s Northern Britain, where they found a noisy and vivid home. Phoenix Court was a grand jigsaw made of many bright, shiny pieces.

I drew the strands of these stories together and I'm amazed now, looking back, and seeing the way that people – reviewers, readers, peers, librarians, booksellers – sometimes threw up their hands in horror. What a freakshow! Poor people! Common people! Northerners! Queers and transvestites! Goths and monsters! Tattooed men and elderly lesbians!

I got told quite a few times by folk at readings: 'Your books are more like soap operas than real literary fiction. One finds in your books the type of character more usually found on television…'

As well as class, there would also be a certain snobbery about Magical Realism. My fantastic effects would sometimes push people too far. 'Oh, heavens, he's already taken us out of our safety zone, into the wild and poverty-stricken cultural wasteland he hails from… and now he wants us to buy into all this magical stuff as well..?'

I had read the South American Magical Realists. I knew my Marquez and Borges. I had also read my Kafka, my Calvino, my Angela Carter. To me, Magical Realism was the genre of the underdog. Magic was the revenge of peasant literature upon cosy Realism… And so it was natural to me to have all kinds of queer goings-on in my novels.

In 1992 I completed my MA in Creative Writing at Lancaster University. I wrote 'Does it Show?' that year, which would turn out to be my second published novel. By 1992 I was studying for my PhD on the books of Angela Carter, in an all-gay household by the old canal, with boats going up and down all day, a piano and a chandelier in our living room, and a cat called Oscar. I was teaching the old ladies in an Edwardian Hotel by the sea how to write their novels and also, postmodern and feminist fiction to the undergraduates on campus. I set about writing 'Marked for Life' thinking, this one I have to sell!

I remember writing it quite vividly, especially that initial burst of sixty pages: a first act in which I set up all the characters and their twisted back-stories and their world of queer melodrama. I was confident enough to show it to a whole bunch of friends at that stage. I was lucky enough to have friends who encouraged me to finish it – to keep going, to keep pushing the story to see how baroque, extravagant and outrageous it could get. I loved the juxtaposition of council estate streets with phantasmagoria.

I loved writing about characters who could reinvent their own worlds through sheer force of personality and imagination. Our hero had turned himself into an illustrated man. One of his ex lovers was so neglected he had become completely invisible. I dropped into the proceedings a lesbian who turned out to be centuries old, a nudist who fancied herself a Valkyrie from the old north country myths…

I set the whole thing during a tumultuous Christmas period, with the snow falling endlessly and blurring and mystifying all barriers… and I turned a screwball farce into something darker, and more decadent and strange, I hope.

I was making up my own genre. I called it Queer Working Class Magical Realism.

I remember, about that time, going to stay with my maternal grandmother – my Big Nanna, Glad – on Tyneside for a long weekend. It was spring and I was about halfway through my book. We had one particular day out in South Shields, where ancient Hadrian's Wall ends by the shore of the North Sea and the remains of the Roman fort were being restored that year.

My Big Nanna and I explored the site and looked down from the grand hill to the whole of Tyneside and the steely sea and the docks and the terraced houses. She had a lot of history in that town, going back to the 1940s (she had arrived on the train with her new husband, in the middle of an air raid!) That day she told me a lot of stories about the intertwined lives of those who lived by the docks and about those few characters she knew still living in South Shields. We visited the town's museum, where they had reconstructed a terraced street just like the one she had lived in, so long ago.

I wrote a short story that night, 'Patient Iris' and it incorporated the images of that day, as well as fragments of family history I'd picked up from listening to my Big Nanna. It was a tiny story, just a couple of pages long. I wrote it for hours, in one continuous flourish: almost one sentence. It was a spiraling, dreamlike thing and when I had finished it, I knew I had written my best story yet. It fed into the mythology of 'Marked for Life' and it felt very much like a gateway into the rest of the novels I was hoping to write.

When I returned to my house in Lancaster I finished 'Marked for Life', full of new energy and attack. I really luxuriated in the magic and the strangeness and set my characters into the very heart of a mysterious adventure, and a wilderness of snow. I realized that I loved novels in which everyone is turned completely upside down and must reinvent their lives by the end of the story.

I decided that my books would always be about people learning to reinvent themselves. All my heroes would come to the conclusion that their life is for living their way, and they can remake themselves into anything they want. That's what I learned from writing that story and that novel that year.

At some point I sent my story off to an open submissions call for 'New Writing', an annual anthology sponsored by the British Council and published by Vintage Books. That year's edition was being edited by AS Byatt and Alan Hollinghurst. As you must always do with these things, I sent off my manilla envelope with my story plus a stamped self-addressed envelope inside, and I promptly forgot all about it.

Then, almost a year later, I returned alone to Newton Aycliffe, to house-sit while my family was abroad. The place had been untenanted long enough for a pile of post to build up in the hallway. When I arrived with my crates of books and belongings the heap (of bills, mostly) was about as high as the letterbox itself. I spent a whole evening sifting them and there, right at the bottom, was an envelope bearing the British Council logo. A grand-sounding lady called Dr Harriet Harvey Wood was keen to tell me how the editors had loved 'Patient Iris' and how they would pay me a hundred pounds for my story. My very first published story!

This triumph was enough to keep me going – spiritually, creatively – through another year of writing and teaching and finishing 'Marked for Life.' It was another year again before 'New Writing Four' was published and there was to be a party in a bookshop on Charing Cross Road in London celebrating the anthology's release. Luckily, that very day there was a rather large review of the book in The Guardian by James Wood, who seemed like a very clever and percipient critic indeed... in that he spent quite a long time praising 'Patient Iris' extravagantly.

I was, as we say in the north, chuffed as muck.

And it made going to a launch party with lots of fancy and literary types knocking around, all knowing each other, wittering away, glugging Frascati, somewhat easier. Knowing that, even though everyone else was already published and exceedingly well known, mine was the story that the reviewer had singled out that very same day - I felt fantastic.

It must be added, I felt fantastic for the first and last time at one of those kinds of parties. I had my secret identity, as author of the story that everyone ought to read first and admire for its bravery, vividness, etc, and if anyone asked who I was, I could tell them my name and they'd know who I was. I'd just have to add – as ever – the right way to pronounce my name (It's a silent G – Mars. It's misspelled Irish from 1898...)

Anyhow, as I saw, this was the first and last time I felt fantastic at such a party. (Though there was that do, two years later, in Waterstones in Islington, for New Writing 6, when the writer chosen to bore us with reading her story out loud went on for so long, I had time to quietly chat up the wine waiter, find the bookshop staff room, have a massive snog with him and return in time to applaud and pick up the wine glass my agent had been holding for me. But that had nothing to do with feeling good about my writing...)

Also at that first book party, I talked to a publicity lady from Random House, and she had read 'Marked for Life.' How was that even possible? I asked. So habituated was I to sealing up envelopes and sending them into the void, I couldn't even remember mailing off my novel, last year's draft, to her boss, the chief editor at Chatto and Windus. This lady from publicity had read it and loved it, and today's review in the Guardian gave her the impetus to tell her boss, and to come to this party organized by her colleagues at Vintage in order to ask me: did I have an agent? Had I sold the book? Would I be interested in 'Marked for Life' being published by Chatto and Windus..?

And that's where it was all happening, in a bookshop – long gone, 'Books, etc' it was called – on Charing Cross Road. In the heart of London, a long way from Phoenix Court. On the day of my first ever review in March 1995. Many things have gone right and wrong with my writing career since then and there are a lot of things I might, in retrospect change… but that first evening out as a published author was one of the best ever times. It was a real coming out moment.

Within eight months 'Marked for Life' was out in hardback. But it wasn't publication that changed my life forever – fat chance!

My life was already changed and I'd done it for myself in the first place. I'd done it by creating this imaginary world for my stories to happen in. Whatever happened after that, I'd always have Phoenix Court to go back to.

New Agent

My new agent is giving me a pep talk.

'Forget everything editors and agents have ever told you about your work. You don't have to try to please everybody. Write just what you want. I'm giving you the green light. Stop trying to hide your cleverness. Stop trying to fit in. You must feel like you're carrying around a big balloon. Stop worrying that it's gonna go pop. It will if you keep hugging it to yourself. Let it float up... Show it off again...'

I was in London to meet her, in Chelsea on a sultry, rainy day, wearing my new jacket and a tie. (A bargain! The jacket was a vintage tweed, very light, from Harrods, that I bought in Cheadle's Barnardo's.) After meeting Charlotte the agent I walked to Earl's Court and took a Selfie with my phone, of me outside the TARDIS they've got standing outside the Tube station. I wanted to mark the moment, somehow. The idea that I felt I could go anywhere again, and do anything...

I'd been sitting with her for an hour in her offices, somewhere in a Chelsea Mews, like where John Steed lived in The Avengers. At the end she went to print off pages of a contract saying, 'I'm happy to work with you, if you're happy to work with me.'

I still had to be sure of what she was saying. I had to get the contract in my hand and look at the actual words. Was she actually going to be my agent?

'We're going to draw a line, today, under all the agents you've had before, and all the editors, and everything you've done before now. You could write anything. You can write in any genre. You can do what you want. The people who've been telling you that you have to change have been giving you the wrong advice…'

My previous agent (before he left the business for something else entirely) had told me I ought to write 'younger, darker, edgier, straighter' and every time he said something along these lines my heart would sink.

My new agent made me coffee and explained how she'd previously worked in sales. 'So, I talk the language they want to hear. If I describe a book I can pitch it correctly at them. They won't be thinking, 'I can't do that – it's too complicated.' They'll be thinking – 'That's exactly what I need to sell.' It's all about the way you put it to them…'

I just now looked again at the model contract she printed off. It does actually say: 'We will act as your literary agency.'

Phew.

But when did I become so unsure of myself?

I'm sitting outside the British Museum feeling like I've had all the stuffing knocked out of me.

I'm relieved, but I'm in bits.

I'm thinking about new things. The TARDIS was waiting for me when I came out of the meeting. I'd talked about how I want to write a novel about settlers on Mars. And now I'm waiting to meet Nick for tea.

Not Wishing Time Away

In March I had that epiphany about not feeling hassled by time. It was a very distinctive feeling – a click that went in my head. I'd been away from my last teaching job for over a month and suddenly I was in a different gear. A whole different mindset. And it was one that told me I was content to be in the month I was in. Even though I usually don't enjoy those early months in the year, I was content to be where I was. I was happy in that precise moment. Content is the word for it, and that's not something I'm used to being during term time in recent years.

And I realized that for the first time since maybe 1981 I wasn't wishing my life away. Maybe it's a familiar thing for teachers – to stay with that childish way of thinking – soon it will be the summer holidays or the Easter break or I can't wait until Christmas. It's a terrible leapfroggy way to live your life – putting on the fast forward and ffing it up.

Another realization this morning – in lazing hot April sunshine and at the end of another week of days spent wholly in the back garden with Fester Cat, in the Beach House or sitting in the sun or under the trees working... with the Turtles on the hifi singing 'Happy Together' and the first coffee of the morning at ten... drinking in that amazing sunshine – that bright blue hot orange juice... with 1200 words of novel written, my day's blog and the rubbish out and the kitchen floor mopped… another epiphany about being happy.

And it's about that luxurious headspace that you don't get when you're teaching. Especially when you're teaching the MA in Creative Writing.

Patricia: 'Of course I'm happy! I'm reading great books instead of drivel!'

And last night I realized that I've cleared off the hard drive and given myself elbow room inside my own head. How else could I have written these outlines and plotted so energetically? Often I would get tangled and thwarted and plot is like a forest of thorns for hacking through with blades and bravery. But in recent weeks I've been writing 1200 word outlines – a sequel to 666, the Mars book, a Brenda my agent didn't like – so I did another the following week. An Iris script outline. And yesterday and the day before – an outline for my epic fantasy – the threshold story I've wanted to write forever. And all the pieces came clicking into place. My agent's enthusiasm helped me to push on and on into the story – right to the end of the whole book. And I like it. It's good. It's the book I've wanted to do for ages. The Aycliffe kids get to go to Narnia. It's important to me. And my agent can see that – thinks it's perfect as a vehicle for me – and he can see its wider appeal to a big audience.

So, sitting in the Beach House with the new laptop and the sun streaming through the garden – watching the squirrels jumping along the magnolia branches, shedding the blossom… and thinking hard and freely.

It's freedom, isn't it? I was thinking of other instances.

I'm back in 1997 and Jeremy's flat in Edinburgh. Using his Mac classic and writing 'The Scarlet Empress'. Sitting with iced coffee in Iguana bar near the university and writing just what I wanted into that book. Juggling that and 'Could it by Magic?' in my notebooks.

When else? Summer 1990 when I was heartbroken because I'd lost Gene (just last night I was thinking about 'wake up sleep, Gene..' by the Monkees and just how excited I was to be mourning the end of my first love affair. And wearing summer clothes and living away from home and reading and writing in the park and at home, smoking, instant coffee, peanut butter toast... typing like mad...)

And the single day when I was alone in Guthrum Place. The family were visiting Janice. I was inbetween a level exams. I had a TV dinner to prepare. I had the quiet. I wrote to the end of my first novel – and it was an Iris novel.

When else have I felt like this about work? About headspace and freedom?

First arriving in Edinburgh in 1995. Scott Walker and Dusty Springfield and the freedom of the city. Living up a fire escape. But I still had a Phd thesis to finish... I was still heavy with other people's work. But I felt very free then, I think. But I got diverted into writing all those journals.

It's only now I feel fully equipped to write novels. After this many I should know how, I suppose. But it's not that. It's about being in a happier place with them. Maybe it's that. Being able to concentrate all my forces on just my own work..?

I'm sure it's that.

On Monday evening – the yellow light of Bloomsbury and black tulips in the park – the sheer delight of being out with Nick – and then June all immaculate, dressed up, like a figure from another age, a fairy tale – and then Katy slowly getting her voice back after imitating fruit for a cartoon voice-over in Soho. Talking about doing your own work, finding new things to do... and how much, how little to compromise... pushing through your own ideas – because they're like no one else's. They're inspiring women – they've always done their thing – and found the freedom to do it.

Notes on The Third Person

1. I love that sense of hovering just beside a character. We are a little to one side, a little behind. We can see what they see, we can feel and hear everything with them. We are often privvy to their thoughts.
2. We are faithful. For this chapter, at least, we will not jump into anyone else's POV.
3. We are inside their personal space. There is an invisible and permeable envelope of warm air around this person. It carries us along and we are buoyant in the slipstream.
4. What I love about the third person - about being this guardian angel in the personal space – is how, as soon as the story opens and time begins, we are privvy to the character's preoccupations. We are living with their obsessions and we are drawn where they are drawn. This is a holiday into somebody's life.
5. When I'm in that hovering, third person mode, I love not having to say very much. I can describe and relate. I can pass on my character's thoughts and sayings and doings just about verbatim. I can tidy him or her up here and there, and fast forward when things are dull or not very pertinent. But won't have to generalise. I won't analyse too much. I won't try to draw out a moral. I'll just hover there, passing on the relevant

stuff. I'll have a light touch. I'll reserve judgement. I'll let the reader make up their mind.

6. Sometimes... I wonder... it's a risk, but is it sometimes worth it? If I let out a little knowledge... just the little bit of knowledge that I have about the future..? Because I do, you know. I know what's going to happen to this character in this story. And just to tempt you, and tease you, and to string you along... I might just let a little of that knowledge out. Hints and foreboding. But that's a dangerous game I'm playing. You mightn't like my tone when it gets high-handed... when it turns to arch and fateful.

7. You'll need to know back-story - and I'm the one that has to supply it. Don't worry. I'll let you know what you need to know. But what I won't do is stop time too much. I won't put my character to one side and put myself centre-stage. I won't bang on and bang about all the backstory you need. What I'll do, I think, is just slip you tidbits here and there. I'll disguise them in the form of... what? Bits of drifting thoughts in my protagonist's head. In the form of dialogue in the present, and I'll sprinkle clues wherever I can.

8. I'll also find the opportunity to drop in flashback scenes. I'll take you travelling back in time - but only when it's relevant. But I won't be too obvious about what the relevance is. Like I say: lighter touch. I'll try not to insult your intelligence - or to go for the easy answers. 'Ah, he was like that with his girlfriend because of the way he had been treated by his Aunty Maude back in the summer he was sixteen. Let me take you back now to a little camp site in the Yorkshire Dales in 1972, where...' NO!

9. My flashbacks will be rich, fully-rendered scenes - I hope - just teeming with the kinds of details that will bring the scene to life. I'll be succinct. I'll make the flashback occur to the character: the scene will swim before their eyes. I'll try to make it rise up - just like memories and reveries do.

10. And the details I pick out - physical, sensual, domestic - I want them to be small, often mundane. I want them to be tenderly-drawn; lightly alluded to. I want them to be the kind that makes you wince with recognition.

11. When I introduce my characters to you, I will try not to do it in scenes where they are alone. I find that boring. I want to introduce them when they are in the middle of a scene with somebody else. I want you to come into the scene just as a moment of tension has arisen between my protagonist and somebody else. I want to draw you into their dynamic and the drama from the off.

12. I will STAY IN THE MOMENT as long as I need to. Obviously, I find these characters and scenes interesting, important, relevant to my story. I want you to be in these scenes, moment by moment. Maybe you won't understand the import of everything I'm giving you yet, but eventually you will. There's method in this quiet madness.

October Blues

Why do you do it to yourself? Why do you keep on at yourself like this?

You're feeling guilty for not writing. You feel bad because you're not progressing on a project, day by day.

Part of the problem is not having a deadline. No one is waiting for this new stuff. You're writing into a vacuum, and so maintaining the daily discipline is tough.

How are you going to make people want your new stuff, unless you keep up the effort to create it?

I had a crashing disappointment this week. My agent read a chunk of new novel I sent her and she said it was 'quiet.' Too quiet. Then she said, 'Everyone's loving psychological thrillers at the moment. Can't you turn it into one of those?'

A couple of years ago, when she first took me on as a client, she said don't ever listen to people telling you to chase the market, and bend what you're writing out of all shape to fit someone else's ideas. Back then I was so pleased she was on my side with that stuff. It gave me confidence back. I was allowed to write what I wanted to write. Of course I was. No one else was ever going to do it. No one else could do it.

But what I've written is 'quiet' and I should think about making it more like 'The Girl on the Train.' (Actually, I loved that novel, but it just ain't me.)

After her messages yesterday and her 'fair enough' when I said I'd put the book away for a while and think about it, I felt like writing absolutely nothing at all. How can I? It all feels foolish.

At home it's too cold now, with our ceilings down and the roof half-ruined. All the doors are left open, men are coming and going, shouting and sawing and banging. So I have to be away and out in town. It's the first day of the year with a scarf and all the leaves on the ground. And all these dead and dying book projects on my hands (that's what it feels like.)

But you know how this works.

A day off writing won't kill you. It shouldn't make you despair. Even a whole week off.

When you've got hold of something, you work like the devil. You can really make the pages fly.

At Levenshulme station you're looking at the gardens and the backs of the houses and imagining when your home's all fixed up and finished. You're picturing yourself in a study – your own study at last. A room where you can close the door. You can have the lighting just as you want it. You can have soft, wordless music playing. And all your things laid out on your worktable, around your laptop and notebooks and tins of pencils and pens: all the talismanic stuff you need to set out around you in order to write what you want to.

There wouldn't be any need to panic. The room would be your refuge and your sanctuary. Something you've been without for so long. (Before the ceilings of our house fell in and the builders made such a hash of everything, your study was the small room at the front of the house. It was really tiny. You're moving to a larger room when the house is finished and you can hardly wait. You've never had a decently-sized study all to yourself, and it's about time. Every writer needs a room they can call their own.)

*

The thing you need to remind yourself is how to look after you and your particular talents and abilities. Only you know how you best work.

You know that the writing only works for you if you don't force it.

What you need is a gentle routine and a feeling of being obsessed with a particular story.

At the same time you need to feel secure and content in your life. Your life needs to be full of soothing regularity and routine.

At the moment your home and your life is in chaos. You need to find any way you can to recharge your batteries.

What you shouldn't be doing is beating yourself up about not doing enough, or doing it wrong.

*

What I'd love to do is be vigorous in my approach to my next novel. I'd like to get into it with no self-doubt and no mucking about.

I'll not fuss about the form or the shape of it.

I'll not fret about point of view or voice or tone or any of those things.

I'll keep it simple!

I'll maintain a consistent view-point. Third person, hovering somewhere over the left shoulder of each character in turn. I won't deviate or subvert my own decisions.

I won't set about reinventing the wheel.

I won't digress or over-describe.

I won't break the fourth wall. Bugger that stuff.

I'll keep time moving smoothly forward. I won't tiddle about cleverly with chronology.

Flashbacks will be kept to an absolute minimum. Forward is the way to go!

If a flashback is really necessary I'll make it into a big, standalone chapter by itself, and label it very clearly at the top, so the reader knows exactly where and when it is happening.

I'm having as little ambiguity as possible. I shall signpost everything beautifully.

I think ninety thousand words is a good length for a novel.

I like doing simple sums so… what about eighteen chapters of five thousand words each?

And I can write each chapter by composing three splurges of writing that last 1,700 words each. That's a good size splurge.

And let's say I have three principal characters. I can keep them in regular rotation, so they reappear every three chapters.

I do think every chapter needs to end with – if not a cliffhanger – some kind of revelation and epiphany.

Maybe it could break into three big 'acts', so that chapter six and chapter twelve both have the really big cliffhangers? Almost like ends of episodes on TV?

If I think in terms of 'acts', like a stage play, then Act One could be all about establishing my world and characters and showing what's at stake for them all. Act Two is all of them running around madly, getting lost and having adventures. And Act Three is where I should start winding it all up into a fever-pitched climax, and bringing them to the same place, perhaps, for a great big barney.

Everyone has secrets.

Everyone is redeemed by the end.

The baddies are punished, of course.

Most of the goodies are left happy. Perhaps one is left feeling rather bittersweet.

The reader must get to know and like everyone.

Use magic sparingly. It needn't be out-and-out fantasy. It might just be a little magical coincidence or synchronicity or serendipity. Just a sprinkling of everyday magic.

At all costs I need to keep my story rattling along.

Yes, that's almost a formula for what I want to do. That's a lovely framework to write a novel inside of.

It's a start, anyway.

What do you think?

Is it possible to write a recipe for a novel, like this..?

When I was writing on Tuesday in Caffe Nero and trying to allay all my panic and guiltiness about not writing… and when I was saying that, really, I know how to treat myself, and look after myself, and do this work, and how I ought to trust my instincts – the very next thing I did was go and spend two afternoons in the library.

I wandered about in the book stacks, browsing and thinking of very little other than what I'd like to read. Then I chose something, and happily lost myself in reading a novel for fun.

I sat in a corner of the basement in the new, futuristic library and just quietly read, until the panic went away.

What I really mean is: it was good for my soul. I know what that phrase really means now. And I know what's good for my soul.

DAYS LATER.

Work on the house is back on in earnest, with the arrival of the electricians, plus the prospect of Jeremy getting to work on the new bathroom floor and laying down sheets of something called 'marine-ply substitute.' (There's all this fascinating language to do with building materials.)

I've fled into town of course, buying another thick, sensible jumper from Primark (the house is freezing and I've been living inside the soft, red and purple one I bought last week.) I also returned my library books and decided that, given my decisions about writing a clear, linear, organized novel, I want to be reading heaps of popular novels. I want to read all my favourite Chick-Lit authors.

Then I'm sitting in the library's new cafe with heaps of books I've picked out.

Is it true that, just when you need it, something turns up in your inbox in order to cheer you up?

Not every time it doesn't. And it's a fool's game to go looking for it, expecting it.

But this time – when I look at email on my phone – I've got a message out of the blue from a man who's editing a big collection of new gay fiction, to be published next year.

It's an actual commission! £250 for a new short story!

It's my favourite kind of commission: something with a deadline, parameters, and a decent amount of cash.

Straight away I'm sitting happily sipping my coffee, scribbling in my notebook, cooking up ideas.

It's delightful to be asked to do something new.

Tuesday.

I've come out to Inspire café in Levenshulme, escaping the house, which is somehow even worse and more slow-moving than ever. We've another week's delay because the tiler has let us down. Jeremy's sitting in a wrecked room, smoking with the window closed, arguing with people about politics on Facebook.

I've stopped keeping a diary. This is the first time in years I've stopped writing in my diary every day. All the entries just dribbled away. Maybe I don't want a record of these head-achey, dusty, soot-covered days?

Maybe this whole year is a write-off. In some ways it really feels it. 2014 hasn't been one of my favourites.

Before you caught this cold (you're giving it three days: it better be history by tomorrow lunch time) and you lost all your energy, you had this rush of enthusiasm for doing Nanowrimo for the first time. You've heard about it over the years and it sounds like a lovely, communal act. Writing a certain number of words every day for a month and getting a huge chunk of a novel's first draft completed in November. You signed on their website and even thought about going to a local get-together in a bar at Piccadilly. It's a global phenomenon, but each city has a chapter that meets up so that writers can egg each other on.

I thought about just taking part, quietly, and not owning up to anyone that I'm supposed to be a professional writer.

I think I was thinking of ways to make it fun, and not seem like a matter of life and death…

It would be nice to meet new people. And it would be good to be involved in a collective project and feel some urgency about writing: a feeling of shared enterprise.

I've lost that feeling this year – of having peers. A couple of years ago a bunch of us had a few retreats. We hired houses in the Derbyshire countryside – in groups of six, eight or ten. We did it several times. We found some beautiful corners of the dales to hide away in, and write pages. We watched old movies and vintage TV. We cooked and ordered takeaways. We went out for pub lunches and walked in the woods. They were really terrific weekends away: very restorative. Lots of talking about writing and planning future projects. We haven't been able to get one of them together for this year yet, and I'm feeling the lack of that kind of support network.

I'm not sure about doing the Nanowrimo thing in November. I like the idea of taking my jellyish, protean story that's still bubbling about in my head and kind-of partially mapped out on paper and then just splurging with it. I love the idea of sticking to a strict timetable and getting it moving. Imagine getting a bright and chatty first draft done!

But right now you've got no energy at all.

It would be amazing, though, to finish the year with the feeling that you've written something useful and good, wouldn't it?

You've been wrestling with this new short story. You think it's working. You hope it is. You were dizzy and aching yesterday, sitting up in bed with the laptop. You kept working on it until the words and the cursor started to swim around on the screen.

Maybe doing this story this week will give you confidence and momentum to crack open your new novel in November? Maybe you can dive into the story and do it just the way you want?

You like the idea of a book that's funny and warm, and has an ensemble cast. That would be a nice place to be right now.

The coffee's not bad in here.

Imagine remembering why it is you do what you do. Not because it's the only thing you can do. Or that it's the thing you do to make money. Imagine finding again that love for doing the thing itself, for its own sake: for making a book exist. A book that would never exist in the world without your dreaming it up. Remember that.

When you spent those calming afternoons in the library you read a slim French novel about libraries. The writer was actually writing about what libraries do for us. She talked about how we go to the library in times of need. We go there in order to be sustained and nourished by books.

It was a dizzingly vertiginous moment. She was writing about exactly how I felt at that moment.

Men between the ages of thirty and fifty, the novelist said, don't use libraries so much. Generally they are busy doing other things. They'd rather own things than borrow them.

It seemed like a bit of a generalization, I thought. But then what she asserted next gave me pause for thought.

One day something goes wrong in these guys' lives. They lose their job. They lose their place in the world. Then they wander about, feeling lost. Until, one day, they find the library again.

She wrote: it's like going to sit in your mother's lap again. That's what the French woman suggested.

I thought that was kind of interesting.

I thought about how Mam used to come with me to the tiny library in Newton Aycliffe sometimes. We would go there after school. (When my father took me on a Saturday mornings he would steer me towards non-fiction. Fiction 'was only for girls', he always insisted.)

When I told Jeremy about my sudden enthusiasm for doing Nanowrimo he looked at me like I was crazy.

I explained: it's writing 1,700 words a day, every day for a month. Until you've got almost a whole novel.

He was still giving me a funny look.

'What?' I said.

'Well, how is that different to what you do *every* month?' he asked.

'Oh,' I said. 'Erm… well, it would be weekends as well. I wouldn't be taking the weekends off, like I usually do.'

'You're crazy,' he said. 'Just do things in your usual way. There's nothing wrong with that.'

In the end, that November, I did Nanowrimo anyway. Just for the feeling of being part of something.

I got a full first draft of fifty thousand words!

I was absolutely *wrecked*.

Old Photos

You have to go home, back to the North East and your mam's house, where the old pictures are unsorted, in plastic bags, stuffed in cupboards. You sort them out a bit. Discover a few pictures everyone's forgotten. You even find a sheaf of shiny negatives no one's ever looked at. Your family at Lake Ullswater in 1976. That was the hottest, sunniest week England's ever had - *officially*, as you all kept telling each other: crowing over the only holiday your family ever took together. In the pictures you're all in trunks and bikinis on a pebbly shore. Sitting on rocks. Squinting into the sun and at each other.

You were seven. You stayed in a caravan in the middle of a farm and every morning at seven you'd all be down at the lake for breakfast. You'd be the first to break the perfect bronze of the water. Your dad would jump in to swim across. There and back. Showing off.

You get the photos developed again. They have to go into the care of trained specialists because they're an old-fashioned format. People don't take square photos any more, or the sorts with white borders. (The white borders are important. They disappeared from British domestic snaps in the mid-Seventies. They put a frame around the moment; made it into a quotation from life. Something very *unmediated* about the pictures that came after: those that go right up to the edge...) When they come back from the specialists, the 1976 photos shock you with their clarity.

They've come up like new. Too shiny and realistic to be twenty five years ago.

And when it comes to talking with the art people as they design the cover for your autobiographical novel, there's the problem you hadn't anticipated at all: the signing of release forms and letters by those in the pictures still living. Ok, you can ask your mam no bother. You can't ask your Big Nanna. She died last year and that set you off on this memoir stuff: eulogizing her in a story in the Times Literary Supplement (the bliss of their banner headline on the cover: 'Here Comes Glad!') But you don't want to ask your father for permission to use his likeness. You don't want to get in touch with him at all.

But there's an elegant solution at hand. One of the episodes you describe in this novel of yours, the one about the summer when you were ten, is how, when your dad left home your mam took a pair of nail scissors to all the family photos. She tore into the collection and, every time it turned up: off came his head. There's a scene in the book where your ten year old self comes across the snaps and finds egg-shaped holes where your dad used to be. So now, in 2002 you repeat the revenge, and tell Simon and Schuster's art department to vandalise and doctor the reconstructed past.

You learned a lot from writing that novel. It covers the time from when your dad left home and you had these weekends with him, when he had a new flat, fifteen miles away in Durham city.

You've written about all of this over the years. In story after story, years of building up to a novel. Still, even now, it goes around in your head.

Sometimes the purpose of these stories, these essays, these books seems to be to exorcise such stuff. Can it? A British poet said on the radio recently that memoir is inescapable, whatever you set out to write. She said that it's like blowing up a balloon. You fill it with breath that comes right out of you; it's all your carbon dioxide and tainted gasses ... but you tie up the end so it becomes a perfect, sealed-off object and floats right away from you. It's got to be separate.

Though fictional, all the novels that you wrote and published before this real 2001 attempt at lifewriting, tended to include elements drawn from your family history. In the first novel, the policeman who comes home blind drunk in a flashback, falls through a glass door and lies bleeding in a bath with his parents and wife watching on, waiting for the ambulance ... that was your dad. He's never told you that story himself. He's never told you any story himself. All the stories you know - all the stories you've ever known - have come through the women in your family.

You learned a lot in writing that autobiographical novel, the real novel about being a kid. People die. Stories are lost. What's the point in getting stuff out into the world if it isn't true? If it isn't an attempt to preserve? To keep all the stories, all the characters who, in real life died and can't come back? Those who'll be forgotten if no one - and that's you, kiddo - doesn't commit them to a form of public rememberance? That's what you've been thinking in recent years.

Is there any going back from this position? Into pure fiction? Well, you never believed such a thing existed.

You also learned a bit about your parents, about all the adults around you, in writing that novel. Those that had the care of you in those tender late Seventies years. They weren't absolutely in control and neither were they absolutely to blame. Your stepdad, real dad, real mam ... all were only in their late twenties. And to be thirty one and writing your first autobiographical book, that's the first time you can fully realise this. They were doing their best - and variously failing, sometimes succeeding - in the attempt. Only now, with a longer time of your own under your belt; a longer personal history of inventing, reinventing a ramshackle life of your own, can you see this: everyone is compromised all the time. Most lives are difficult. Not many people really set out to ruin your life on purpose. They're just doing their best and mostly causing upset.

Only writing about all of this at thirty one, doing your best to recover your own voice at the age of ten, can you work this out. You step away from the manuscript and you see - just children, forced into the roles of adults, all because they've got children of their own. That's the generational problem. In the late Seventies – the time of *Grease, Star Wars, Starsky and Hutch* - they had kids. In the generation since, in the late nineties, not many people had kids yet. They learned - even the straight people you knew - to stretch out that childish part of their lives (now they call it Middle Youth...) and not to procreate too rashly. Now the twenties and thirties are a time to wear retro clothes, get nostalgic for old TV shows, do further degrees, buy records, write novels, concentrate on a tricky career, get stressed, take recreational drugs, live in cities, get to know lots of other people. And you think - you were thinking, when you were doing all of that - at your age your parents were divorcing, organising access weekends, working hard to keep all your bodies and souls together.

This will make you feel guilty, of course. But it takes the sting out of blaming them for being hapless with the lives and feelings of those in their care. What did they know? Barely kids themselves. And they lashed out at each other, like angry kids, when things went wrong.

In writing, you were only trying to keep all of you together.

That's what writing a novel - even, writing an essay - seems to be about. Reflecting on who brought you up and how. That isn't always going to produce a flattering picture. It's natural history: red in tooth and claw. But it's a true picture. True as you can make it.

You do want to say ... to all of them ... at least I waited till my twelfth book. I held off all the fire and heat of the young novelist before turning onto the truth for material. I could have turned around at that first instant, at twenty one, not thirty one, and set our shared past alight. I don't think the burning is destructive. It should be brilliant. It should be incandescant.

I waited for the balance of being just over thirty. Like Jean Cocteau said in that poem he wrote at the same age. About sitting here on the roof of my house ... surveying all the property front and back. What's been, what's to come. I can see all around.

Why not upset yourself?
Get drunk and flip through old photo albums.

Out of Office

Getting some time away from your desk is good for you.

We get so stuck in our rooms and at our computers. It's such an artificial way to work. Sometimes I think I sit at my desk like this – from eight in the morning till teatime most days – and it's out of some misplaced working class guilt. I have to look as if I'm doing a full-time job and putting the hours in.

Well, there's always plenty to do. When you write professionally there's a lot of stuff to get through. A lot of admin, a lot of correspondence. Organisational stuff, invoices, queries, even fan mail. And then there's all your social networking gubbins – the Facebooking, Blogging and Tweeting that every writer needs to do these days, just to remind the world that you're here.

I sometimes think I'm pretending to be in an office, with lots of people in offices, at desks, all around me. I'm proving I'm at work by working too much. I'm evidencing my busy-ness every day.

But when did that happen? Was it when I went freelance?

I used to feel much freer, I think.

I'd pack my bag and head off into town. I'd go off on a walk or catch the train. I'd wander the city streets and pop into shops. I'd find a café and sit down for hours. And naturally, when I was there, I'd write. Out would come the journals and the notebooks and I would start scribbling and stay there for hours.

Guilt is an awful thing.

Maybe I think that, when I'm writing, I'm enjoying myself too much?

Except, that can't be it, because I often find writing hellish and difficult and horribly hard. I'm sitting there cudgeling my brains, cutting and pasting and crossing out and losing my patience.

Or maybe it's feeling guilt because I'm free when I'm writing? Especially the kind of writing I do when I'm sitting out in public, in a café or a park. I deliberately clear the space to write any old thing I want, and I realise that's not something everyone can do.

Complete creative freedom, even for an hour or so, is a breath-taking thing.

I mean, sometimes when I sit out in the world and I write, I'm getting on with the Work in Progress. Sometimes I know the bit I need to write and I go straight to it and get it done. Like that marvelous summer in 2002, when Wayne and I met every day on Canal Street in Manchester. We had a pact that, every weekday afternoon we'd sit in a bar or a café and write for two hours and get a thousand words each of the novels we were writing. And we both got to the end of draft one by the start of autumn. It was brilliant fun and felt like solidarity.

Similarly, I spent a summer in Edinburgh writing my first Doctor Who novel. I drank a lot of iced coffee and I blame that book's dizzying surrealism on the frosty caffeine that fueled it.

Mostly, though, when I'm writing away from my desk and my home, I'm taking a holiday from the ongoing projects – the so-called serious work. I'm doing my journal-writing. My notebooking. My writing in situ. My experiments.

Now, I'm not proposing in this chapter to come up with some perfect recipe or guide to how to write in your notebooks while in the field. Everyone is different, naturally, in how they approach such things, and your own perfect method is best developed by yourself, over time. It takes time and dedicated practice – and lots of cups of tea and biscuits, cakes and sandwiches. And hours and hours of avid people-watching.

Some writers go off to remote areas. Some wander into the wilderness. They go up mountains or seek silence amongst the trees or in the desert. All that is fine and dandy. It sounds amazing, actually. Communing with nature. Having epiphanies all over the place. Meeting with the sublime. Like Wordsworth and all those Romantic Poets did. Yeah, terrific, if that's your thing. And I've had my moments with nature too, over the years.

However, my preference is to be among people.

Books – my books, and the books I love – are filled with people and their chatter and clatter; their emotions and adventures. So, what I like to do is wander the streets and spend time eavesdropping. I visit different shops and public buildings. I love galleries and museums (mostly for the echoes. Voices – even whispers – carry so well in those temples to culture.) I love going into Charity Shops and perusing the bookstands. Yes, for the bargains, obviously – but also for the craic. You can hear some startling things when you listen to the people who volunteer to work in Charity Shops.

Above all though, I love cafes. It's all about sitting still and relaxing. It's about having a nice cuppa and taking stock. Slowing your breathing. Keeping calm and still even with the streaming mass of humanity bustling around you. It's finding a way to slow down time to a pace that suits you.

Maybe that's the guilt thing. And maybe that's the purest enjoyment in this writing life.

The thought – even the illusion that – in those moments of writing we have learned to master time.

No longer are we surfing through it – keeping ahead of our deadlines and all the things we have to do. No longer are we drowning in it and waving feebly as we realize that we can't keep up. And no longer do we feel we're being left in its scummy wake. For those moments of sitting with our notebooks and writing the good stuff – we are moving time at our own pace. We are controlling the flow of time in our own world.

It's a powerful and heady feeling. A very addictive feeling.

What I love to do is start off my writing in these café situations by tuning into the conversations around me. I take careful notice of who's around me. I see what kinds of characters are sitting all around me. I try not to make assumptions about who they are, what they are like, or what kind of lives they lead.

What I really want is for them to surprise me somehow.

I tune myself in like an old fashioned radio. Remember them? With the dial and the numbers and the Short Wave and Medium Wave bands? And the way the white noise used to whistle and scream out of the speakers. Voices in all kinds of languages would whisper tinnily and surge forward and then fall back as the dial went round. You'd search for the voices and it was like spinning a globe around. An invisible world of sound would be rolling under your fingertips.

It's the same when you start eavesdropping on a crowded room. All these lives and all this energy can be overwhelming at first, and it's tricky to pick out strands of actual conversations. This takes practice. It's like being a pickpocket. Remember Fagin and the Artful Dodger teaching Oliver Twist the various ways in which to lift the goods from unsuspecting victims? This is a bit like that. Don't let people realise you're lollygagging. Don't stare at them. Don't look too conspicuous as you scribble down their every utterance.

And, for me, it's not about catching every utterance anyway. I just want a few snippets. A few leading, intriguing sentences or fragments. That's all I need. I'm not trying to rob everyone of their life stories. I just want – in these journal afternoons – a bit of local colour and flavour. I just want to sketch in a few crisp details. I want the sense of the language as it is actually spoken, clogging and colouring the air.

Do this. Go out this afternoon. Or if you can't, at your earliest opportunity.

Don't set yourself targets. Don't put any pressure on yourself with goals or pre-conceived ideas about what you might write. Life is full enough of those kinds of deadlines.

Just award yourself an afternoon out – with your notebook.

Wander and wander. Absorb all the details you can. Look at the tops of buildings, not just ground level. Have a look at the faces of people as they talk to each other. Have a look at what people are buying, and the way they stand and walk. Look at the statues and the public art. Look at the wording of signs. Pay attention to colour. Tease out the smells that surge around you as you move through the city. Could you draw a map of your walk and tell directions just by the aromas you encounter?

After a bit, find a perch. Find a corner in a café or a bar. Get your notebook out straight away, and your pens. Have them ready right from the start, so you won't feel self-conscious later on. Also, you're not sitting here waiting for inspiration to strike.

God, I loathe that phrase. 'Waiting for inspiration to strike' sounds like the worst kind of writing. People who've never written creatively assume that's how writing works. How all art works. We drift around waiting for lightning. For god or a muse or some such rubbish. Nope. We just get on with it. We start making marks on a page without even thinking about it too much. If we've got any sense, that's what we do.

Just write anything. Any overheard fragment. Or anything that's floating up from your own mind. Just don't sit there with a blank page. Don't save yourself up to write stuff that you deem is great. If you wait for the quality stuff to just drift along you run the risk of writing nothing at all. Of sitting there crossly and impatient, waiting to be a genius.

Hmf. Much better just getting on with it.

Have a listen. Tune in. Ravel up a few thoughts, a few lines of dialogue. Something that draws your attention.

Learn to follow your interest. Learn to trust your attention.

And see where it leads. Free associate. What do these opening remarks lead to? What do they suggest? Perhaps, if someone's talking about their upcoming holiday and their dread of flying – this could trigger a memory of your own. Write it down. Where does it lead? To an old friend you've not thought about for years? Who were they? What were they like? What became of them in the end? Where were you living then?

What you're trying to do is to follow the dance of your own mind as it moves from subject to subject. You're trying to follow it with your pen. You can't help it moving like this. It will do this dance, whether you're actually listening or not.

The point of this exercise is, in many ways, getting you to tune into other people. But you'll find that, in the end, you're really tuning into your own mind.

And the point is also to gather up some great material. And to surprise yourself with what it consists of.

I promise that, if you give yourself up to this practice and do it as often as you can manage, you will AMAZE yourself with some of the stuff you will write.

WHERE DID THAT COME FROM? You'll ask. And, when you read back through your journals – which will be chockablock with scribble and coffee stains by then – you'll be able to see exactly where the material came from.

So. Off you go.

Have a LOVELY afternoon.

And I think I'll do the same.

Over write

Over write! Go on, be embarrassing! It's allowed. At least, at a first draft stage.

In fact – as it happens – *anything* is allowed.

So you need to free yourself up, and stop feeling so hampered, worried and tense. That internal censor you've got inside your head: you've got to stop it squawking away, as soon as you set pen to paper. Don't let that angry goblin that sits on your shoulder have his own way. He'll tell you to pack it all in; that you're really no good; that it isn't worth you trying anything at all. You're bound to fail. You're bound to make a fool of yourself.

You'll cough your guts up on the page. All your most intimate feelings and thoughts. Your most private desires. The ideas that you dared to think profound. And people will laugh at them. Or be embarrassed by them. Or politely ignore them. Who are you to think you can be a writer anyway? Who do you think you are? People like you can never be writers. You aren't the right sort at all.

All the best writers are dead and long ago. There isn't a thing worth writing about in the world any more. All the great tales have already been told. Who needs even more stuff to read? No one takes fiction seriously these days anyway. No one really wants it. The only stuff that sells is trash and crap. Why beat yourself up trying to write good work? Who cares?

Okay. Get all of that out of your system. Let the internal censor and the nasty goblin have their say. Let them tire themselves out in telling you all the reasons why you shouldn't even imagine that you can write anything of any worth.

Now let them be quiet.

I think, in order to gain some confidence in overcoming those persuasive demons, it's a good idea to splurge. To really let rip. To write like a bastard.

It's important for you to realise that no one has to read your early drafts. You can write as much as you like, and try out all kinds of mad things, and you needn't show anyone a single line. Not until you're ready. This is all at your convenience. You're allowed to fail and overreach and overwrite and experiment and fall flat on your face. You've got to really push the boat out.

I like the word 'splurge' for these grand, splashy first attempts. These writing routines, in which you simply let go, and write down everything that comes into your mind, attempting to keep your pen moving as quickly as your thoughts – they are like snapshots of your mind at work.

You have to go where your ideas lead you – one after another – letting them skitter and bounce. You have to see where free association takes you. You might be surprised to learn something about the way your mind works: the way you curl one idea up inside another, and the range of textures, emotions and sensations that you draw upon. You're not going to get the full effect of that if you constantly edit and reshape each and every sentence as you go along.

Allow yourself to write some messy drafts. Splurge to your heart's content.

What you end up with is a mass of writing that's a bit like a lump of dough. All the ingredients are in there, sticky and heavy and clagged together. Now you have to set to work with the rolling pin and the pastry cutters. You've got to shape and refine and tease out the strands.

I love overwriting as a means of getting the good stuff out. Yes, it'll go too far and get too splashy. You'll shove in a million adjectives and a hundred adverbs. You'll Jackson Pollock your pages with a hundred extraneous words for every seven good ones. But that's okay – specially in these days of the magical delete button. (He's like a Pac-man going along your lines: munching up ghostly letters.)

Some people get too mealy-mouthed and safe with their writing. They like to keep it clean and tidy; agonising over words, one at a time. They don't push themselves on. They like to keep it decorous and neat.

The brilliant thing about writing is that you're not wasting materials. You aren't cutting diamonds or hammering gold. You can't cost yourself a fortune with one tiny slip. All we need is cheap exercise books and pencils, really. We can rip pages out and chuck them away. We can even snap pencils in fits of pique. (There's always the rain forests to make us feel guilty, of course… but if you're going to think like that, you might as well give up the idea of writing right now. If you write fiction, you're going to use up a lot of the world's paper. And anyway, other people will make far worse uses of it than you will. Just think about some of the things paper gets wasted on.)

So let yourself spread out a bit. Enjoy yourself and be bold and ambitious.

And – you know - you're allowed to go against the grain of every piece of advice about writing you have ever heard.

Write about what you don't know.

Use loads of adverbs and adjectives. Use completely inappropriate ones.

Be verbose and over-rich, over-ripe; tangy and slangy; potent, pungent and raw.

Try using every terrible, hoary old cliché you can think of. Get them hopelessly wrong!

Have completely unbelievable, ridiculous things happen in the middle of your story.

Be blasphemous.

Be utterly un-PC.

Be utterly PC.

Be savage and kind and sarcastic and woeful and rhapsodical and idealistic and solemn and pompus and sentimental and barbaric and juvenile and fogeyish and pure and filthy and tender.

Be obscene.

Be schmaltzy and sickly-sweet and sentimental.

Be cruel.

These are your notebooks and no one ever has to see what you write here, unless you want them to. Here you can be anything that you want. And, in order to limber up, and stretch yourself, you'll need to write things that will, afterwards, sound a bit bonkers.

But that's all right.

Parlour Games

'I'm not staying here for this! These are just parlour games you want us to play! I've got better things to do! I've got my novel to write!'

I let him go. He stropped out and slammed the seminar room door behind him. I asked if anyone else in the class felt the same, and his girl friend got up and left, too. What can you say? This was a postgrad course. They weren't kids. In fact, they were older than me. If they didn't want to stay, they couldn't be compelled to.

What I'd tried to get them to do were writing exercises. Warm-up writing routines, like piano practise. Like warm-up in the gym, or a good jog around the park. I always do these, with every class I teach. I do them myself, as a practising novelist, and I always have. I'm not arrogant enough to believe that I can start work – and produce brilliant work – cold, first time, without warming up, without playing around. Without playing parlour games first.

Such affrontedness in the little fella's tone! 'Just games you want us to play! I won't stay! I've more important concerns! My novel! My grand, important novel!' And off he went to tend to his novel. His little bit of tortured bonsai.

Oh dear. I've met a lot of people who are very, very serious about their novels. And their novels are very, very serious things. And they go about them with utter seriousness.

Actually, I'm spoiling the word 'serious'. 'Serious' is a good thing. It means important, vital, and of value to the world. What I actually mean is that I've met people who take themselves and their novels far *too* seriously. Who tie themselves up in knots trying to be especially profound all the time. This little fella, storming out of the class, felt that writing exercises and games were too trivial for him. He'd be wasting his fantastic talent in indulging them.

I talked to my fellow tutor on the course about this business afterward. 'I think exercises are very good things for beginners and undergraduates,' I was told. 'But perhaps not for the more experienced novelists on our MA programme.'

Wrong!

I still think he was dead wrong.

People doing MA's are writing their first, maybe second novel. Rarely have they published more than a little bit of fiction. They need to practise, practise, practise! They need to experiment and try things out and fail and tear things up, and shock themselves with what they produce. They need to learn humility. They need to sit in a room with other writers and write things there and then, and read them out afterwards. Even – shock, horror! – unpolished work.

I think they need to get their hands dirty. Mess around. Act up. Be silly.

They have to remember the joyfulness of playing.

So, whenever I feel that I'm getting too serious about my own work – or anyone else around me is – I remember that pompous little bloke. Shuddering and stomping out: 'Why, this is a parlour game! Not real novel-writing!'

What did he think real novel writing entailed? Sitting up a mountain in a blanket, waiting for brilliance to descend from the skies?

Something I've learned in the years I've been in the Lit World: those who get pompous about the writing of novels don't know how to do it. They have never really done it and they never will. They monumentalize the idea of writing novels and make it something special and terrible because they fear it. They'll never get there.

The people who can do it and who are really good at it, deal with the process much more lightly. Not because they think it's easy or unimportant. It's a different kind of seriousness they have. An earned one.

Watch out for pretentious, pompous people. The Lit World seems to attract them. They're usually useless, and they tend to go stomping out of the place, if they think something's beneath them.

It's just snobbism, really. All of fiction doesn't have to be gloomy, profound, self-consciously 'Literary.' And as a novelist you don't have to go round wearing a big black cloak.

What is it about writing that attracts these personalities? Who can't enjoy fun for its own sake? Who think they don't have to practise or experiment?

At one point – at the end of the last century – I worked with the novelist W.G Sebald, who wrote some of the most gloomily erudite novels in the world. The photos in his books were dark grey, smudgy and the text seeped with gentle despair. He touched on some of the really serious, profound topics. He touched on the real biggies. And what was he like in staff meetings?

He messed about and giggled and twinkled mischievously. He had a big moustache and it always seemed to me like he was pulling faces behind it.

Some of the more pretentious students I've had seem to think that, in order to be a writer, they have to be like Dirk Bogarde in *Death in Venice*. Nice hat, slouching about on the continent, coughing into a hanky and being queasily miserable all the time. Having great thoughts they can occasionally jot down in a tiny Moleskine notebook.

What a life!

This is what I was getting them to do, the day that fella took himself off to tend to his novel.

Everyone chooses a fairy tale or simple story they already know.

They write in five minute bursts. The tutor times them and issues instructions between every 'round' of writing.

Each five minute round has a set of conditions imposed on it.

Here they are:

Start the story. Five minutes. You can't use articles – the, these, a, an, etc.

Continue. Use articles. You can't use conjunctions.

Continue. Use articles and conjunctions. You can't use verbs.

Continue. Use articles and conjunctions and verbs. You can't use nouns.

Continue. Use articles, conjunctions, verbs and nouns. You can't use words with the letters 'n' or 'd.'

There are lots of other, obvious things to disallow, and this can go on for a while.

It can produce some very strange effects.

The conditions and the restrictions they set make the writer think around corners. The writer has to abandon their usual, habitual choices. It makes them work harder and have to think laterally.

Each burst of writing should have its unique flavour. Some of it will be gibberish – and interesting nonetheless. Everyone will produce something startling, at some point, almost without knowing it.

Sometimes effects have to be randomly, spontaneously generated, through experiment.

Sometimes you have to give yourself up to the process.

Sometimes you have to not know what you'll end up with before you set off.

Sometimes you have to learn that you can't be in control all the time.

Hardly any of the time, in fact.

Photos of Strangers

Something I love collecting is old photographs of strangers. In junkshops I've found old albums and once a very small, ancient suitcase, brimming with tiny photographs. Sometimes you can find the history of several generations of a family. Everything in the wrong order. Holidays, weddings and Christmases all mixed up. You can sit for hours with the jigsaws of other people's interlocking lives and never quite figure it out. The scribbled names and dates on the backs sometimes help, other times they just complicate things.

It's heart-breaking, in a way. These pictures have ended up in a junkshop. If I don't rescue them, then who will? No one wants to remember these people anymore. These Edwardian folk. These war-time families. These 1960s people. New cars. Reunions in Civvy Street. Fairgrounds and Father Christmases. Babies who are probably old people by now. Dogs and cats who could never sit still.

Over the years I've built up quite a collection. When I go and teach I pass them round very carefully. Some of these pictures require delicate handling. I should get them scanned in order to protect them.

If we don't already know who these people are or were, and we have no way of finding out who they actually were, then we are free to make up new stories for them. We can give them new names. Really, it's no different to catching glimpses of people still alive, on the street in everyday life and wondering about their back-stories and inner lives. It's the same kind of work. Photographs are sometimes better to base stories on, because you get a wonderful access to a frozen moment of time. You get very specific expressions and quirked eyebrows and the curious way people sometimes look at each other and the camera catches them…

That's part of the skill of collecting amateur snaps, I think. Having an eye for the intriguing ones. There are a billion billion photographs out there, but most of them are boring. Certain pictures, however, contain accidental magic. They encapsulate the real magic of ordinary people, and that's what you're looking for. That's something that can trigger your imagination.

I'd far rather use amateur snaps of unknown people for exercises like this. I've seen people teach workshops using the work of famous photographers and well-known photographs. This can be good and useful in its own way, but it only allows the writer to go so far. They are taking their cues from the things that a skilled photographer has provided: the story is already told. The experience has already been aesthetisized by an artist. In a way, all you're adding are footnotes. It's hard to own the work.

But when it's a photograph that's been forgotten and lost in the junk rooms and old albums, then you can go to town. It can become as good as your own memories. There's more to play with, I think, in the anonymous pictures.

Here's some instructions.

Have a good long look at your set of photos. A set of about five is good. From any place, any time. Colour, black and white.

Groups, individuals. So long as there are people somewhere on show, it's all good.

Write for twenty minutes – loose-writing, without thinking too much – around the idea of 'the family album.'

See what you come up with. What does the phrase make you think of?

Now, read it back.

Circle any interesting phrases or ideas that leap out at you.

Have a look at the photos again. Did you write about any of the people? Is anyone becoming interesting to you? Do you have any ideas about them?

Have a good think.

Choose one person.

I'm going to give some writing prompts and, for each one, you should respond in character, as that person. Write for five to ten minutes. Build up a pile of sentences responding to each idea.

What's your favourite place in the whole world?

What has been the darkest moment in your life so far?

What was the best trip you ever went on?

What was the best meal you ever had, and who with?

There's a ticking clock on your happiness. What is it?

Who is that stranger who just arrived in your life?

Tell me about a moment of real jeopardy in your life?

When were you happiest, and who were you with?

What song is on the radio? What does it make you think of?

If there was a movie of your life, what would the title be?

Have a read back at what you wrote. Is the character coming to life yet? Are they starting to give their secrets away?

Here's a next stage. Now you can become another character. Is there someone else in your photos you can choose to be? What relationship do they have with your first character? If they're in a picture together you can learn a lot from their position and body language towards each other.

Now I think your second character should ask your original character some searching questions.

Let them ask the big five W questions:

Who are you?

Why are you here with me?

What are you doing with your life these days?

When did we first meet?

How do you see life panning out for you?

Or if you have better questions, let character two ask those, as well.

Then you can respond, as character one, in a few sentences per question.

Don't think too hard. Let the character speak.

It's almost like having a séance. The answers may surprise you, if you let yourself open up to writing what comes into your head.

(Don't freak yourself out, though!

Or maybe: do!)

Perhaps your first character gives two answers. One answer they say out loud, to their questioner. The public, polite answer. And the other answer is the one they give inside their head. The secret answer. Which is the most truthful, do you think..?

For me, this is the real stuff of writing. This is mucking about inside strangers' heads. Or rather, the illusion of mucking about in strangers' heads. To me, it's endlessly fascinating. And this is one of the ways I go about it: by degrees. By letting characters ask questions of each other.

Here's a few more instructions for small 'routines' of writing. Brainstorm from these prompts. Write a few lines, a whole page, or five hundred words, based on these suggestions. They're all ideas that will push your static photograph into action. They could well get the story moving…

Focus on one figure. Perhaps one you haven't looked at properly or written about yet.

They are at the heart of your story. You're going to begin a story and they're already in the middle of things happening, all around them. This photo has been snapped in the middle of a complex tale.

Your character has a secret.

You can see it in their face, can't you?

What do you think they are hiding?

Think up a scene in which the secret is revealed to other characters.

Now think up a scene in which a stranger turns up.

Who is the stranger? What do they have to do with the secret?

Just write the dialogue of a scene between your character and the stranger. Maybe fifteen lines of dialogue.

Then add detail to do with location. Atmosphere. Smells, sounds, colours, furniture. Build up the whole scene carefully.

What's the subtext?

What's the atmosphere like?

Who's hiding what from who?

Does the secret come out in this scene?

Something big interrupts the scene. Something unexpected. What is it?

Pull all these elements together. You needn't include every little thing you invented. Just compile all the best bits. Fill it with tension and clues.

Turn it into the first page of a story.

Keep looking at the photo.

Cut it down so it's really tight and economical.

Keep everything 'on camera' – ie, keep it all happening in real time, so that we see it all. Make it move along, moment by moment. Let us hear the beats in the air.

Tension. Keep it filled with tension.

Now. How does it read..?

Plotting in the Hipster Cafe

I'm sitting in the Fig and Sparrow in the trendy Northern Quarter in Manchester. The coffee comes in glass tumblers and they sell upcyled craft geegaws, too. The music is lovely and calming: Fleet Foxes, Nick Drake, the Velvet Underground. All the young guys have hipster beards and it's overcrowded on a rainy August afternoon. But that's okay. Everyone crams in and it's rather pleasant.

Okay. Down to work. Plotting your novel.

Are you any closer, then?

In recent days you've filled pages of your notebook with plot ideas, twists and turns, timelines and lists of character names and potted biographies. You've written sentences and notes-to-yourself that say things like, 'Not sure you should even be writing about writers…' or 'Maybe I need a clean break from these characters, otherwise I swerve down into the same story grooves and want to re-hash and re-write earlier drafts?'

Oh, I like the idea of 'story grooves' and I've underlined it later, several times. It's like some of these characters are on predetermined courses and not even their author can break them out into new destinies. They swerve out of your control…

In these past few days you've been mulling gently over Haruki Murakami and Batman and romantic bestsellers you've dipped into. You might have become dizzied and derailed from your own story as you've thought about these other things. Or maybe they've fed in usefully to your thinking about your own story? You truly believe that everything is grist to your mill. Sitting in this café and observing the details: that's useful, too. You'll set a scene here, maybe, at some point. The hipster café.

You can't be derailed from your story if your characters are bold and strong enough. That's what you think.

The thing is, though, not to be too caught up in ideas you had at the start of the process. Have some of those elements gone stale on you? Are you sure they still fit the story? Don't be scared to ditch them.

I start scribbling furiously, forgetting where I am, almost.

I still like the idea… and the tale of Dodie chasing her mother all the way to Paris… and that story was going to be about Helene cruelly faking a dreadful illness, wasn't it? Like in that old movie… or was it a short story? A classic short story, where the hotel staff claim never to have known the woman: she was never here. You must be wrong. What *was* that story..?

This has become a thing for you, it seems. This trope of characters who lie and who almost get caught out in the lie. And they're really big lies. And they have to go on lying, in order to save face. They end up making their fantasy come to life. Yes: that's become a big theme for you.

By roving over and over the story twists and ideas that fill your pages, you start to realise what your obsessions are.

What do you like? What do you enjoy about this roster of characters you have picked out?

What is it you want to really write about? What are you actually getting at..?

I list the names of my three main protagonists, and sketch out a handful of attributes, and make a few notes about who they relate to in the book I want to write.

For example…

I want to make the heroine – Cath – married, and her husband works away. She wants a baby. She's a reader and a book club member. She works at a local café and is a friend of Dodie's.

I want David to run a small shop beside the café. It sells old junk and paperbacks. No way it's ever gonna work out, but it's what he's always wanted to do. He meets an older bloke, who proposes to him. He's in two minds about marriage.

Dodie is my third character. Her dad has died and her mum is carrying on with this blimpish poet and everything is changing. She finds a boyfriend of her own – a sci-fi fan she meets in David's shop.

Now, when I take a step back from these characters I'm looking at people in their thirties. They're all highly-educated and they're all working in cafes and shops and trying to make their way. They've all got their secret projects and ambitions and they're all on the hunt for love, in various forms.

So… that's my world and my fairly ordinary characters. So far, it's nothing but set-up. I want to set them in motion. I want to put stuff at stake for them.

I've got a story in mind already for Cath. It's to do with her finding out from an old magazine her mother has kept, that her father had to give her up. There was a custody battle and he lost. You read something similar in an ancient issue of Woman's Own in the library the other day and it touched you. It's stayed with you. You imagined what that girl might feel, decades later, finding that story and discovering that her father really had wanted to keep her. He didn't choose to be frozen out of her life forever. You want to use this moment somehow.

What about David? You want to tell a straightforwardly romantic tale for your principal gay characters: you've decided this already. So you want to have him whisked off his feet by an older suitor, who proposes respectable marriage, now that such a thing is legal. This brings David into the world of academics and eminently respectable professional folk. They're all ten years older than he is. Is this the world he wants? At the same time he's still carrying on with a scally lad from Longsight. It's a casual thing that's been going on for two years… ever since they met during the riots down town in the summer of 2012. Yes! You wrote a fragment of a story about two such characters! While they were in JD Sports the riot kicked off and they hid in the fitting rooms and ended up having sex to pass the time while Market Street burned. Now's your chance to use that fragment of story! This is where it fits..! (See? Hardly anything gets wasted. Most things find their place in the plot…)

And What about Dodie? You've had this shy, homebody character in your head for a while. You want to write about someone who is just a good person. You want to have really horrible things happen to her. You want to see how far she can go on being good-tempered and nice, before she snaps. You want to write a story in which she comes up with a brilliant story idea and her sci-fi loving boyfriend nicks it, and also this saga of her mother faking a deadly illness just to mess with her daughter's mind. Poor Dodie is going to be a bit of a victim, but you're going to show her overcoming all this stuff, I hope.

Inevitably, Dodie's mother is appealing to you as a character. As soon as you start inventing wicked things for her to do, she starts leaping forward, wanting to be written, wanting to take up more space in the text.

She's going to be called Helene, and she fancies herself a bit sophisticated. When the novel starts she is in the process of reinventing herself as a widow. 'Who can I be now, after all these years of marriage?' I think she must get involved in local politics. She'll be one of those who wants her part of town to be gentrified and invested in. She's in her sixties and part of the generation who came through the Sixties and Seventies, and she's very frustrated with her daughter, who seems to lack get-up-and-go.

'Sitting in a park in Paris, France…' Ahh, now there's Joni Mitchell playing through the speakers, here in the Fig and Sparrow on Oldham Street. That song could be Helene's anthem. 'They won't give peace a chance / That was just a dream some of us had.'

You need connections between these characters. So they live close by each other. But that's not enough. They need to be linked by means that will entail the choices of one character impacting on the life of the others. What if… Helene's self-reinvention takes the form of her doing an MA in Writing at the university? She enrolls on the course at David's new boyfriend's department. I think she'd be a truly horrible, demanding, selfish student. She would be a ghastly writer, who can talk the talk and get through interviews, but writes all this gushing nonsense…

Maybe I should nip out and buy some of those index cards? Then I could lay out chapters and scenes… and make a wall-chart, perhaps.

What I've got are a number of lives. Three, maybe four main voices. And I want to braid their stories. Yes, braid is a good word for it.

A good way to bring them all together is to put them in the same book club, say. They meet at the café, at David's boyfriend's fancy house, or in Helene's jumbled, artfully bohemian kitchen.

Now, what about imposing an artificial shape on the book? What about making it last a full year? Summer through to the next summer? With Christmas falling in the middle of the novel, and bringing it to a close with a wedding? People like a nice wedding at the end.

A big issue for having separate voices is how to keep them separate and distinct. A good way might be by giving a different form and shape to each one. Perhaps Cath's could take the form of letters? She is alone at the start. She finds the magazine amongst her mum's things. Is she house-sitting for her mum? Are all the letters to her mum, accusing her..?

I think David might tell all his own chapters in the form of dialogue only. No description. He loves pulp novels, TV drama and comic strips. He wouldn't mess around with anything but pure dialogue. Pithy and succinct. His chapters would read almost like screenplay.

And Dodie? How does Dodie write? What would her chapters look like? Are they in her actual voice? Or maybe she's presented in third person? So we have a little distance from her? Or does she even have distance from herself? Has she always had that feeling of watching herself living her own life through several panes of glass? That weird disembodied feeling?

But maybe that would make her too drifty and not heroic enough? Could she be a main character in my novel and be as passive as that? Would everyone think she was a drip..?

Something that would be lovely to write would be a character who everyone thought was lovely. Someone who always comes across as much too nice for this world. And the reader sees all of that. But we also have access to her diary entries and her own, innermost thoughts – and they're horrific..! What if she was secretly really hideous, and thought evil things about everyone all the time. It would be a sweet sensation, to let the reader see the contradiction between how she is inside and outside at the same time.

But, no. I think, in this story, Dodie has got to be a good, decent person. That's how I want her to be. She is perplexed by other people. Mystified by the world around her. And trying her best, the whole time, against the awful odds.

Thinking further about the form of chapters... some might just be lists of stuff. Highlights of days and weeks. Because there's just too much to catch up with.

What about a chapter of texts sent between the characters? Or Facebook messages or discussions to do with the book club meetings that connect them? Book Club, or as they privately call it: 'Drinking Wine and Gossiping Club.'

I think you should think about the café as the heart of the novel. Come up with a name for it that might stand as the novel's title, too. It should be the great, good, safe place that is at the centre of their lives, in different ways. It should be the Greasy Spoon equivalent of 'Howard's End'. It should be the eye of the storm of the novel. As things go wrong for each of the characters, they know that when they get together in this café, in their gang, they're okay for a while. Maybe it only happens once a month.

What they're all looking for is a life – a partner, a job, a preoccupation, something – that will make them feel as content as they do in that café.

The outside world is violent and silly and outrageous. Only your friends make you feel safe. Is that enough?

Yes, these are the kinds of themes and ideas you love.

But what about betrayal?

Betrayal comes in and causes massive ructions. It might not even be on purpose, but it still happens.

David realizes he's betraying his fiancé because he's still carrying on an earlier affair. Dodie is betrayed by her new boyfriend nicking her ideas. And she is betrayed by her mother, who perhaps sells the café out from under her and runs off to Paris with all the money?

And Cath is betrayed by her husband, who is off having a thing (and kids!) with another woman in another city.

(Now I'm not sure that Cath is as essential to the story as she seemed before. Do I really want four main characters? And yet she was the first one. Can I abandon her..? She feels less tied into it all than the others…)

So… that's my team of characters, and a sketch of each one, and a sense of their entanglements. We have a feeling for how they'll be brought together, and what the shape of their distinct chapters will be.

I'm getting a feel for this novel.

But does it feel too schematic and worked-out? Everyone is betraying or being betrayed somehow. I wonder if that's a bit too obvious, the way I'm laying that out? But in the actual telling of the tale, it should all feel a bit more natural, shouldn't it? It'll be about bad things happening to nice people, and how even nice people end up doing bad things. That should feel like real life, I think.

Here's a thought. What if Dodie's chapters are florid and fairy-talish? What if she has this idea of her own world as far more dramatic and heroic than we know it really is? We could counterpoint her sweeping romanticism with a bit of bathos from the other voices.

That's the key to this business of braiding the lives, I think. You let the three different voices contrast amusingly. Dramatic irony. So you don't – as author – have to go pointing stuff out to the reader quite so obviously. Just let the differences stand.

LATER.

I left the café and walked through the rain to Piccadilly Station.

I'm fretting slightly because I've made all my characters quite bookish. They're all readers, book-clubbers, bloggers, would-be writers, scribblers, MA students, poets, etc. Is there anything really wrong with that? They're just bookish people who are drawn together. And people do like novels with a bookish bent, don't they? It might be fun to tap into that vibe.

Also, it's what you know. You are familiar with that world in which people are connected by their love of the written word. Other writers set their books in particular worlds and professional milieus. Why shouldn't you describe this loose affiliation of writers and readers in a novel?

You don't want it to seem too contrived. That's the thing.

That's the whole business right there, isn't it?

It's the art of being contrived, without making it *look* contrived. That's what the plotting business actually *is*.

And pages like the ones you've filled up today: these are your pages of working out. The writing itself will erase them. These are your guidelines, scribbled in pencil. You'll approach the actual writing via the eyes and ears of your characters and the things they actually say. When you write the new pages and the actual chapters themselves, you'll say *everything but* the things you've been writing today.

You've got to hide all your working out.

But you've got to do the working out first.

Go and sit in a café full of attractive people and drink strong coffee and make stuff up. Do horrible things to the characters in your head. Plan their triumphs and love affairs, their highs and lows.

Work it right through and wonder about giving them a happy ending or not.

But hold off writing actual scenes just yet. Don't let yourself start writing too soon.

That can wait for tomorrow.

Today was a day for plotting.

Now it's teatime. What time's the train? We're done. Let's go home.

Putting on Airs

The thing to avoid is believing that writing seriously means having no sense of humour. A lot of first time writers try desperately hard to sound serious. Too serious. They don't allow themselves to be funny, even if they are in life.

I'd ask people – especially those doing MA courses, 'Why are there no laughs in your novel? Where are the funny bits?' And they would look at me oddly, as if jokes and laughs weren't proper things to have in novels. Like they were downmarket somehow.

Where did that idea come from? What about Fielding and Austen and Dickens and Thackaray? Even Henry James has funny bits. (Madame Merle and Henrietta Stackpole in *Portrait of a Lady*! Monsters!)

I think there's something about embarking on a first, 'serious' novel – especially in the context of a university course – that makes people lose their sense of humour. They start putting on airs. Comedy becomes something beneath them. But comedy has always been intrinsic to the novel. There's nothing downmarket about it at all. If you can make someone laugh out loud when they're reading – then you've got them. They are yours.

I'm not necessarily talking about belly laughs, here. I'm simply talking about the humour implicit in good observation of human behaviour.

But I think those novelists who put on airs and think humour beneath them, aren't often very interested in observing human behaviour. They aren't watching other people. They aren't bothered about other people – which seems very odd to me.

I'm talking here about the narcissistic novel. I think it needs to be avoided at all costs.

I've dealt with a lot of narcissistic writers and their boring novels, over the years. They tend to be vain, self-regarding, and stuffed with fake erudition. There's not a jot of life in them.

I think the narcissistic novelist shows off with fireworks and tricksiness, in order to deflect our attention away from the hollowness at the heart of the novel. There's no story here. There's no centre. So… look at this! Gymnastics! I'll turn somersaults and cartwheels! I'll kick my legs in the air!

This tricksiness – this rather hollow aping of Pynchon, Rushdie, Eco, Chatwin, Carter, Calvino (or whoever else they have recently read, revered, half-digested) – is a set of charades. It's an avoidance tactic for not taking responsibility for telling a story, with characters we can believe in. It's an avoidance of trying to write about anyone else, other than the writer him or herself.

The narcissistic novelist puts up defences: arch formality, fussiness of tone, deliberate difficulty and obscurity, and diversions in the form of arcane knowledge and made-up quotations.

What I'm saying is, beware of using effects for no purpose. Beware of showing off for no reason.

I think about getting into reading and writing – obsessively – in my early teens. I would go through my parents' novels in the living room. There was a real jumble of paperbacks on the wall unit shelves: literary fiction (Lawrence, Hardy); horror (King, Herbert); romantic blockbusters (Cookson); sexy bestsellers (Jackie Collins!) I remember scouring them for mucky bits. For hints of real adult life, and what that might be like. I was fascinated by the adult tone of these novels: third person free indirect narration and its hint of closeness and complicity. The way that tone draws us close to the characters and whatever it is – horror, sex, romance – that they get up to. That tone has a frank insistence that this – the series of events of this novel – is what life is like and the shenanigans of these characters are vital, important, and need to be disclosed to you. That's what good fiction writing – in any genre – insists.

There is no clean, easy divide between 'Literary' fiction and 'Genre' fiction.

Whoever said there was? But that's what people setting off often think. If a book involves generic effects or tropes – space ships, detectives, werewolves, guns – it doesn't make it second rate. Why should it?

What is 'Literary' fiction? Books that can't be said to belong to any genre? Books that argue seriously with the messy stuff of life? Books that articulate the liberal qualms of the middle classes? Books where nothing much happens? Books about art and truth and beauty? Books about the way people think?

I think 'Literary' fiction describes a kind of fiction in which each book is the unique product of one single author. Only you could have written this book. It is watermarked all the way through with your particular stamp. No one else could have done this. Without you, this book would never have existed in the world. There is no reason that it exists, other than the fact that you went out on a limb and wrote it.

So it can involve werewolves and guns and unmarried mums; and spaceships and time tunnels and shopping precincts and trips to the continent; paintings and bumblebees and last wills and testaments. Those are just the trappings, the bits and pieces.

The earliest novels in English were road movies and sexy romps. *Moll Flanders* and *Tom Jones* were great, funny, racy sagas. Don't put on airs. Don't go thinking you're classy just because you want to write a novel. It doesn't make you posh.

Read some fiction in a genre completely new to you.

What have you dismissed in the past, and never dreamed of reading? Space operas? Shopping and Shagging? Novels with historical portraits on the cover? Novels with the name of fruit in the title? Novels set abroad? In the past? Russian novels in translation? Novels about psychos and serial killers?

Have a think. What would you automatically steer away from, assuming that there's no pleasure to be found there; nothing to be learned there?

Steer yourself purposefully towards the books you'd never usually touch.

Take notes in your writer's diary as you read. Don't read dismissively. Enter into this other world. See how it works. Listen to the way it moves and takes the story forward. Is it what you were expecting?

Timed writing: write a long list, elaborating when necessary on this topic:

What makes good writing? Or, what makes writing good?

Give yourself fifteen minutes, brainstorming on that idea. Keep writing – don't edit or change. Let your first thoughts get onto the page.

You might surprise yourself with your ideas about *good*.

Reading is Always Escapism.

I love it when science fiction is mind-expanding and slightly psychedelic, and I *catch* the idea of it. I don't quite grasp the entire concept perhaps, but I get enough of it to keep me intrigued. I'm in pursuit of understanding the whole, crazy thing. I'm trying to fit it all inside my brain. That's what reading science fiction is like for me, when I'm enjoying it.

Now I'm reading Roger Zelazny for the first time, his 1973 collection, 'The Doors of his Face, The Lamps of his Mouth.' The first, long, Venusian fishing trip story didn't do much for me, but 'The Keys to December' is wonderful. Lurid and moving and full of astonishing imagery. We get a palpable sense of the life of the planet flickering by as the sub-zero cat people go in and out of hibernation, watching the world and its people evolve.

Giant woolly caterpillars..!

It reminds me of the sensation of reading science fiction when I was fifteen – 'Dune' by Frank Herbert, especially – when I felt I got maybe half the idea of it. I was grasping at the strangeness of the book, my imagination in overdrive. (Thinking all the while: is this really happening? Have I imagined too far? Can a book from Newton Aycliffe town library really be as weird as this? Wouldn't other people have noticed? Am I getting it wrong and making too much of it in my own head?)

I would spend a morning, an afternoon, a whole day marinading myself in 1960s science fiction. Druggy, apocalyptic, surreal, mystical. And I'm doing the same today with my first foray into Zelazny's world. It's a yellowing, falling-apart Corgi paperback with an outrageous cover. It was twenty pence from Barnardo's ('Five for a pound!' A sure sign no one really wants them but me…) It's a very rich and heady reading experience. My mind fizzes, like a Vitamin C tablet dunked in a glass of water. This will perk me up. Give me energy. Turn my pee green. Give me *ideas*…

Maybe I'm forever grateful to weird science fiction because it will always have the effect of making me feel fifteen?

(Today it's an ambiguous feeling. Being fifteen again and thinking of other things I loved. Not just strange novels. I loved Victoria Wood's sketch show, 'As Seen on TV.' I recorded each episode on cassette tape and listened and listened again, memorizing and trying to find out just how she wrote like that. And I also loved the albums of Prince. Both these people have gone and died this week, one after the next. Both have journeyed to that planet you fondly imagine, where everyone wakes up like it's a Philip Jose Farmer novel. This week the actress Anne Reid was on Channel Four news and she talked about Victoria Wood, her anecdotes giving you a new picture of heaven – when she described Christmas parties at Victoria Wood's, her friends singing with her round the piano and doing their party pieces… 'Oh, the Christmas parties..!' she said, on the news.

It's a sad week, with chunks of my teenage loves disappearing into the ether. But how lucky I feel to have been that age when those shows, those records and these books were published. To have been enriched by this stuff at that age – it feels a great privilege.)

And so, with Roger Zelazny. I wish I'd read him back then, in a way. But you can't read everything. That's something you learn from reading over the years. There's only so much time and you make your choices. But that's not to say that books won't wait for you.

And so here I am, with Zelazny at last. And all these tales are astonishing… The cat people debating whether or not to help the humanoid race evolve and survive ('Erm… *no.*') And the one with the sentient wild cars and their desperado bandit leader. And now the man who's reading Martian history in a gilded temple. There's an incredible piece of imagery to do with having a flashback:

'And at night the elevator of time dropped me to its bottom floors…'

It's very simple, and very fine. Amongst all the baroque stuff, it stands out as true.

Later we meet the space societies and religions that will be changed forever by contact with human beings, and also a space rock who is sentient and longing – we are told – to *deeble*. (We come to understand this means something like his desire to transcend to the next stage of being, once he has accumulated enough atoms.) But he learns that his visitor is planning to take him home, for his uncle's collection…

Zelazny has these polite, bemused, highly articulate beings – rocks, lizard princesses, talking cars driven to commit murder – and they must have explained to them the things that devious human beings intend…

He seems to specialize in the bafflement of exotic creatures in a universe of humans.

Later that day – the sun was out – I was thinking about my Beach House full of books and my determination to read all of them and how, really, it's imitative of holiday reading experiences. It's a way of making yourself feel holidayish all the year round.

Real readers know that one of the best things of all about going on holiday is planning ahead which books you will take with you. Packing for vacation is a delicious process of making early choices, deselecting, honing, changing, editing, adding, starting again. And then all the fun of wedging them into your luggage. How few items of clothing and other practical things do you really need? Making room in your bags, in the car boot. How many books can you actually physically carry? On a plane it's all to do with weight. Do you go so far as to fetch out the scales? And then doing more sums: how many pages do you expect to read in a day? How many hours can you spend? You read slowly, only about thirty pages an hour. Ten thousand words. The exact speed of reading aloud, like four Radio 4 Afternoon Stories, one after the next. How many days are you going away for? Calculate: if you spent every waking hour reading, what's the maximum number of books you would get through? But it doesn't work out like that, does it? You read even slower. Sometimes you speed up. Sometimes you dwell and reread and go back. Sometimes you get bored and ditch a novel halfway through (though you resist doing that, as much as you can…)

Some would say that all these considerations have now been obliterated by the advent of the e-book. If so, then that's a shame. To me, it's no solution to the delectable quandaries outlined above, to simply carry with you seventeen thousand books on a machine. Seventeen thousand books, all lighter than air. To me, that's all the fun gone out of it, right there.

I have tried for five years to grapple with the e-book. It's just another way of reading, and that's all very well. I don't see why it should replace or supercede anything. It suits some people, it suits some occasions. That's all fine and dandy.

But… reading my Beach House books as a project is very much about the book as physical object. As the actual thing. It's about the burden of books and lugging them about, piling them up and making a mess. It's about the dusty and smelly books themselves: the very illusion that their content is indivisible from their soft or brittle pages and their tacky, fading covers. They take up space in your life and that's good. So do partners, family members and pets.

I love the very idea that just picking up a pile of books and weighing them and putting them beside your bed can make you feel like you're on holiday all the year round.

We never got to have many holidays when I was a kid. The ones we did have were magical. In a caravan park up a hill by Lake Coniston, I'm still there reading about Mrs Frisbee and the Rats of Nimh and Worzel Gummidge and Saucy Nancy. In a sense, summer 1982 has never ended. Dexy's Midnight Runners are still number one with 'Come on, Eileen.'

I can flash straight back to being 26 in 1996 and the bungalow in Wales with a whole bunch of friends. While they went swimming in the sea I immersed myself in Mary Stewart's first novel, a funny, romantic mystery story called 'Madam, Will You Talk?' and also Georgina Hammick's novel, 'The Arizona Game.' I'd found the first in a box of cheap paperbacks in MacNaughton's bookshop, across Leith Walk in Edinburgh, from where I was living at the time. The second, I'd been sent by my editor at Chatto and Windus, who knew I would love Georgie's novel, which he had worked on with her. What I love about this memory of that Indian summer on the Nefyn Peninsula is that both books were amazing and instantly became old favourites for rereading, but they also, both, led to friendships. Almost immediately, in the case of Georgina Hammick. I wrote her a fan letter from my makeshift desk in the back garden of our rented bungalow and she wrote back – kindly, and somewhat mysteriously - promising that we would soon meet in person. I was at a conference the next month in Potsdam, Berlin – and there she was! At a table in the foyer of the space-aged hotel, wearing dark glasses and a mac, watching the new arrivals. Like something out of John Le Carre, peering at me over my own novel.

The Mary Stewart book from McNaughtons led to a friendship with Roy Gill, only many years later. It was via my blog, where I was remembering visiting that shop, and he popped up in the comments, giving me some info about it. We talked and I ended up reading a chunk of his first novel – all about werewolves in Edinburgh – and we became friends.

This isn't all just about wonderful reading experiences and favourite books (though these things are enough in themselves) it's also about how books are somehow linked to friendships. Friendship is something I value as much as I do reading.

Books are doorways and you step through them with the assurance and excitement that you are going to meet new people on the other side. Imaginary, but also real, people. I always wrote to authors I enjoyed, even as a kid. I always assumed they'd want to hear from their readers. (I was right, I think, too.)

Later holidays, in recent years… I'm thinking of being in Paris with Jeremy. We went several years in a row to the same hotels and restaurants round St Germain. I limited myself to just a very few paperbacks, only two or three for a week's visit or a long weekend. Many days over the past thirteen years, spending August afternoons in the Jardin du Luxemburg with John Irving, Anne Tyler, Jacqueline Susann. I remember one whole day, enthralled in the blazing sun, seeking shelter and hardly taking my eyes away from the more brutal and breathtaking chapters of Haruki Murakami's 'The Wind-Up Bird Chronicle.'

On those holidays I would play that game of DELIBERATELY RUNNING OUT OF BOOKS. It forces you to find English language bookshops. It becomes a quest. Every visit to Paris I duck into the close confines of the San Francisco bookshop, where everything costs five Euros. And then there were the secondhand stalls outside Gilbert et Jeune at St Michel, though they've now gone.

Why is it so lovely? That anguish of almost running out of things to read? The pleasurable eking out of the last chapter and the final few pages before you need to run to a bookstore and find something new (or old.) I suppose real readers love that feeling because they know it's an illusion and they love toying with it. It's not true that there's nothing left to read, and it never will be. (Historically, Coleridge was the last obsessive reader on the planet who could feasibly have run out of books to read. It's probably complete apocryphal crap, but it was one of the most interesting things I learned during my first literature degree. I was fascinated by that idea. Coleridge lying on his sofa in a cottage by Grasmere. Waiting for someone to write something new and send it to him. Being forced to write (God help him!) poems to pass the time…)

For us in our times, however, there will always be something worth reading. You will never, ever let yourself become bored. It is impossible. It will never happen.

Remember thinking (how old were you then?) about people who didn't read? Remember thinking to yourself, 'But what do they do with all their time?'

I remember thinking that they loved to spend all their time on the mundane, doing practical and physical things. They liked football or mending stuff or going places. They did housework or DIY. It seemed to me like they were keeping themselves busy and involved in external things in order to avoid the mental, the imaginative, the interior worlds. It was as if they were avoiding meeting their own imaginary selves. To me, it was not reading that seemed like the escapist act.

Even though she loved nothing more than cleaning out kitchen cupboards and tidying round, my Big Nanna did enjoy reading. (I can picture her with 'Jaws', 'Mommie Dearest' and anything by Catherine Cookson, who came from the same dockyard terraces where my Nanna had lived during WW2 and after.) But she also said that it was possible to read too much. You could let yourself think about things too much. You could dwell and drive yourself crazy and depressed. She put warnings out about these things and how you ought to keep active and busy to prevent them.

On the other side of the family, the Magrs side, nobody read. My Mam said, when she briefly lived with them, when I was a baby, she never saw a single book inside their house. Only the Catherine Cooksons she brought with her. They had the sports pages from the Shields Gazette, which my Granda brought in with him after work. Trilby, ciggy, sheepskin coat, Shields Gazette rolled up in his hand.

They preferred to play games of darts in their lobby at the side of the house to reading. They preferred to have long, noisy arguments about politics and football over the dining table.

Of course, though, I think of reading itself as an escapist act. The most thorough one. A deeper, more compelling illusion than film or TV or anything on the stage. I've always read to block out the real world, even when I'm sitting somewhere wonderful, like the Jardin de Luxemburg on a hot August afternoon. Under the swaying branches, on one of those green metal chairs, my shoes off, drinking iced peach tea. It's a very particular pleasure, to block out the world when the world around you is gorgeous.

Tricky days are worth blotting out with reading whole books in one go. When I was a kid and there were parental fights at home. Or my first night at college, when I was so nervous and shy I wouldn't take my free beer tokens to the college bar to meet my peers, I stayed in my campus room and read 'Dracula.' I still have the same 1950s Pan paperback, with all the pages loose and the hilarious cover (Dracula with his tongue hanging out and his fangs bared, as if *he* can barely restrain himself at the thought of Freshers' Week.)

Books have always helped me to escape, sometimes with very little notice: I can dive right in. They staunch panic. They make life simple. They fill your head with other people's worries. Life becomes containable. Controllable.

It seems to me nowadays that deciding to study English Literature in your late teens is just like going off somewhere to learn how to take control of your own life.

Becoming a writer is taking it a stage further.

A kind of shy and gentle megalomania. That's what reading and writing is about.

It's that feeling of being at home, wherever you are. You're in control.

All you need is this book.

And the next one, of course.

It's something to do with seizing the heart out of a story. Reading the hell out of a book. That's what I'm thinking about.

I'm lying staring at the piles of everything I've read in this first third of 2016 and I'm thinking: 'I *get* these books.'

I've seized the heart out of them. I've grasped their essence. I know how they hang together. I could show you a diagram. I could draw you a map. I could show you how to get into them.

That great phrase: how to get into a book.

That's what writers, critics, reviewers, teachers do. That's what they ought to do, anyway.

They show you how to *get into* a story.

The story belongs to all of us. Anyone can go there. But sometimes the path needs pointing out...

(How many times though, do we hear that teachers or reviewers or critics have put readers off ever setting out on their journey?)

When I was a boy, and a slightly lazy reader with weak stamina (it's true!) I tended to fall back into reading the known and the familiar – all those Doctor Who novelizations that were generally 126 pages long. Or Marvel comics or albums of Peanuts cartoons. Some books – longer, more challenging – would seem insurmountable. They might seem boring and stubbornly resistant to being read. And yet I owned them. I was cursed to carry them around… from home to home… all my life. Even when my stamina increased and I unearthed a fathomless desire to read and read all day, every day, there were still some books I had that seemed just hopelessly unreadable to me.

I was carrying them about almost as a kind of punishment. My punishment for not tackling them was guardianship over the books themselves.

I never devoured them.

I couldn't 'get into them.'

Some of them are in the Beach House at the bottom of the garden right now, waiting there. As if they know better than me. As if, some day, I'll crack and start reading the hell out of them and fall in love. (Tom Jones. Lord of the Rings. Tristram Shandy. Sins.)

Maybe one day.

But right now, I love looking at these immaculate heaps. The books I have read so far this year. The books that I not only own (ownership is beside the point): they are the books that I have *got*.

It's about getting to the heart of something. That's what I love.

Residential Course

I'm sitting at a plain, sanded table in front of my bedroom window looking out at fields that go on for miles. It's a brilliantly sunny day at the end of summer. I'm here to start a residential teaching course. Sixteen students are here to study with me and another writer, Joan. It's a week about how to write for children.

After unpacking, and before going downstairs for the first introductions and our dinner together, I sit at my desk with my journal and scribble for half an hour. I need to orient myself a little, after several hours travelling by train to get here. I'm gathering my thoughts and writing down everything that comes into my head. I'm thinking about all these courses I've taught before. I first did one in 1996, when I was twenty-six. I count up and this must be my fifteenth residential course.

Do I still have the zeal that I used to have twenty years ago? Back then I thought it was an amazing, life-changing thing: everyone ought to write! Go on, get writing! Give it a go! You can change your life! Anyone can do it!

I taught these courses in residential centres in the countryside and at festivals and town halls and classrooms. I taught courses on university campuses. I taught them in all kinds of ways and my conviction never altered. They were a good thing to do. Writing is good for you. By taking hold of language you're taking control of your life. By learning to tell your own story, you can learn to tell the stories of others. If you free your imagination you can start to free yourself.

Am I jaded yet? Have I forgotten all of that? I'm sitting at my wooden table with my notebooks out and I'm sharpening my pencils and starting to write lists of exercises and ideas for the week.

I still think I believe in that stuff. Yes of course it's good to be able to write and to instill a love of writing in others.

But what I found tiring over the years was the demandingness. Everyone wanting to be published. Everyone wanting to be the next big thing. Everyone thinking they want to make a fortune.

And then – of course – some of them actually did turn out to be the next big thing! Some of them actually did become tremendous successes and they made a fortune!

And then everyone wants to know how they did it. How did they crack the code? There must be a secret. There must be a lesson plan. Can you give it to us? Can we learn it? And of course, there are no rules. Everyone makes up their own. Everyone has to write their own books. Whether they become huge and well-known or they are never seen or read by anyone: they have to be the books only their individual writers could write. There is no other secret to impart.

All we teach is this: the confidence and the throat-clearing and the space-making and the resilience-building and stamina-creating that you need to write these singular works of your own.

And that's what I'm here again to do this week.

I just need to build up my own resilience and feeling of stamina and confidence first. By sitting here for a while and scribbling some pages. And in some ways it'd be natural and preferable just to have stayed at home. I could be quietly sitting in the Beach House with Fester Cat. I could be quietly writing my words for the day and not showing them to anyone till I'm ready. And not talking to anyone else at all, unless I want to.

But I'm not. I'm teaching. They're paying me and so I've got to put on a show.

It seems so long since I taught anyone anything. When was it? Last year? Am I out of practice, now that I've gone freelance? Now that I'm out of the headlong dash of lecturing full-time?

I spent all those years convincing people to have courage. All that time eking stories out of them, line by line. Teaching them the patience to go over and over them, making their pages better. What is it you really want to write? What kind of story do you think it will be?

The trains lasted forever coming up to Scotland. Apart from the stuffiness and the slight overcrowding it wasn't all bad. I was sitting next to a miserable lad who'd forgotten his Railcard and who'd had to pay sixty quid extra. He phoned his mum to complain and the signal kept breaking up. He told her to find his Railcard at home. It would be in one of four places, and he got her to check them all. The final – but he admitted, most likely - place was 'The Important Things Box under my bed.' It was kind of the last place he wanted her looking, but he wanted to know the card was safe. And it was, it was there, but he was cross at himself for the waste of sixty quid, and he was hoping his mum wouldn't poke around anymore than she needed to in his Important Things Box under his bed.

NB.

Don't write awkward, lumpy sentences.

Don't shove too much stuff into a story, too quickly.

The reader needs to feel established amongst your characters right away, as things start to happen. We need to feel we know them all, somehow, right away.

Stabilise your point of view. Make sure you know where it's coming from.

All the key moments of action and transition and things changing: make sure they are dramatized sufficiently.

All these bullet points really boil down to this: make sure the reader knows exactly what's happening.

These are good questions about your work in progress. Whoever you are. Whether you're a student having a one-to-one tutorial in a wooden hut or whether you're the tutor, also thinking about your own work-in-progress.

Do you need a point of view character working as a focaliser, guiding the reader through your story?

Do you need more narrative drive?

Is it a bit one-thing-happens and then-another-thing-happens? How can you make it more cumulatively dramatic?

And this is a good question for writing kids' books in particular. The fluffy factor. Do you need more darkness to counteract the sweetness? Even Winnie the Pooh (especially Pooh?) had a calamity and some scares now and then. Often they were to do with being lost and stuck and unable to get home again. Counteract the fluffiness! (Actually, not just kids' books are guilty of this. Stories for grown-ups can be filled with too much fluffiness, too.)

Basically: sort out your point-of-view and remember to pile on the tension.

Out of coffee in the tutors' cottage, so I'm over in the main kitchen before 8 a.m pouring myself two large mugs of strong coffee to take back to my room. Interrupted by the Australian woman who tells me she's just been for a run. I congratulate her. She tells me: 'I just find it impossible not to move my body. I move my body so much in my everyday life.'

I nod smilingly and take my two mugs of strong coffee and schlep all the way back up here to my desk.

Last night was a pretty late one. My fellow tutor and I were left in charge of the Visiting Writer. The visiting writer was an extremely famous one, who was very nice. The night went a bit strange, though. She stood in the living room and told us the story of her whole career. Then she put on a pair of furry mouse ears and went hopping round the coffee table. She roped all of the students in to wear tails and ears and other furry bits and pieces she had brought along. They all played their parts in acting out the rhyming lines and repetitions from her most famous children's book. Everyone was enchanted. It was the weirdest author event I have ever been involved in (and that's saying something.) 'Marcus, Marcus, I'm a little mouse and you're a big fox! Chase me round the coffee table!' It was like a party for Plush and Furries. I had visions of someone getting over-excited, tripping up as they trotted round and banging their heads. We really are in the middle of nowhere here.

I tried out my write-a-first-page and a-killer-first-line exercise again. It worked again! It even worked for the dreaded Maisie – who has been the most difficult student all week. (She came with her own fixed ideas and is damned if she's going to learn anything new. And she smiles very fiercely as she challenges you to tell her something she doesn't already know…)

It turns out that, it's usually the seventh sentence on the first page that proves to be the best sentence to open with. That's the rule of thumb we discovered today! I guess by the seventh sentence you're nicely warmed up?

Everyone said they had written much better than they had expected to. That's good to hear as you get towards the end of a course. The idea is always to make them less precious. And sometimes you have to use sleight of hand in the writing exercises and you have to trick them into being brave. Sometimes you have to make it look easy. Or at least, you have to make them feel that writing – and making their writing better – is not something to be scared of.

As ever, I hope to take all those lessons I've learned from them – and my fellow tutor – home with me.

We all had our photo taken together and I played for a while with the house's Border Collie, Cashew and her burst football. She is adorable: laughing and leaping to catch the ruined ball in mid-air and flomping down, exhausted. Her ears pricking up at the least sign you're willing to play again...

Looking forward to being home, though the journey seems daunting. Picturing being home with Fester in the garden and a mug of tea with Jeremy. Then Nick and Jon will arrive for the evening and we can fetch fish and chips which we'll eat with lashings of vinegar and tomato sauce and we can open those bottles of freezing Prosecco and then maybe watch 'Terror of the Zygons', say? And then next week I can think about starting to write my own book...

Funny, convivial final evening, with a young girl piper coming in with the haggis and mash and creating a huge hullaballoo. Round about midnight people go disappearing outside to look at the stars. It's a night for the Pleiades. I keep on talking about books with those left in the kitchen, making some licorice tea.

And then I go out to the garden where Joan and Jill and others are looking at the extremely vivid night.

'So, what are we supposed to be looking at..?'

And then: 'WHHOOOOOOOOOOSSSSHHHHH!!'

It even makes a noise!

It's the biggest shooting star surely anyone has ever seen? It's marauding across the Scottish skies, directly over the farmhouse.

'WOOOOOOWWWW!!'

It was great!

And off I go to bed – knackered, now, at the end of our week.

PART THREE

—

KEEPING ON

2011 Sytear 2015

Sayso

People always ask about dialogue. They want to be taught how to write it. They find it difficult to get right and so they want to know how to make it sound real. What do they have to do?

I love writing dialogue. I'd do it all day if I could. I like it much more than all the other stuff – the plotting and the descriptions. I always feel a bit silly when I'm describing things. Especially weather.

When questions about dialogue and-how-to-do-it come up, it's the one time that I resist. I don't want to give the answers away. I think: maybe there aren't any answers anyway. Maybe dialogue is one of those things where you've either got it, or you haven't. You've got to have an ear for dialogue. It can't be just down to technique. It's a talent. It's a gift.

It's also something to do with having an ability to actually listen. To take things in. To hear what someone is saying, and to start to enter into their world view. To start to experience their world as they do.

You have to hear what their spoken words are saying at lots of different levels at once. You have to hear them give the truth of themselves away.

That's the tricky bit. Actually listening.

Don't be one of those writers who are so keen on the sound of their own voice, that they've stopped listening to everyone else.

Develop those listening skills.

And start to develop the technical skills of rendering dialogue on the page.

Here are some pointers for capturing a particular voice:

It's about being concise. You aren't writing everything down verbatim. Dialogue is a distillation of speech.

It's about taking out the small clumsinesses of everyday speech. We all go 'errr' 'ummm' much more than we'd like to admit. Compress and edit all of this. You can leave a few hesitant bits, a few little slips, just to add flavour and authenticity.

It's about not making it too perfect, either. Gone are the days of novels inhabited solely by nicely-spoken professionals and their roughly-spoken comedy char ladies.

Decide what to do with dialects. Render as a phonetic patois like Irvine Welsh does? So the reader has to learn the new language as they go along? Or just include a *flavour* of the dialect? A few giveaway words and phrases to supply enough clues?

Decide about using apostrophes to indicate missing letters. Is it patronising? ('Sit yersel' down over 'ere…') Those flecks of punctuation are there to indicate where these spoken words are 'deviating' from the standard, received pronunciation. Is that what you want? I prefer to present things just as they sound, and not include those intrusive inverted commas. I also avoid neologisms such as 'cos'. They look rubbish on the page.

The idea is to be accurate and succinct.

A good method of sharpening a scene of dialogue is to translate it into a different genre. You could take a scene of dialogue you have already written and set about turning it into a short play. Pull away all the descriptions and gestures and moments of reflection. Just give us the dialogue: stark and bold on the page, and set out like a play script.

This is like giving your work a good shaking. Or, as in the olden days, when they would take rugs out into the back yard and beat them till the dust came billowing out. Translating your work like this allows you to see what superfluous bits drop off, and lets you examine what's left. Does the dialogue that's left stand up on its own? Does it work hard enough? Does it tell us enough about the characters? Are their voices distinct enough from each other?

Are your characters too articulate? Are you – as writer – intruding too much, and using your characters as vehicles for what you want to say?

Is it too smooth, somehow?

You must remember: dialogue looks like naturalism, but it isn't. It's always tampered with. It's always heightened. Every line of it has to do two things it once. It has to tells us things about the characters, but it has to move the story on, too.

Take your page of dialogue and roughen it up.

Cut out every other line.

Cut the opening line, and the final line. Top-and-tail your scene.

How does it look then? A little less smooth and articulate. A little less controlled.

Think about the gaps and misunderstandings in everyday speech.

Half every line of dialogue you write. Have your characters interrupt each other.

Have a look down the page. Do your characters speak an equal number of words and sentences each? Are they very organised turn-takers? That will sound very bland and unrealistic. Let them vie for air-space. Let one of them hog the conversation. It's all about power.

When you've got a page of dialogue you're really happy with, turn it back into prose fiction. Give it back those trappings: the description of visuals, sounds, smells, textures. Gives us clothes and carpets, tea cups and eyebrows. Give us colours and music.

You can even give us the thoughts of one or both of your characters. You can start to demonstrate the gap between what they say and what they are thinking.

Working this way, and using your spoken words as a framework, and gradually bringing in the rest of your special effects – it's very like turning the sound up, or turning up the brightness and colour contrast knobs on your TV.

Let the lines of dialogue sink in. There are beats between the things they are saying. In those moments, allow your characters and your readers to absorb the import of what's being said, and what's being implied. Fill those moments with tension. Play those tensions out through very palpable, physical means: someone butters a piece of toast, very slowly. Someone slams down the lid of the piano. Punctuate your dialogue scene with little bits of business, like an actor would. And, like an actor would, get your small gestures to speak volumes.

In dialogue, you want to say as much as possible by using the smallest possible number of words.

Should I be in the South of France?

When I was twenty-one I had a lovely affair with an older man, an academic. He was clever and worldly. I must have been very naïve-seeming, very gauche. He made gazpacho for lunch one day. I'd never had cold soup before. He made me stand on the balcony of his flat when I wanted to smoke. The ashtray he gave me had never been used. It was decorated by a Cocteau drawing of Orphee. He was an intellectual, a Francophile. When it came to the summer he wanted me to go to the South of France with him…

And this was one of those turning points. Did I turn left or right?

At the time I chose to turn right. Going with him on some fabulous holiday would have meant him paying for everything. I was a student, going from my undergraduate degree to my MA in Creative Writing. I had less than no money in the bank. I had no business letting someone else pay for me. He would have seen it as an extravagant gift. He'd have enjoyed it. It would have moved our relationship onto another footing.

Also, I knew that I'd have to tell my family. I wasn't coming home to them because I was off to the Mediterranean with an older man. It would mean coming out to them in a pretty dramatic way. (I was still about six years shy of actually coming out to them.)

So I said no. I ended up breaking up with him. I used the excuse that it was moving too fast, too seriously.

I went back home to Newton Aycliffe in the North East. I caught the Primrose Coach with all my belongings in lots of bags. The coach crawled over the moors and hills between Lancaster and County Durham. I stared at boggy landscapes and bored sheep and wondered what it would be like being in the South of France. It made me think of Scott Fitzgerald, Noel Coward, Colette, Pink Panther movies.

Instead I was spending the summer in our council house. Too full already.

But I could remember the year before - 1990 – when I stayed away for the summer – and there had been trouble. Mam wanted me to come home, to spend time with them. I suppose she could sense that I was moving gradually away and would be gone forever, soon enough.

The summer of 1991 was muggy and hot on our estate. I remember everyone sitting in their front yards and all the doors of their houses open. Tempers ran high and there were fights and frustrations, in our family and in others, and between neighbours.

I sat on our front door step with my notebook.

I was making notes and thinking and doing writing practise all summer. Come the autumn I'd be back at Lancaster University, and I'd be doing my MA. I'd be expected to start a novel. It's what I'd applied to do. I'd got on the course and I'd got the funding. Now it was time to start my novel proper.

Would I write about the young gay intellectual who goes to the South of France with his much older lover? Was that the kind of story I would tell?

Or would I get caught up in what I was seeing right now? In these streets of semis and maisonettes and terraces?

There was that terrible afternoon and the rough family over the street. How they were baiting the old man who lived next door. They were getting him riled with their screaming kids, their blasting music and their barking dogs. His wife tried to stop him going round and they all laughed when he shouted at them over their garden gate. Everyone came out to watch.

Then they let the pitbull out and set it on him. He panicked and – before anyone even realized what was going on – the old guy dropped dead of a heart attack in the street.

And then there was the brothel on the terrace, which got raided in the middle of the night. A mother and daughter were entertaining a dozen Caribbean gentlemen who were all dragged out by the police, while all the neighbours watched from their windows and gardens in their dressing gowns. The mother and daughter were screaming at the police.

Other, less dramatic things were going on around us, too. Just everyday stuff for the families in the houses all around us. I talked to them, and they talked to me. Even though I'd been away somewhere down south and at a university and got a First and my mam was telling everyone about being at my graduation and all, they still could talk to me and it wasn't like I'd dropped from some alien planet.

I could always talk to people. Right from a very early age. And people always told me stuff. Confided in me, even.

That summer I started writing stories about people from our estate. I picked up threads to do with the lives around me and I began to fictionalize them. I changed their names, and some of their circumstances. I started reaching into their thoughts. Or imagining that that was what I was doing. The poor family who always smelled dirty, but who were the kindest souls around (who kept rabbits that ran free all over their house); the single mum who was addicted to romance novels, who spent every afternoon drinking tea with my mam in her kitchen. The poor put-upon woman next door whose husband was drinking himself into oblivion every afternoon and leaving her to cope with their four kids and just as many ferrets.

There was so much going on around me. In such a small space. Less than a square hundred yards. It could feel claustrophobic and hemmed in and sometimes that summer I longed to escape. I thought about the Mediterranean and how the water would be the same blue as sun-faded denim. I thought about being somebody's lover and being cherished and taken out to places. Here, I was just a grown-up child. I was there to do the shopping and keep Mam company and help with things. I was there to be glared at and ignored when my stepfather was home from his job abroad. I was there only as an echo of myself, really, and not really myself at all.

I was still in the process of making my own self up.

But I think I knew how to do it. I would do it through turning this whole place – all these homes and lives around me – into the stuff of fiction.

I was reading Anthony Burgess, A.S Byatt, Ian McEwan. I was going to our tiny library in the town precinct and taking out these fine hardbacks and reading contemporary literary fiction. But 'Possession' was no help. Neither was 'The Company of Strangers.' They seemed to posed, somehow. Too self-regarding. Their characters seemed to live in a very rarefied atmosphere. The atmosphere of literature, where they had finer feelings and shared deep thoughts and wandered around in a hazy fog of their own self-importance. When I later read all of Iris Murdoch's novels through one summer, one after the next, I recognized her work as the epitome of this rather soggy cloud of literary fictionality. It was a world in which hazy, slightly unhinged and well-off people drifted about the place being vaguely at odds with the world.

I was trying to measure my own experience and my own stories against it. I was trying to find a place inside it.

I knew that the lives and the characters I was inventing – drawn from the lives all around me that summer – were epic. I knew everything about them was huge and important. Their thoughts and the rhythms of their speech were lyrical and true. And it was important to me to catch hold of them and to make them into something.

By the end of that summer I had a clearer idea about what I was going to write about, for the next few years at least. I was finding my own way into literature.

I might have found it in the South of France. I don't know. It might have worked out much better, even. If I'd written about intellectuals in France – I'm sure that would have seemed far more fitting for 'literary fiction' to its middlebrow gate-keepers.

The first thing that many people said about my work in those early years was, 'Hm, these women and these working class characters… they're more like characters in soap operas from the TV, aren't they? Is that fair to say? You write a kind of soap opera?'

It was just sheer prejudice. Unthinking prejudice, and it came from some very clever and thoughtful people.

However.

Literary fiction isn't just about posh people.

When working class people appear in fiction, they aren't just chars or druggies or criminals.

If they are, then you're reading rubbish.

Broaden your reading. Broaden your outlook.

Get out of the house more.

Listen to people.

Listen to everything around you.

All those voices.

Tell me about where you come from.

Whose voices do you hear?

Go back to a street you lived on at some point in your life. Perhaps when you were twenty-one and wondering where your life was going to go, and which people you were going to live among. Were you longing to leave? Or did you want, more than anything, to belong?

Who was living beside you? What do you remember of the circumstances of their lives? What kinds of dramas were going on for them, parallel to yours, intertwining with yours?

Every street you live in is as big and as complex as Middlemarch.

It's so important to remember that. Wherever you are. You're just a part of a huge, ongoing, rather messy novel.

You aren't bigger than your own material.

Tell me about those neighbours and their tales.

Silly

I always knew as a kid that people who went on about being serious and grown-up about things were completely full of bullshit. I remember certain teachers when I was really small telling me that you oughtn't to be frivolous in stories, and you shouldn't send up adults for their foibles because it was disrespectful. You shouldn't answer back, do silly voices or take the piss. Even when you were grown up. Especially then.

I always knew that people who were *never* silly and never frivolous and who were scared of being satirised were full of shit, and usually, they were trying to put one over on you. I feel the same now, and I feel the same about writers, too, and I avoid books that are determinedly grim and earnest in an attempt to be taken seriously.

When people find it impossible to embrace their own essential silliness, it's tragic. Also dangerous. There are too many deadly serious, destructive, hypocritical people getting listened to these days.

Spare Paper

I'm remembering summers when I was a kid and school would break up for the holidays. To me those last days were exciting because we were allowed to take home books, projects, models and drawings from the classroom walls. We brought home leftover stuff. I could show Mam what I'd been doing. (She didn't go to many school Open Nights, 'Oh, I know you're doing fine. There's nothing they need to tell me about you, is there?')

I loved the thought of having school stuff at home: the smell of rice paper and exercise books and poster paint. I could pretend to have my own school at home. Or rather, I could have at home just the bits of school I liked. The paints and crayons and paper and writing and reading parts of school. And I could take all these parts down the Burn and sit in the trees and the long grass, filling in more pages and reading. Taking books home from school was exciting in itself. For some reason I preferred books that other people had read before me. I liked that the paper edges and corners were soft and smooth.

One of the first class rooms I remember was Mrs Payne's, when I was six. The divine, inspired, rather old-fashioned Mrs Payne with her shock of silver hair and dark eyebrows. Her occasional severity and her brilliant ideas. On the very last day we had in her class, I could have sworn that she told us to help ourselves to the contents of the spare paper cupboard. This was too exciting. I had no resistance to that store cupboard and its heaps of multi-coloured off-cuts of paper and its reams of creamy pages. Everything was stacked higgledy-piggledy.

Mrs Payne knew I used up a lot of paper. More than anyone in the class. I went through multiple Busy Books – which were the blank books, half-lined, half plain – which she doled out and told us to fill during our spare time with simply anything we could dream up. I wrote stories that went on for ten, fifteen, twenty pages at a time. That final day – having somehow got the message that we should help ourselves to a supply of loose paper from her store – I stood on a chair to take a daringly deep stack and stowed it away in my satchel. I went through the day looking forward to going home and imagining what I could fill all the pages and the empty days of summer with.

But I was caught out. My satchel was extra heavy and suspicious-looking as we all filed out of her classroom for the last time. To my shame I was forced to show what I'd purloined. On my very last day with Mrs Payne my beloved teacher was unhappy with me. The school bell was ringing and everyone was filing out happily, rushing because it was the end of the week and school was breaking up and I had an awful pang of misery as I understood that I'd done something wrong.

Every writer has a thing about stationery, I think. We all like talking about our notebooks and pens. We like to be engaged on that search for just the right materials. I always think that the cheapest and most obvious are the best kind to have. People can freeze themselves up by buying things that are too fancy or expensive. They save them up 'for best' and don't do anything at all with them.

As a kid at school I really loved using up paper, and I still do. My happiest memories are to do with the smell of sugar paper, and cutting out shapes and making friezes for the walls.

We used to do these great displays with pages of handwritten stories stapled to the walls with cut-out shapes of characters and monsters and extravagant lettering.

Stories were something that were writ large and they were papered over all our walls.

Everything we read together as a class was represented and I'd be helping out: standing on a chair or kneeling on a table, pinning tissue paper to notice boards or glueing sheets of coloured card together. Creating Narnia and Middle Earth and the outsized world of the tiny Borrowers. I remember standing on a ladder all one afternoon when I was eight, while the rest of the school was running about having Sports Day and I was constructing Smaug the dragon out of pink crepe paper across one whole wall. Tissue paper flames were shooting out of his nostrils.

Or maybe it was that other thrilling dragon we'd read about? The one that came from space and sat on Australia? In the last of Ted Hughes' 'Iron Man' stories?

It didn't matter – it was every dragon we'd ever read about, rendered in pink crepe and tissues of flame. Books became something you heard read aloud, you internalized and dreamed about, and you turned straight into drawings and stories of your own: that's what we were taught and it stayed with me. We rarely heard a whole book in class, of course, because there was never enough time. Bits got skipped. So I joined the library in town and looked for a copy to take home and to read alone and it was wonderful to find that the story was still there: still marvelous.

My own copy of Ted Hughes' dark, mystical 'Iron Man' I bought in a school jumble sale I visited with my Big Nanna. I was delighted to have a really old Faber copy from the 1960s, just about falling apart and date-stamped all over its first page. With Glad I ate candyfloss and rummaged through the bring-and-buy stalls. I think it was the first rummage sale I'd ever been to and a new obsession was born that day. I've never been able to walk past a heap of secondhand books ever since. I just know something wonderful is lurking there, probably right at the bottom, smelling of old paper and costing about fifteen pence. Something as good as a 1960s copy of Ted Hughes' 'The Iron Man.'

That day we wandered off with our candyfloss and our bargains to watch a disco dancing competition in the schoolyard (it was 1978.) The kids were dancing to 'Kung Fu Fighting' and then 'I was Made for Dancing.'

'Is that John Travolta singing?' my Big Nanna asked.

A scowling little girl standing next to us butted in and told her: 'No, it's Leif Garrett. It's nothing like John Travolta.'

Glad pulled a face, like all those names meant nothing to her. She wasn't really interested in disco music (or 'moosic', as she said in her Norfolk accent.)

What she did know about was wildlife and birds and trees and flowers. She could name them all as we walked back home through the Burn.

Starting Again

If you're going to write you must get used to starting again. I mean this on the small scale and the big scale.

You must start again with every project. You get to the end, start again. Edit and rewrite. Put it away. Take it out again. Are you happy yet?

On a bigger scale, you must start again with every new project. You must build it up from the ground again, whether it's a standalone novel or one in a series. I've written a number of series now, in different genres, and each new volume I've approached as if it were the first. Each new book must be a doorway to new readers.

Then, on a wider scale again, you must be prepared to pick yourself up and dust yourself off and start again from scratch throughout your career. You have to be resilient and resourceful. If you want to go on as a writer, then you must be prepared to reinvent yourself repeatedly and move on.

I've been dumped by several publishers over the years. I've been sacked by editors and passed on by agents. These things happen. That's just how it is.

And I've always been good! Never in trouble at school. Always worked hard and played by the rules as an adult. I got qualifications, I wrote, I revised and I invented stories and styles that were true to me and like no one else's. I always did my very best. Having found my own, unique voice I practiced it and sang for all I was worth. I sang my head off. I delivered books on time, did the edits, took the advice, rewrote, did everything I was told, performed at readings, festivals, taught workshops, smiled and signed and answered questions and did everything that was expected of me.

Even so. Being good has nothing to do with it. Being lucky is something else. That's just how it is.

And so you must reinvent yourself, if you want to stay in the game.

I was lucky, at times. I published my first books when I was in my mid-twenties, with the highly-respectable literary imprint, Chatto and Windus. I got in there simply by writing in and asking if they'd like to read my work. I was delighted to find they were interested in novels about working class council estates in the North East. And what's more, they were interested in magical realist goings-on in those places and amongst those characters. And they really were! For a year or two, anyway. But the books didn't sell, and I was dumped.

I then wrote Doctor Who novels for BBC Books in the 'Wilderness Years' before the show was brought back and became hugely successful. I wrote wayward, experimental, crazy Doctor Who novels and, when the show returned I was told I'd have to calm it all down if I wanted to carry on writing for them.

Be more conventional.

That's just how it is.

That was the reinvention wished upon me by various editors and agents over the years, especially as I went through my thirties and they despaired because I still hadn't 'broken through' (as they call it) to that commercial success they all wanted.

Why couldn't I write like other people did, they wanted to know? Why couldn't I have a success of my own by modeling my work on somebody else's?

I just couldn't. I didn't even know where to start. Why would I want to change anything in order to be like someone else?

I'd tried so hard to be me. Not being me was the only kind of reinvention I couldn't manage.

When I started writing children's fiction I put gay kids in because I'd been a gay kid and no one told me you weren't supposed to. (I gather this has changed somewhat now?)

When I wrote Science Fiction I made my heroine a drunken old woman who swore and smoked and drove a double-decker bus and who lived in Darlington, and I put in more jokes than science.

When I wrote Gothic Mystery I made my heroine the Bride of Frankenstein and she was like your favourite aunty, but hopeless at solving mysteries. She and fellow sleuth Effie usually ended up making situations much worse and the books followed none of the rules of the Gothic, nor Mystery, and were sold in the Science Fiction section of bookshops, for some reason.

When I wrote a memoir I wrote it from the point of view of our recently deceased cat.

When I wrote a book of literary criticism I did it about the Doctor Who Annuals: books which even Doctor Who fans think are unreadable.

That's just how it was.

With each new reinvention and change of genre and style I've only ever become more myself. These books and stories I write have only become more like me. I always thought that was the point. And though my books appear to belong in different genres and though they seem to be firing off in all sorts of directions, I see them as belonging to the same world, all interconnected.

And that's what the job has been about for me, through these twenty odd years and thirty odd books. It's about creating a body of work unlike anyone else's. It's about changing direction not so that you pander to someone else's duff expectations or silly guessing games about where the market is going (those kind of predictions never work anyway.)

I've changed direction in order to remain true to what my writing is all about. My books are always about picking yourself up and starting again. Reinvention has always been one of my most abiding themes.

I go my own way.

That's just how it is.

5 tips:

1. Begin a writing session with ten minutes of writing any old garbage. It's just to clear your throat.
2. Write in longhand first, in notebooks. Valuable editing goes on when you transcribe onto computer.
3. Only ever set out to write for a finite time. An hour or twenty minutes. Or a target of a thousand words, or 500. Don't push it too hard. We're in for the long haul, when we write novels.
4. Email your work to yourself at the end of the day. It's a useful back up, also it means you can read it back later on your phone or whatever device you carry about with you. Rereading your work with fresh eyes is vital.
5. Don't read other people's work forever thinking: 'I'm better / as good / not as good as this writer.' They couldn't write your stories, and you can't write theirs. You can only write your own.

Stockport in January 2015

That afternoon I was down the precinct in Stockport, and drawing the golden carousel from the window of Costa coffee. On rainy days in January the concrete walkways and paving slabs of that town centre can seem a little dreary and dim. There's still that hungover, faded feeling from the end of the festive season. That afternoon I'd walked all the way from Levenshulme just to get out of the house and now I was sitting with a coffee cup almost as big as my head, staring out of the window at this merry-go-round in the middle of the shopping arcade. A few kids were sitting on the gaudy ride, watched by their parents. The kids were going round and they were sitting on things like a dragon, a miniature double decker bus. It was a pretty good carousel if you were that age, but it had to be said, the whole effect was depressing.

As I was drawing the scene outside the window I became aware of an oldish lady sitting at the table to my left. She had frosted hair and her anorak still on. She was trying to catch my attention, I realized. She asked me, smiling: 'Is that part of your job? Drawing?'

Drawing merry-go-rounds in town precincts? Capturing the expressions on the faces of people hunched over their lattes?

What kind of job would ever involve things like that? 'I'm afraid not,' I told her. 'It's just for fun.'

She nodded, as if she thought doing things just for fun was a good idea.

I thought about this as I went back to my drawing. The world in January is particularly grey and harsh. I wanted to spend some time each day – even if it was just an hour each day – thoroughly enjoying myself. And I was lucky that, round about New Year, I had rediscovered my habit of drawing-whatever-the-hell-caught-my-eye. Also: colour. I love colour. I love splashing it about. I love turning up the colour dial as bright as it will go. What I really love is finding the brightness in the dreariest of town precincts and drawing the golden dragon as it goes round and round on even the rainiest of days.

That's why I was there that day. I was having fun.

Also, I was sick of trying to write.

The old lady was looking at me again. She was peering over her glasses and revving up to ask me something else. 'Do you ever wish that drawing was actually part of your job?' She studied me and put it another way, shaking out the thought: 'Do you wish that you'd become a professional artist?'

I answered without thinking. 'Yes, of course.' It was the instant, obvious answer, and I surprised myself by bursting out like that.

It was only January and already I had learned – or rather, remembered – that nothing makes my heart sing like being happy with a picture I'm doing. Being in the middle of a picture is one of the earliest, most vivid states of being I remember. Saying that it makes my heart *sing* sounds soppy and sentimental, I know. But by that I mean that I feel my heart beat faster when I put colour down or when I'm feeling confident letting lines go where they want. My heart beats faster and it expands in my chest, too. That's how it feels.

The old lady was nodding. I wondered, should I tell her that I'm a writer? That I do for a living something that other people dream of doing? And it's something that I dreamed of doing myself, and it's still one of the most amazing things in the world?

No, I thought. We're not talking about your writing. Not today. This was actually a novel idea. Here I was, having a conversation about life and art in a café, and it wasn't about my writing, or anyone else's writing. I almost felt liberated as I sipped my frothy coffee and watched the rain.

'Yeah,' I told her. 'I would have loved to draw for a living. When I was a kid I would have been amazed by that idea. But, as it is, drawing is my hobby. It's a pastime. It's something I love doing when I make time to do it, which, this year, is every single day. And if it was my job… well, what would my hobby be then..?'

I was very pleased with my answer, but I was probably talking too much. She'd think I was crazy, and wished she'd never started this conversation with a stranger, interrupting his joyful scribbling.

But what I'd said was exactly what I thought about the matter. This really was my glorious hobby. My miraculous rediscovery, at the age of forty-five. I was teaching myself to draw again, properly, for the first time since I was a kid of eighteen. And I would draw for at least an hour every single day of this year. My idea was to reconnect with who I was back then, when I could draw easily, without even thinking about it, without words getting in the way. I used to draw as naturally as breathing or as running around…

The old lady in the coffee shop was still looking at me.

'What would be your hobby then?' she mused. 'If you did your drawing for a living? Well, you'd find yourself another hobby, wouldn't you? You'd find something else that you longed to do.' She seemed to be giving this serious thought, digging down into her own ideas about what would make her own heart beat faster. 'Why, you could do something else again. Something wonderful. You could... you could... *sing*!'

When you draw in public, people come and sit next to you and tell you surprising things. When you write, they don't do that. They keep apart and try to give you the peace they assume you want.

Drawing brings me closer to other people than writing does. And it's made me feel part of the world around me.

Twenty years as a writer made me feel strangely alone.

But I'm still doing both, of course. I'm writing my journal and drawing my pictures. I'm just using up even more paper.

Summer Reading

It's just about the end of August and I'm thinking about what I want to be reading in the autumn already. I'm looking back on a summer during which I read a whole load of novels – perhaps more than ever before.

This summer began on the first of June, when Bernard Socks moved in with us and I was going through a phase of Richard and Judy novels. I read one after the next and thoroughly enjoyed most of them. Three months on, though, it's interesting just how much they've faded from my memory, or coalesced into one big shiny-covered blockbuster. All those long afternoons in the Beach House with Bernard Socks exploring the garden around me – I was inside some vast, page-turning miasma. Of course, some of them I completely adored and would read again – books like M.L Steadman's 'The Light between Oceans', 'Secrets of the Tides' by Hannah Richell and Paula McLain's 'The Paris Wife.' However, because they were brought to me by a very famous and popular book club they don't feel like *mine* somehow. I don't feel invested in them in the way that I do with books I have discovered for myself…

Books that I discovered for myself this summer will stay with me longer, I'm sure. The strangeness of Sam Savage's well-read rat, 'Firmin', or the warmth and wit of Sebastian Stuart's 'The Hour Between.'

There were only about seven or eight books that I wish I hadn't picked up this summer. For some reason I've forgotten how to abandon books unfinished. It's something I need to learn to do again. I won't go on about the things that I didn't enjoy so much – I want to stress the stuff I loved.

And I loved Julian Clary's 'Briefs Encountered' – which was a romp with real heart; I loved Jenny Colgan's 'The Loveliest Chocolate Shop in Paris', which was like having a marvelous holiday, a fabulous affair and eating as much fancy chocolate as you could manage – all on the Ille de France. And at the moment I'm loving Jo Baker's clever revisiting of Jane Austen, 'Longbourn' – which I'm sure I'll carry on thinking about as the leaves turn.

So – the moral seems to be – FIND BOOKS FOR YOURSELF, PAUL. Yes, book clubs and promotions are all very well and make you feel like you're part of a gang – for a bit. But the reductions make you feel queasy. You feel coerced into reading what everyone else is reading. You can see that the price-drops are ruining the very idea of choice and diversity and individuality. For every author and book raised up to dazzling heights of non-obscurity, dozens are cast into the fiery pits. After a summer's reading and thinking about it, you've decided that BOOK CLUBS, PROMOTIONS AND MASSIVE DISCOUNTS are unequivocally JUST BOLLOCKS, REALLY.

You're best off following your heart.

Every time.

So – here comes Autumn. What do you fancy reading?

I'm thinking about some Golden Age Science Fiction, actually. The type I really like has monsters and spaceships and exotic worlds. And, of course, autumn will bring ghosts and earthbound monsters and more detectives. There's nothing coming out new that I'm particularly bothered about – save Susan Cooper's 'Ghost Hawk', which is winging its way from

Amazon as I write. Other than that, I'm content to slalom the stacks of novels I already own... I'm loading up my To Be Read shelf right now... hoping to attain the perfect mix of thrills, thoughtfulness, and getting carried away by it all.

Limefield
Terrace.

The Big Top

I used to tell myself, 'I can't plot.' 'My mind doesn't work that way.'

I thought that, in order to plot, you had to be logical, precise. It was like a mechanical, mathematical thing. It was a very commercial thing, for Hollywood movies and stuff like that.

I used to think real art was about intuition solely, and you had a duty not to plot your novel out fully, in order to let the magic and mystery into it. In order to let the novel live and breathe...

Hmmmm.

I've changed my mind about that.

Novels and short stories are about intuition and magic and mystery and art... but they're also about craft and mechanics, logic and plans.

We've got to start making some plans.

Some people can hold the shape of an entire novel inside their head, and they don't have to make notes. My memory is terrible, and I find that I have to write everything down. Sometimes, to see the whole shape of a piece of fiction I'm planning, I have to construct flow charts, graphs, timelines, all kinds of diagrams.

I like to be able to take an aerial view of the novel: to see where it's all going; to see where the characters are heading to; and where they cross over and intersect with each other.

There's no set, perfect diagram for the shape of a novel. Each novel might have its own diagram, completely unique, like a snowflake or a thumb print. I think it's useful to get into the habit of being able to talk about the shape of your novel, as if it was a piece of sculpture.

Wowee: to be really deep... maybe that's what a novel is... a four dimensional sculpture? A sculpture in time?

Some writers use architectural metaphors. I'm sure I've read about Henry James's *The Portrait of a Lady* being described as a magnificent cathedral. We walk into these vast, echoing novels of the past, all hushed with awe, flipping through our guide books, watchful for special features... (wrinkling our noses, at times, at the musty, disused smell...)

When I was trying to teach ideas about plotting to a class recently, I came up with a metaphor that I'm happy with – for now, at least. And that's the circus tent.

It's a bit jollier than a draughty cathedral. Less determinedly sublime, perhaps – and committed to entertainment and a certain raffish glamour. So circus tents are good.

(I also like novels about circuses: Angela Carter's *Nights at the Circus*; Paul Gallico's *Love, Let Me Not Hunger*... but they're irrelevant to this chapter, really. This is just about the circus tent and its construction as metaphor.)

It's an image I invoked in a workshop, in order to stress the effort required when building a plot. As in putting up a great big circus tent, in order to put on a show, you can't leave out any of the stages. You can't rush it or bodge it. Otherwise the whole lot will collapse. The tigers will burst free, the trapeze artists will fall from their wires, and the dancing horses will trample on your disappointed audience.

You need to get everything right and in its proper place, to make sure it will stand up.

The *premise* of the novel is the clear wasteground where the circus is going to set up. This is where they park their caravans and motors and they lay out the sawdust ring and bleachers. They mark out that space very carefully.

This is the *conceptual space* of your novel. That means, the very simple idea behind your story: the world of the book and how you define that. (For instance: a dystopian future society in which – I don't know – the only currency is ice cream. And cows rule the earth.)

You might be raring to go, having created your premise for the novel. But this is only the starting point. It's the sawdusty ground and the banks of seats. It's the circus ring without the tent. It the wind gets up or the heavens open, there won't be any show.

You need to have a plot. The plot involves knocking in poles and pegs and guy ropes. It's strenuous and complicated, and involves knowing what goes where. It involves sketching out in the air, the shape you want your tent to take: being able to gauge how wide, how high. How roomy.

Last of all comes the canvas tent itself, and only when all the structure and framework and skeleton is strong and fixed underneath. Then you can get your strong men and clowns and tethered elephants to pull together, and draw the canvas over the top. Will it hold? Will it stay up? Will it be in the shape you imagined?

At the very end you can pop a little flag on the very top. You can string some bunting around it.

People get the order of this construction very mixed up.

I've watched them mark out the ground and then try to put the flags out on top, when there isn't even a top there yet.

I've watched them mark out a huge amount of ground and come struggling in with a tiny, perfect, shiny piece of canvas, that they dump in the middle, in a heap.

And I've seen a tiny piece of ground and one huge pole, reaching about twenty times too high. Little straggle of bunting hanging off it.

What I'm saying is: get your plans and proportions right. Just enough premise. Just tall enough poles. Exactly enough canvas. Room enough inside for your performers and your animals and your cheering crowds...

In terms of getting that skeleton of wooden poles together, I think it's useful to erect the tallest ones first. They become the highest points in your tent. All the other tight ropes depend upon those points. The whole circus tent radiates from those apexes. These are the poles that the trapeze artistes go shinning up...

And those highest points represent the ultimate dramatic moments in your novel. They are climaxes. They are where everything comes together. Everything depends upon them, and they are what everything tends towards. All the characters are there at the climax; their eyes trained towards that highest point. Something is imperilled, everyone is alarmed. There has been shouting and drama leading up to this. Now everyone holds their breath.

I like this model of plotting. It's one that gets used in TV serials a lot. I heard Russell T Davies describe it ten years ago, and it struck me then as a useful method. You imagine your dramatic high-point first – you invent the most fantastically exciting collision of characters and circumstances you can picture – and then you work backwards from there. You tease the stories of all the characters back towards their starting points. Then you can start to figure out what (separate / tandem / parallel) journies they each have to endure.

I find it useful to have these very visual, tactile metaphors to hand, when trying to construct stories or novels. I find it too much too keep in my head, and I find synopses and bullet point pages confusing. I need to be able to grasp an image in my head. Then, when I'm working on the novel, I don't have to carry the whole thing at once. I can work on it a piece at a time. If I'm writing a circus tent, I know when I'm stringing the bunting up.

If I'm doing a cathedral I know when I'm fiddling with flying buttresses, or deciding where the gargoyles should go…

Think about the novel or story you want to write. Have you constructed enough of it, before you go blundering on with it? Have you just got a premise, or have you got a plot as well?

Write a few sentences for your premise, and then a few sentences for your plot. Make them gripping. If they aren't very, make them *more* gripping.

Don't elaborate too much: just give us the bare bones of plot.

Now develop your climactic moment. Who will be there? What will their conflict be? What huge, dramatic event will transfix your characters and readers, and bring your novel to a crescendo…?

How will you work towards that?

Think back through recent novels you have read. Think about their construction.

Draw the shape of them. Construct a diagram.

Are there are as many shapes as there are novels in the world?

I once wrote a dissertation about *Wuthering Heights* having the same Chinese box structure as *Frankenstein*. Maybe there are only a certain number of shapes that novels can be stretched to?

Try to work out what a satisfying shape is.

Try to construct something completely unique.

Is it possible to create a story shape that no one has ever thought of before?

The Fellow Reader

A friend was on the phone that night, and we talked about reading. About the compulsive kind of fiction reading we both go in for. Hungry reading, she called it.

We had got onto the subject because we'd been talking about technology and the things that can go wrong with it. Technology has always scared me, I think, and books seemed like things that couldn't *go wrong*. They would never spontaneously blow up, or wipe their memory out. I was safe with books, in a way that I wasn't safe with tricky, electronic things.

Technology reminds me of Christmases when I would receive expensive electronic toys. My gruff, aggressive stepfather would be the expert: setting them up and getting them going. I would sit and watch him playing.

That very night, as my friend and I were talking, Jeremy was having a situation with our computer just-about crashing. He kept rescuing it from the brink, just to have it fade away again. It was like the iMac was having a nervous breakdown.

Jeremy loves fiddling with that stuff and getting annoyed with it. He's the kind of man who takes the backs off things in order to have a look inside: to blow dust off the circuits and to tug at loose bits of wire.

I'd be frightened of blowing myself up.

My friend was saying that she hadn't really known anyone who went in for that voracious kind of reading until she was forty, and she enrolled on the Creative Writing MA at Lancaster University. That was where we met in 1991 and became best friends. All her life she had read fiction in that way. When she was a child her mother used to say: 'Who are you being *today?*'

For me, it was such a relief to have someone like that in the workshop. I hadn't really met a reader like me, either – not even through an English degree. It was lovely to have someone else saying things like: 'That's just like the wolves in Angela Carter's stories!' or 'Have you read *The World According to Garp?*' And mostly, we had read the same books.

We had both read scads, and took immense pleasure in recognising a kindred bookish spirit. Because we had certain novels in common – *Wise Children, The Hotel New Hampshire, The Passion, Saint Maybe* – we had a shared vocabulary. Our bookshelves matched: with the spines of the books all nicely cracked and the covers similarly weathered.

It's such a relief to find readers. To know what somebody means when they say they want to read a book that, 'tears the flesh off your bones.' Or one that is 'consoling and chocolatey.' Or that contains the kind of mundane, everyday, embarrassing detail that makes you 'wince' or 'flinch.' These words are a sort of shorthand between you.

Even at university I'd never really been surrounded by many readers. In the late Eighties, amongst my peers, it wasn't the thing to be. Theatre was their thing. But I was the one, during Freshers' week, getting over the trauma and guilt of leaving home by sitting in my room and reading my lurid Pan paperback copy of *Dracula*. It still makes me smile – with embarrassed recognition – that Bram Stoker was my consolation.

That autumn term I was keeping a very involved diary. I was burning incense and lighting candles in Chianti bottles. I was playing David Bowie, the Cure, Lou Reed. I had brought my ten favourite novels, for comfort's sake. I made a ritual of setting them up on the single shelf in my 'study bedroom' (bare yellow brick walls with green splashes; chilly linoleum floors. BTW Linoleum was invented in Lancaster. Down at the docks, someone accidentally spilled hot tar on a roll of carpet. Hey Presto!)

Even at university I felt odd for being bookish. A group of us would convene in my room after lectures, and we would try to make sense of all the advanced linguistic analysis stuff. They were panicky meetings, with some people crying. Even I didn't much like the stodgy stuff we were given to read in the first year.

In my second year, though, English Literature with a capital E and L kicked in. We English Majors went back in time to the seventeenth, eighteenth and nineteenth centuries and we had five set texts a week. And then, after a winter of Oscar Wilde and Frankenstein, I met my first boyfriend.

That spring I met someone who called himself a novelist. He was exactly the same age as me (I mean *exactly*: we found we were born on the same day.) He was from New York. He was unapologetically gay, unapologetically a reader, and unapologetically a writer. All of this was very novel to me.

He had a clunky word processor. State of the art, then, of course, in 1990. The screen was small, like looking into a periscope. But the print was black and confident. Clean, sharp prose. He was introducing me to contemporary American fiction.

He said: Had I read Armistead Maupin? Anne Tyler? Amy Tan? We went round the Waterstones in town and he was buying copies of new novels by these people. During his year in England he had gotten out of touch with what was coming out. And here they were! He bought them up. I had to read this! And this! And this one! But only after he'd finished them.

I hadn't read any of these people. They were contemporary. They were set in Baltimore, New York, San Francisco. They were *wonderrrfuullll*, he told me. I just had to read them. They were written to sound very much like real speech. Everyday language. Ordinary people.

When I read them, I was astonished. In my reading I was stuck somewhere in 1917, thinking Virginia Woolf and Forster were flashy and brand-spanking new.

Also, crucially, I was still thinking that characters in books always had to be posh. In serious books, anyway. 'Literary' fiction was about what posh people did and said. And that thought had depressed me. And I'd got stuck.

It was the rhythms and the casual music of contemporary American Lit that got me unstuck.

He also asked, had I read any *gay* fiction? Any Edmund White? David Leavitt? I hadn't, of course, and all I could offer were Christopher Isherwood and E.M Forster. They weren't good enough. 'All that old, country house, closety stuff is fine,' he said. 'But you never *see* anything! You never find *anything* out!' He mimed exasperation, sitting crouched on the floor of his study bedroom. He was small and rangey, with these pale, expressive hands. His face was long, with dark hair brushed to one side, in a self-consciously English style, for his Junior Year Abroad. His beard looked almost blue, when it started to grow through, during a long night awake talking about books. 'You need the *real* stuff,' he said. 'The *explicit* stuff that tells you *exactly* how it is. In gay fiction, and just generally. That's *important*.'

There was a freshness to all of this for me. I was delighted with the idea of clarity: of making the prose seem easy and colloquial. And I was delighted by the idea of being able to say anything with it. There were no holds barred. I didn't have to be closeted, cramped, writing in code.

My hand-writing got bigger. Really! That was a measure of my loosening up. The writing I had been doing that year, until then, had been all these small, scrappy, unfinished things, in the tiniest handwriting possible. I was writing in one of my stepfather's technical workbooks, filched from home. Those books had thin, onionskin paper, and I wrote in fountain pen. I wrote descriptions and snatches of conversation: everything very oblique. It was very laborious. I let my new American boyfriend have a look at some of the things I had written. That was a huge step for me. Letting someone else look at that stuff! He gave it his considered attention. 'Hmmm. You need some actual *stories*.'

At that point I don't think I had ever got to the end of a story.

I was learning to do that now. That spring I was learning that prose fiction had to follow a scene, moment by moment. The writer and reader had to inhabit every moment as fully and richly as they could. The writer had to keep the reader there, in the moment. The writer had to seduce the reader and make them want to run time back. The reader had to want to go back through these scenes and rooms again and again. The moment had to be perfect, like a dream. It had to be something you could always go back to.

Think about the novels that have made you want to write. What was it you learned from them? Why did they make you feel brave?

Who were you then, when you were deciding you were going to write? Were you a different person to who you are now? Have you changed at all?

What do you look for in the fiction you read? Can you see a line of continuity in the books that are important to you?

Do you want to write like the people you read?

Who do you write for anyway? Yourself? An ideal reader? Your lover? Your best friend? Your mother?

Is your work still private? Is it public yet?

Choose a number of these questions. Brainstorm responses to them.

Make lists of books that have defined your life. Give them to people.

The Green Door

I was very lucky with the teachers I had.

I think I grew up in an era when there seemed to be more time about. Whole hours or more were given over to reading, and teachers reading aloud to the class. The last part of every day was when we'd all listen to the teacher reading the latest chapter from our class book, whatever that happened to be at the time.

We were lucky to hear so many great children's books read aloud to us. Reading aloud lets the air into a book. It lets the breeze run through it. The first time I knew about 'The Hobbit', 'The Wind in the Willows' and 'The 101 Dalmations' was when they were read to us, chapter by chapter.

Also, they were complete books that we heard. Serialised, day after day, until the books were done. Building up reading stamina is so important, as is learning the ability to listen to an ongoing story. So much of teaching these days seems to rely on snippets and excerpts of things. Bits and pieces, as if all of literature could be turned into easily-digestible chunks or Chicken McNuggets.

But books aren't really like that. You have to spend the time.

I don't think it was a programmatic and thoroughly-planned business, this delivering of the children's classics to our tender ears. We just happened to get the best, one after the next – 'The Secret Garden', 'The Lion, the Witch and the Wardrobe.' No one was sitting there, at the Local Education Authority's offices or in

Whitehall, deciding which books we should be exposed to, and how much good they would do us.

The teachers themselves decided. They brought in books they themselves had loved. Novels and stories that had turned them into readers. They brought all of that enthusiasm with them. So even a spectacularly unsympathetic teacher who looked after us one year – harsh and difficult though she could be – still had fantastic taste in children's fiction. She introduced us to Narnia and Cruella De Ville and because of this even that whole tricky year (the year of my parents' divorce!) becomes blessed in my memory.

That same year we had a stand-in teacher for a little while. A lovely, hippyish Barbra Streisand lookalike who usually taught music. Mrs Saferi wore a poncho and lived on the same council estate as most of us in our class. When she walked home she had a big gang of kids walking along beside her. It was like the Jewish 'Sound of Music', in Newton Aycliffe, County Durham. She walked along the country lanes to our estate making all these kids sing rounds with her.

And, when it came to the end of the summer term she made little goody bags for all my classmates and we queued up at the end of the final day so she could dispense these bags of sweets.

When it came to my turn she gave me a brown paper parcel. Rectangular and bookish and tied up with string. 'Don't open it now,' she told me. 'Wait till you get home. These four books were my favourites when I was your age. The very summer when I was the age you are now. I want them back, of course! They're my very own copies from the 1960s and therefore very precious. But I want you to enjoy them this summer as much as I did back then.'

She didn't make a fuss, singling me out in front of the rest of the class. She did it very discreetly, watching me stow the book parcel away in my satchel.

I walked home feeling like I'd been entrusted with something very special. I got a bit of teasing from friends who'd seen her giving me the parcel, but I didn't care.

When I got home I took the parcel upstairs and opened it so carefully, like it was a time bomb ticking under that brown paper. Inside were four Puffins. Sun-faded covers from summer afternoons. Soft, yellowing pages. 'The Horse and his Boy' by C.S Lewis; 'Five Children and It' by E. Nesbit; 'The Borrowers Afield' by Mary Norton and 'Worzel Gummidge and Saucy Nancy' by Barbara Euphan Todd.

It was a long, warm summer of reading. It was the time of my stepfather moving in and all kinds of upheavals. He was a glowering presence. He would never speak to me. He didn't have a name I could call him. He wasn't 'dad'. Dad lived in Durham city. And calling him by his actual name would have been impertinent.

I concentrated on my reading and on my Petite toy typewriter, which only typed in red, for some reason. I worked on sheets of paper half the size of A4 and wrote stories about Cruella De Ville, Doctor Who, Mr Tumnus and Worzel Gummidge. Almost straight away I was burying myself in Further Adventures for the characters I was getting to know.

Mam and her new live-in boyfriend were fighting almost straight away. Turned out she never really asked him to move into our council house. Just one day he turned up with his hi-fi equipment and his collection of leather coats and vinyl albums.

I typed and typed and read my books.

Once they were fighting through supper, as we ate pies from Greggs' bakery at the smoked glass dinning table. 'Well, we don't need you to support us anyway,' Mam yelled at him. 'Paul's writing a book, aren't you, Paul? He's writing his first novel and it'll be a bestseller and he'll be able to earn all the money we'll ever need! So we don't need you here anyway, do we?'

Her boyfriend just glowered and wouldn't even look at me. He went back to his pie and gravy, grumbling and mumbling. On the telly it was the local news and I imagined myself being interviewed on there about my book. It was a book about witches, I remember, and I'd even drawn a cover for it, and I was discussing it all quite confidently on the TV.

Sometimes it seems to me that the whole course of my life was set for me during that summer. Somewhere between Mrs Saferi and her bag of books and my clattering away on that toy typewriter with its frayed red ribbon.

Much easier exercise this time.

I want you to do a bit of memory-work. Think back. Close your eyes.

What are the books that were important to you when you were a kid?

Writers most often become writers because they were obsessive readers. They had the ability to be caught up completely in somebody else's imaginary worlds. They know that it can be done, and they want – through their own writing – to recreate that feeling of magic. Even if the things they read and write about aren't magical in the least. The very act of them coming to life from the page is about magic in its purest sense.

So – think about being read to at school or by someone at home.

Think about using the school library, the town library, the bookshelf in your living room. What books fell into your hands? Which books did you find for yourself and read to yourself?

What did you get from them?

Take a little time jotting down answers to these questions.

When did you read a book that made you think, I want to do this? I would love to write stories like this?

Who was the character who first fired your imagination?

Who did you want to be?

Which characters scared you? Which stories were actually frightening?

Which books did you read under the bedclothes with a torch? (Yes, this is a whopping cliché – but only because it's true. Some of the most delicious reading in childhood is that through-the-middle-of-the-night stuff, when you're supposed to be asleep. In our house there were transom windows above each interior door and so any light spilled onto the landing and Mam would see. So the torch and the tented bedclothes were absolutely necessary for night-time trips to Skaro, Wonderland, or Middle Earth.)

Think about where you were and what you read when you were:

In the final year of your Primary School.

In the first year of Secondary school.

When you were doing your exams.

What's the first ever book you recall reading for yourself, by yourself?

Which book first made clear sense when you were learning to read in the first place? When did all the words suddenly click into place?

Also, are there any particular afternoons that come to mind? Any days when you were completely stuck in a book?

I'm thinking of my obsession when I was twelve with 'Danny, Champion of the World' by Roald Dahl and how I read it several times in one week. Yes, it had been set as the book for an exam we'd be taking and it was part of my revision timetable to just about learn it off by heart. But even so, that book opened itself up like a whole, wonderful world of its own. It's a book drenched in nostalgia and a book full of love. I don't think I was reading it again and again simply because I was going to get a test on the plain facts about it. I think I was reading it because I was burrowing into it. Wearing a path that led right into its beating heart.

Our footprints stay inside books we've read. Sometimes we forget where we've been. We pick up a book and we find our footprints are still there. We can recapture who we were when we first read this story.

This can come as a real surprise sometimes. A delightful surprise. Going back to Enid Blyton's strange 'Faraway Tree' books when my much-younger sister wanted to be read to was an amazing business. It was like opening a door into earlier days. Like instant sunshine. Like drinking very fizzy pop.

Sometimes when you go back to reread the things that were important it's like meeting old friends – the characters, yes. But also ourselves at a younger age. Rereading these books we read when we were young is like being introduced back to our younger selves.

This is a hugely important thing for a writer to do. To become young again. To stay young inside your head.

So many people make themselves old deliberately. They think about old things and talk about old things. They don't let themselves be silly any more. They don't go anywhere inside their heads when they shut their eyes.

Now I'd like you to draw up a list.

Think about yourself at all those ages. Every age up to, say, twenty.

How many books can you remember reading?

Everything. Write down everything you remember reading. The classics and the modern books and the TV tie-ins and film novelizations and fairy tales and the series books and the find-your-own adventure books and the adult books that you snuck from your parents' shelves that you weren't really allowed to read. Rack your brains. Ask old friends and schoolmates and contemporaries, siblings and parents. What have you forgotten? What did you take out of the library during the winter holiday when you were eleven? What did you have with you every rainy lunchtime at school when you were fifteen?

Sometimes the ones you have forgotten will suddenly come back to you.

And things like the internet and book bloggers can make things easier for you.

A couple of years ago I was trying to remember a particular book I had adored when I was about ten. I took it several times out of the library in Newton Aycliffe and disappeared inside it. But I couldn't remember its title, nor its author, and so I assumed it was lost to me forever.

All I knew was that it was set in New York, in an apartment building, and there was a girl, her best friend and her irksome little brother. And they had a magic silver pencil that could bring to life anyone who was on TV. Pirates were involved and they were all running about this apartment block and Central Park, causing havoc.

I happened to mention this to a new friend, whose book blog I was reading. He specialized in children's books and knew incredible amounts about them. It took him about an hour on the internet to find out what it was I was half-remembering.

I was amazed by what he told me.

I was actually recalling two books and had mistakenly fused them into one. One, about those New York children and their magic television set. But it was a set that broadcast tomorrow's TV and its magical foresight is what causes their adventures. It was 'A Billion for Boris' by Mary Rodgers. The other was 'The Captain Hook Affair' by Humphrey Carpenter, in which a girl in a children's home and her best friend get hold of a silver pencil, which can be used to bring characters from books to life – and that's why the pirates and other fictional creations are running rampant in the story.

Well, both books were floating about on the internet, it turned out. I found copies through Amazon Used and New and they were with me within a few days. Lovely, worn-out old library copies. The very epitome of forgotten books cluttering up someone's shelves. Precious as anything to me.

And when I reread them they were just as good as ever.

I found my own footprints all through them.

I remembered being there, when I was ten. I recognized the rooms and the conversations and the exciting bits and the jokes.

One of the best gifts ever.

Having books returned to you like this.

Is there a similar book or books in your reading history?

Something you can't quite put your finger on? A magical book with a title and author you can't remember at all? Maybe you just have an image.

The same friend who did that detective work on my lost books talks about a similar case of his own. All he remembers is a green door, and how it was important in a story he once read. But he doesn't know what it was, or where it led.

I think we've all got one of those doors.

So, take some time and make some lists. What did you read and what did you love? Do you know why you loved some of these books and not others?

Then try to find out what that elusive memory of a book is all about. What's behind your own particular green door?

And maybe narrow your list down to just four all-time favourites you haven't read for a very long time. Just four titles – enough to fill a special brown paper parcel at the very end of the term and the start of the summer holidays.

Make your assignment the rereading of those books.

Lie in the long grass, in the branches of a tree, or in an attic, or in the town library as the rain sheets down outside. Or hide under the bedclothes all over again.

But make some time to recapture those feelings.

Remember how you felt when you were first discovering that stories really do come to life. And you don't even need a magic silver pencil to help them do that.

The Kernel

People like to ask: 'Do you plot your novel out to the end? Do you know where it's going to when you start?'

With each novel I write I find that I'm making more and more elaborate, comprehensive plans. About six novels into my career I discovered what it was like to work with a fairly rigorous synopsis. At the start I used to jump on board, like a novel was a roller coaster and I didn't even wear the safety harness.

But everyone works differently and they change throughout their writing career. There are no hard and fast rules about how much you have to plot and plan. Iris Murdoch used to reckon that she had the whole thing worked out in her head before she sat down to write even a word. The actual writing of words was the least of it. That seems very alien to me.

I mentioned what Iris Murdoch had said in a recent workshop, and someone said that they would feel that the actual writing had become futile, in that case. Having worked a whole plot out in their head, they would feel as if they had already been there and done that. The novel, in other words, would never get written.

Some people like walking out into the blankness of the page. Setting off into the unknown.

Other people are terrified by that idea.

A few years ago, the brilliant short story writer and novelist Georgina Hammick came and talked to a group of students I was teaching in Yorkshire, for the Arvon Foundation. They were pretty practised writers, all of them embarking on novels, and quite soon, during the questions and answers session, they were onto this question of how much can you and should you plan?

Now, Georgie is a very dry, ironic soul, and very self-deprecating about her own work. She isn't given to grandiose, sweeping statements about life and literature. She always gives me the sense, though, of secretly and quietly knowing *exactly* what all the answers are. I think the students saw that too, as she sat in the living room, by the fire, giving the question all of her attention.

She told us that she herself couldn't plan things out. She talked about Planned Novels and Unplanned Novles. She told the group that she makes up her stories and novels very slowly, bit by bit. She *encroached* on the novel. A very organic process, whereby one characters' actions and reactions will necessarily lead to repercussions through the lives and doings of all the others.

She told us how slowly, slowly, slowly she works. Lots of thinking, lots of carefulness. But not intellectualising. Not being schematic, programmatic, scientific.

Letting the story have its way. Going where it needs to go. And, above all, sticking to the truth of your characters. Georgie gave the sense of caring very deeply for her characters, and getting their story *right* was the most vital thing of all.

I think my students were very pleased with that. I'd been in the grip of a sudden enthusiasm for inventing plotting exercises and synopsis-writing. I'd given them recipes and charts and encouraged them to get away from the page and to take an aerial view of their novels: to see the lie of the land. I'd asked them to draw diagrams and flow-charts and to colour in huge sheets of card.

It's useful sometimes for writers to get away from words. You should draw and paint and cut out bits of paper. Use origami and graphs and clay models. It doesn't all have to be words. Fiction's raw materials, it seems to me, are space and time, people and ideas and emotions, and words aren't the only things that can represent those.

A useful way to think about plotting is this:

Begin with the kernel of the story. What's at the heart of this drama?

What theme? Which characters?

What climactic scene of conflict brings these characters together?

Decide on that. The emotional high point – or points – of your story. And then work backwards. Rewind all your characters back from there.

Where would they all have to start from in order to reach that point?

The kernel can be approached from all different directions. You can approach the emotional heart of your novel in lots of different ways, trying out different routes. Drawing new maps to take you into the heart of the forest.

Try out writing whole chapters from different view-points, or scenes from unusual angles. You don't have to use all of these. Think of these sections of text as jigsaw pieces that you might or might not place together, in order to build up the big picture. You can collage them together later.

You don't have to write a novel in strict chronological order.

People often make the mistake of thinking that you write a novel like you read one. IE, that you start in the top left hand corner of page one and continue – blah blah blah blah – until the bottom right hand corner of page 350 or 240 or whatever. It doesn't have to be like that.

You need to do that tricky, conceptual work – of creating a shape for your story, your chapters, your novel. And then you need to fill those shapes with broader strokes, bolder colours, and build it up in layers, coming to finer details gradually.

That's not to say you can't write the whole thing at the micro level of perfect sentences, one after the next – but that way is the harder way, I think.

And whether a writer plots and plans the whole thing out, or whether they just make it up as they go along, I think they have always got to have the bigger picture in mind. They are moving out into vast, open spans of time and space, and they have to lift their head up from the confines of the page, now and then, just to be able to take it all in.

What I'm saying is: Make plans! It's not as hard as it seems! Give it a go!

Here's the plotting exercise I used that week in 2000, teaching in Yorkshire. I've refined it a bit since. This works really well with a group of about ten writers. What happens is, you have a hat (or, in our case, a pudding bowl) in the centre of the table, and with each 'round' (as described and listed below), everyone puts their folded bit of paper in, stirs it round like a tombola, and takes out a slip of paper at random.

There are six rounds to get through. You can do this with fewer or more people. There must be a way of doing it by yourself. Maybe using slips of paper you've put in the hat ages ago and have forgotten about: you could maybe plan this way in advance and do this exercise alone.

The point is the *randomness* of it. You should inherit specific details that you MUST include in your story synopsis. They should be completely random factors, coming out of left field, that will push you in directions you would never have expected to go.

This is always profitable. As is the exercise – whether the synopsis develops into a fully-fledged story or novel or not. It's good, stretching practise to make stories up. We used to do this all the time, as kids. They were grand, splashy adventures. Growing up cramps our style, sometimes. It stifles our imagination. Even people who want to write novels have cramped, confined, hampered imaginations – and need to exercise them and make up stories – even (especially!) – silly ones.

Okay – six 'rounds' of writing. In just a sentence or two, on a small slip of paper, describe the following story ingredients:

Round one. Two characters. Names, short physical and temperament description. One on each slip of paper.

Round two. A third character. The stranger, who comes into the lives of the first two.

Round three. Two settings. Anywhere you like. As weird or as homely as you want. One will be a starting point, the other will be the place the characters will end up.

Round four. An object. Maybe it has a symbolic dimension. It might even give the story its eventual title. 'The Frantic Hatstand.'

Round five. A disagreement. What might people row about? Give us the kernel of their argument.

Round six. A moment of danger. Something physical, tangible. Be as action-packed as you feel like. (Sometimes, writing 'literary' fiction, people forget to be at all action-packed. They end up writing novels with people just standing around talking. Imagine!)

Now, each round should be written in three minutes max. Don't dawdle. Don't get too clever. Put someone in charge of the tombola. (The most cynical, disruptive person, perhaps. They'll do a good job of seeing it all comes out right. They'll be keen to see how the experiment works. Because they don't believe it can: 'You can't use a recipe for stories! No way!')

Once everyone has their slips of paper, they should be given time to examine them all together, and put them in order, and think about them – and usually end up hooting with laughter. That's how it should be. They're laughing at the ridiculousness of the combinations: the juxtapositions they've got and the impossibility of making this thing work out.

But their minds are already ticking over. They're already making up stories.

They should check that they each have eight slivers of paper. (Two characters, one stranger, two settings, an object, a disagreement, a moment of danger.) They should check that they haven't received back any of their own, original pieces. If they have, a swap should be quickly arranged with someone.

I've tried this workshop with ten year olds and everyone up to the age of eighty. Everyone fusses over the tombola – someone always takes too many by mistake. There's always a slight kerfuffle that has to be sorted out. Everyone always descends into laughter and giggles. And, at first, no one thinks they can actually do it.

At this point I get everyone to read out their slips of paper. This takes a while, and lets everyone see that everyone has a tricky task ahead. Lots of laughing in this bit – but also, lots of minds racing. Stories are starting to form themselves in people's minds: connections are being made. Imaginations stirred. People are thinking of tales they would never have come up with before, without the stimulus of the exercise and the randomness, and the prompting of other people's inventions.

The idea is to give them some time to write a story synopsis. Forty minutes is a good length of time. Write maybe a thousand words. Now everyone has to thread all their elements together in a chain reaction. The two main characters begin their story in the first setting; the arrival of the stranger; the addition of the – perhaps symbolic – object; the travelling to the other place; the argument between them; the climactic moment of danger. And then – how does it all get resolved? Here, of course, I've suggested the ordering that feels intuitively, obviously right (It describes Frodo and Sam and Gollum taking the ring into Mordor, I suddenly realise.) You can, of course, combine the elements in any order you like.

Give it a go. String these items together like beads on a necklace. Make the wires connecting the items quite taut: like the wires between telegraph poles. You must make sure that one event leads inevitably to another.

I think it's our nature to connect random elements and events and to make a story out of them.

And that's just a way of saying that, once you get going with this exercise, you'll find it much easier than you thought. And you'll surprise yourself with what you come up with.

The Killer First Line

We all know that feeling of being grabbed by a fantastic first page of a story or a novel... and we also know the feeling of failing to be hooked by those crucial first paragraphs. This exercise is about looking at brilliant and terrible examples of fictional openings - and trying to pin down some of the elements that draw us in and make us want to read on and on...

Hopefully by having a go at this, you will have composed something completely irresistable.

I tried this out originally in 2011 at a workshop at Halifax library. It was a new exercise I'd dreamed up, and I had no idea whether it would work out. But I was willing to experiment and take the risk. I was very interested in finding out what people made out of these prompts, and what they thought constitutes a really good beginning.

I chose a bunch of first pages from novels. They weren't all classics, and they weren't all brilliant. I photocopied a sampling of different kinds of books. Some were pulpy, some were literary, some were recognizable, others obscure. They weren't quite random. I had my own ideas about which I thought were instantly gripping and intriguing and which I thought were hopeless.

Doing this exercise at home by yourself, you can go off and explore your bookshelves. Have a good hunt around for a memorable first page or two... Which ones stick in your head? Which surprise you? Do any make you want to sit down and read further right now..?

What do you really want from a good first page?

When I first did this in Halifax, and then later at the Ty Newydd writing centre in Wales, I got a good list of some of the things people like to be drawn in by on page one, and some questions, too:

Snappy dialogue. Starting in the middle of a scene. Starting in the middle of something exciting going on.

A funny, pithy line from a character.

A line of gorgeous description?

Something more abstract, warming up to the theme of the story, like a kind of overture?

Something more plotty and intriguing? Characters onstage from the start, or off?

A sense of being baffled. Or maybe stark clarity?

A chance to find your feet in the fiction. Do we like being disoriented?

What else..?

Do we need to know exactly where we are on page one? Do we need to be in the middle of a major event? Or can we sneak up on the action, with something more banal and everyday?

Is what we really want a great hook?

Puzzles and questions? Sympathy? Something eye-catching? Jokes? Immediate tension? Drama?

Is the look of the words on the page important to drawing the reader in..?

All these questions came up straight away as we looked at the sample first pages. We all talked about which pages made us want to read on, and which didn't.

Ok, now it's time to write.

Don't think about it too much. This is just first draft. It's about getting down a smattering of ideas.

Think about the story you most want to write today. Forget about any other, ongoing projects. Think of something new. Or a memory. Grab hold of a thread of new story.

Take some time to write down about five hundred words. Fill about two pages of your notebook. Do it now. I'll give you... half an hour to do it.

Are you back?

Right. Now, spend some time reading back through your two pages. Cut fifty words out. Some of the redundant words and expressions and sentences. Get rid of the flab.

Now. Look at your first line.

Is it good enough?

Does it do the job?

Maybe, maybe not.

Pick a line from somewhere in the middle of your piece of writing. Would that work as a first sentence? If you just chopped everything that came before it? Or reorganized everything to put this first? How would that look?

Remember: you're in charge of the fiction. You can control time itself! These events and sentences can happen in any order you decide!

What about... say, the seventh sentence? How might that work as a first line..?

Any good?

Compare the different options. Which is the best opening? The one you had at the start? The one picked from the middle? Or the seventh line?

In workshops it can be fun at this point to get people to write the lines out and show the person sitting next to them. If you ask someone with a fresh pair of eyes: which is the best opening line, you get some interesting replies. Often we found it was the 'random' seventh sentence.

(If you're working alone, you can get the 'fresh pair of eyes' factor by putting your work away for a whole day, and doing something else in the meantime.)

I think the reason for that is that, by seven sentences in, your writing has warmed up. Your controlling editing eye has switched off. Your story has started to flow, hopefully.

I think when people set out to self-consciously write a killer first line, it can get a bit precious and over-controlled and self-conscious. We're all trying too hard to grab attention. Much better to let it sneak up on you, I think. Let it be real and proper intrigue, rather than bogus stuff.

The first line breaks open time. It's a voice that comes out of nowhere, jarring a story into life. It has to feel natural and spontaneous, I think.

This is a great experiment to try out on all kinds of writing. Look at some of your old stuff. How's that first line? How's the seventh? How's the thirty-seventh?

Have a look at some published fiction, too. Would they be better off choosing line seven? Is the first line they've got trying just a bit too hard?

Looking as if you're trying too hard is like death in fiction. I think the whole point is to hide all your working out, hide all the sweat and strenuous activity.

You have to make it look easy.

And then the reader feels free to focus on the story. They feel confident to step into your world.

Think of Three People

I'm setting myself a writing exercise today… I'm thinking of particular people from my past and then imagining them at the heart of a story about themselves.

Here's a quick list of three people who – for no particular reason – pop into my head.

Rini's husband Reg, who was so dodgy.

Rupert H, Lorna's second husband, who was an expert on Michelangelo.

Roger, who was Dean of the English department when I moved to Norwich.

The way your mind skitters over people from the past, and alights on them. I wonder what makes you think of them today? For some reason they have lodged in your thoughts. They all begin with the letter 'r'. Is that all that connects them..? Or perhaps they're three people you've never actually written about: not yet.

Something about them makes you want to incorporate them into a story. They're unfinished characters, somehow. (This really is the selfish way writers think about real people. Isn't it awful? It's completely utilitarian. 'What use can I make of you? Which parts of your physicality or your personality can I cannibalise and mash up with bits of someone else? How can I adapt, distort or mutate you..?) Perhaps there's a mystery there? Perhaps you don't know where they are now, or what they did after you knew them?

If certain people are still in your mind like this, it means that something about them is still intriguing you. Perhaps you want to investigate them further. Perhaps you want to fictionalize them…

Who are your three people? Don't think too hard about it. Every time you try the exercise you'll choose another three people, I think.

Choose one and write three pages about them. Anything you can remember about them. Any fragments of scenes or episodes your were involved in. Any anecdotes you heard about them. Were they a legend, somehow? Were they a person other people told stories about? Did they accrue stories about them? Or were they a modest kind of person, who kept themselves to themselves?

I don't think anyone goes through life with no stories at all…

I tried out this exercise for a few days, in the summer of 2013. I wrote about Reg and how he was Rini's late love. How they returned from Australia in 1986 and they were like lovebirds. He was a creepy little man, all her family thought: it seemed certain that he had brainwashed her. He was after all her money, perhaps. Then she was ill and she was wearing a wig and he had to help her round the place. He couldn't understand how or why she had a brain tumour. He sat crying in our living room and said: 'Why would she have such a thing? It's not like she ever had a bump on the head! It's not like I ever hit her or anything!' And I remember watching my mam and Big Nanna look at each other, open-mouthed in shock at what they both felt sure was an admission of guilt.

And Rupert! I'm thinking of him on the terrace in Florence in 1999, in the house he shared with Lorna. Nights that were swarming with insects in the summer heat and the air fierce with citronella. The two of them telling us how they were both fantastically allergic to insect stings of any kind, so if they were stung, there were syringes loaded with adrenalin, stashed all around the house... And then, after Lorna died and Rupert went back to Italy, nothing more was heard from him. Years later we heard that he'd died, only two years after she had. Heartbroken, I guess. He was devoted to her: I can see him bumbling along two steps behind her, with two carrier bags, one filled with books and papers, and the other clinking with her bottles of 'special water' as they always called the gin and tonic supply. There was a tiny cameo moment for Rupert, though. Just before he died our friend Stephen was on holiday in Sicily and, sitting outside a café on a brilliant day, he heard a loud, fruity, upper crust English voice braying and showing off for a bunch of American tourists. And lo and behold it was Rupert, still holding forth and lazing about on the continent. I was amazed at Stephen when he related this for not going over and saying hello, but I was delighted, too, that this was the last known sighting of our silly, tipsy, erudite friend.

What struck me, each time I tried out this exercise, was that I found myself veering away from the person into other realms. The person was a stepping stone into a subject or a story I hadn't anticipated writing about.

This is something I've noticed before. If there's something you want to write about, it's best to approach it obliquely.

It's also a good way of tricking yourself into writing about a big character in your life: to choose someone who was related to them, or standing to one side of them. Perhaps choose someone who never really seemed like the true hero of the story, and start to tell the tale with them at the centre, for a change. How does the story look from that vantage point?

By focusing to one side and looking at the big story slantwise, from the view-point of a secondary character, it's interesting the effects you can achieve. It means you leave the obvious centre of the canvas or the stage quite blank. And sometimes this means you can coax into the limelight the idea that you really, secretly wanted to write about. For example, in my case, with the characters I chose above, I might have ended up writing about my step-grandmother's cancer, or my friend Lorna and her stories about literary London in the Seventies. If I'd begun a story with these ideas centre stage I might have found them shriveling away, or even becoming too daunting. Beginning by looking to one side of the main subject and creeping up… this can really work, I think.

I find that the little nuggets of memory that I really want to rake over and think about and turn somehow into a part of a story occur to me when I'm not expecting them to. I need to have that journal beside me at all times – in my bag, at my desk, on the bus, beside my pillow – for when flashes of intriguing moments come back. And I write them down in - at most - a handful of sentences only, if I can.

For example:

The Radio One Roadshow in Ambleside in 1982. We were on holiday and keen to see it. When we got close the crowds looked a bit rough, so we went to The World of Beatrix Potter instead.

Old Mr Magrs standing outside his bungalow, waiting for us as we went up the garden path. I was wearing a red velvet jacket and felt like it was a bit too flash for after a funeral.

Fred, my Big Nanna's ex-husband. After she'd fled from his

house, he came up to her months later in a supermarket. 'Am I allowed to talk with you, Gladys?' He kept following her around the aisles until she shouted at him to leave her alone.

What I find is that, if I have a few days deliberately not writing anything at all, and having a kind of holiday from my own voice, these little moments and fragments start suggesting themselves.

It's as if the people want to be written about.

It's almost like being haunted.

So I make sure I write down quick notes about these people and these moments so that later, when I need to write something longer, just to stretch my legs and my memory and my writing muscles, I can find out where their cameo appearances might lead me…

A good next exercise, to follow on from this, would be to take two or more of these remembered characters and imagine a meeting between them. Characters based on people who never met in real life. How would they respond to each other? What if they were waiting for the bus together? What if they were caught in a hostage situation together? What would we learn about them that we don't already know?

Time, Friendship and Love

An eight o'clock start, giving Fester his pills – his thyroid and his antibiotics, wrapped in bits of meaty chew. Making tea to take upstairs and begin work. Smooth 70s on the radio, 'Baker Street' by Gerry Rafferty. That line about another year, and then you'll be happy.

Even as a kid of eight years old that line would catch at my heart. When I was that age it was always the message from my mam and Charlie that things weren't perfect at the moment – far from it – but maybe next year they would be okay. Maybe looking ahead they'd be happier or have more money. Things would work out by then. In 1978 I suppose it was when they were thinking about Australia and emigrating. I was sick with dread when I imagined it. I mentioned it to my best friend at school and he just took the piss. He held up the cover of a Ladybird book about aeroplanes in the school library, taunting me that I'd be going on one with all my family and all our stuff and we'd never come home again. I felt sure that our going to Australia would work out horribly… And also, what about Dad and his side of the family? I was forbidden from mentioning the emigration plans to him.

In 1978 I was still spending weekends with Dad's side of the family. On Sunday nights he'd pass me back to my mam and Charlie. The handover would happen in Durham city. Charlie would park in the town square. It was always dark and misty and completely deserted, the way I remember it. Mam would walk by herself down the long, curving cobbled lane to Old Elvet Bridge and she would stand at the end, while Alfie stood at the opposite end of the bridge and let me go to her. I'd walk across through the mist, under the watchful gaze of the cathedral and the castle and even at that age I'd think they were being ridiculous. They were acting like we were in a movie about the war, or spies.

I suppose it was carry-ons like this that set me off hating having to rely on anyone at all.

Why am I writing about this now? First thing on a sunny, hopeful morning? Digging over the past again. All the most upsetting bits of the past... Mam in her long brown coat on autumn nights on that bridge, walking over the cobbles.

Hilary Mantel was on the news last night after winning the Booker Prize. What snagged in my head was her talking about Henry VIII being constantly in pain and how that affected his behaviour. Mam has an illness and she's constantly in pain, and I wonder if I take that into account enough. How does it affect her mind, her behaviour, her personality? When we watched Hilary Mantel I couldn't help thinking about this. Am I being cruel by not phoning up and making peace? Shouldn't I just give in after every argument and outburst? Shouldn't I just put up with it? Let them do what they want? Do I have a duty? Do I owe them, as they say, everything? And are they really bothered about seeing us anyway? Do they just like mixing up trouble and causing anguish? What do I really want to do?

I don't know.

Hearing 'Baker Street' just now as I made my tea and Fester nibbled so daintily at his cat food, I couldn't help thinking of those Sunday nights in the Seventies. When I'd go from Alfie's endless questions about my mam and Charlie, over the bridge to weather Mam's questions about Alfie and his family. I was the go-between.

I was nostalgic for other times. I was hankering after the future. In another year, perhaps, we'd all be happy.

I was wishing my life away at eight years old. It seems ridiculous now, but I was. And now I'm in my forties I try to imagine how wonderful it must have been to be that age.

All of this stuff has fed into my writing over the years. I wouldn't have written any of the things I have – I wouldn't be this writer – if these things hadn't happened to me.

When I write fiction and I'm putting stories together I am constantly trying to reverse these separations. All my novels are about reunions.

Time, friendship and love – that's what I write about. It's always about how those who can remember are doomed to try and put things together again. It's always about how to be hopeful and trying not to be bitter. And how to understand people and listen to them. I always assume I'm great at listening, but I'm not sure I always am: my head gets filled with too much other stuff and my thoughts drift away. But I'm always trying to listen and pay attention. I hope I'm always trying to be kind.

Also, when I think about it, I'm also always writing about being left out in the cold and never fitting in well enough. I'm always writing about creating your own family so that you won't feel left out anymore. I write about giving the unlikeliest characters another chance. I write about outsiders who want to be able to join the gang and take part in the dance.

This sounds a bit too much like analysis. I must stop and write my daily words…

I'm about to finish this notebook. I look back at the start and there's an account of being in the pub with Simon Barnard, and he asked me why I tend to make my stories cross-over with each other. Why do I take characters from one place and introduce them again, to other characters in another world? Why am I building a ramshackle but vaguely consistent universe of my own?

At first I put it down to growing up as a fan of Marvel Comics and loving things like 'Team-Up!' and 'Marvel Two-in-One' and 'The Secret Wars', in which heroes met and interacted with each other all the time, crossing lines of continuity with every passing issue. But really, more than comic book characters, it was about separations in my family. I can see that easily now: being at the centre of two sets of characters who will never meet again, of course I longed with all my might for easy interactions and parties once more. Growing older and more conscious of the adult world meant living in a place where there would be no more crossovers into each other's universes. The universes stand quite separate and alone. I think I invented my own stories from the beginning to integrate the pieces of my life.

'Crisis on Infinite Earths!' is what DC comics used to call that universal team-up and conflict stuff and that really does fit my childhood as a title, in many ways.

I've ended up with a desire to write stories about reunions and making amends, rapprochement, crossovers and juxtaposition. I love the idea of people and characters and how they make guest appearances in each other's lives. That's what fiction is, for me. All the great stories are about surprise collisions and conflict and, despite your complicated backstory, still hoping for the best.

Trashy Books

You know I can't stand snobbishness. I saw a great list on someone's blog about reading, of the fifty greatest 'trashy novels of all time.' They all sounded great! Every single title was alluring. Every description made me want to read them. I'd prefer to call these books just fantastic, bestselling examples of popular fiction.

How many trashy books have you read? It turned out of those fifty I'd only read seven – and I really felt the need to fill the gaps. Why had I never read 'Gone with the Wind' for example?

One of the happiest summers I ever had was in Edinburgh in the late Nineties, and it was the summer that cargo pants were in. They had those deep pockets down both legs? Very practical for an addicted reader of paperbacks. I went up and down all the charity shops of South Clark Street (and there were a lot!) and kept myself entertained with yellowing blockbusters with gold-foil embossed titles. I had 'Sophie's Choice' down one leg and 'A Woman of Substance' down the other – and I stopped in every other café and tea room I came to in order to pile through some more pages.

Actually, neither of those books appear in this list of fifty. Thinking about it, neither do 'The Rats' or 'The Winds of War'. I was a teenager in the 1980s and lots of the big, popular novels were made into ludicrous, nine-hour long mini-series that were filmed all over the world and starred actors of dubious vintage and quality.

For me the concept of 'trashiness' transcends quality, genre and other definitions of dodgy taste. It's about content. They are books on a grand scale - even when confined to one town. They're usually a bit saucy and feature characters whose behaviour might run the gamut from questionable to downright evil. A whole host of taboos are shattered and worlds usually hidden to the general reader are gloriously explored.

I think 'trashy' books are all about having the veil lifted on something you've never experienced and would like to, vicariously. It's about hoping to be shocked and not being able to put your book down. That's 'trashiness' to me – it's all about being compulsive and even, perhaps, a little ashamed of yourself. And long may it continue.

Voice

I was an early talker. I loved words from the start. Mam says that she'd lose track of me, and when she found me again I'd be deep in conversation with someone. Someone like the milkman (whose squint I'd copy as I stared up at him in the doorway) or the postman, or the doctor's wife next door.

We shared a hedge at the back with the doctor and his wife. I loved to eat the berries. Mam says they were bitter, rancid things, but when I was two years old there was nothing I liked better than wandering off down the garden, filling my plastic pail and cramming my face with blackberries. I'd get covered in dark juice and come home looking pleased.

One day Mam came to find me and she heard an adult voice. The doctor's wife had found me purple-handed.

'I don't talk very well yet,' I was saying.

'I think you talk very well indeed.'

'I pick all your berries.'

'You're welcome to them. There are hundreds.'

'I wait till you can't see,' I told her. Mam had warned me: if you must pick them, make sure the doctor's wife can't see.

The doctor's wife was laughing, just as Mam darted out of the hedge. 'Come here, you.' She scooped me up. 'I'm so sorry,' she said. 'He's such a chatterbox. He'll be getting me into trouble.'

The woman from next door – older than Mam, careworn, dowdy – looked her new neighbour up and down. She hadn't had a good look at her till now. The new neighbours tended to keep themselves to themselves.

Earliest memories. Do we actually have them, or do we create them out of bits we've heard from family members? Stories get embroidered through retelling. There are things we vaguely remember... and then get them confirmed by parents or siblings and they take on a life of their own.

When I think of earliest memories now, they are fleshed out in all kinds of ways. Telling that story above, I start introducing glimpses of the doctor's wife's point of view. I introduce aspects that I could never have observed and remembered from being that age...

We fictionalize ourselves.

What's your earliest memory?

How did you learn to tell stories about yourself?

When were you first aware of stories as something that existed in the world..?

From the very earliest age I talked to anyone and everyone. Perhaps it was because I was the first grandchild. No one was used to talking to children and they just spoke to me as if I was another adult in their midst? A miniature grown-up, who managed to keep up with the things they were saying, and sometimes enthusiastically joined in the talk?

On one side the family was noisy and enthusiastic in everything they did. The other side – my mother's – was quieter and more modest, though no less verbal.

I became aware of myself as a person in my own right, in the middle of all this chatter and gabble. Early on, I was wrapped in blankets, or in my push-chair, or I was sitting under the kitchen table. I was listening to endless talk. It was talk that made the world go round.

Mostly it was women's voices that I heard. The loud, braying tones of my dad's sisters and mother and aunts, and the quieter gossip of my mam, her mother and her sisters. There were fewer men on both sides of the family and those there were kept mum. They sat in front of the TV and watched football scores or they vanished behind the evening paper.

Words were important. Right from the beginning I found myself chasing after them, trying to make sense of them: earnestly attempting to catch the drift of everything that was said around me. The adult world was a complicated and perplexing place crammed full of words and stories, the meanings of which I could only sometimes guess at. Thrillingly, the best bits were when the adult voices dipped lower – when the more salacious or scandalous secret details were divulged. Or when anything too personal or medical was mentioned. Then the female relative would simply mime the offending word. I'd learn to prick up my ears and concentrate hard on divining the meaning in those moments.

Best of all, though – even better than listening in to adult gossip – was when the grown-ups would talk directly to me. I was read to by my Mam and my Big Nanna, mostly. Bedtimes, for hours. Way beyond the point of tiredness for both reader and listener. The object of the exercise – sending me quietly to sleep – would be forgotten as Mam became engrossed in the tale she was telling me. I'd listen and blink my way through sleepiness and out the other side, into complete wakefulness. I'd be listening, agog, as she told me another story we both already knew really well: the Gingerbread Man, the Magic Porridge Pot, or the Wolf and the Goat's little kids. Somehow the stories came up fresh and exciting every time.

I had a collection of those fairy tales – slim hardbacks from Ladybird Books' 'Well-Loved Tales' series. They contained a pleasing mix of fairy tale princesses, wicked wolves and a variety of talking beasts. Elves and pixies fascinated me.

Every time we went to the shops, right from me being in the push-chair to me walking down the road of my own accord and old enough to go to school – we'd go into the newsagent's and Mam couldn't stop herself buying me another Ladybird Well-Loved Tale. She could hardly afford it. She was justifying it to herself before she even left the shop, as if my dad or her mother were asking her how could she throw money away on such fripperies, so frequently, for the bairn. He'd grow up spoiled and demanding, always wanting something new, every time he was taken down the shops... But he's building a collection, Mam would think. It's good. It's books. It's never a waste of money. He's hearing all those wonderful stories. It's not like buying sweets or silly toys. They're *good* for him.

No matter how she rationalized it, though, it all boiled down to the simple fact that she liked to buy these storybooks because I loved them so much. I loved to hear them again and again in her voice and, when I realized how it was she actually managed to draw these words and stories up out of the pages, I loved to watch as she underscored each line of print with her fingertip as she read. I understood what she was doing now and it amazed me. The pictures were wonderful, but the left hand pages – mostly white, but for these dark letters – that was where the true magic was stored.

Mam loved the hours of reading, too. When she read to me she had a companion, and someone who was hanging on her every word. She'd never had anyone do that in her whole life. She was the quietest in her family. She had an older brother, and sister and a twin, who were all louder and pushier than she was. Her mother was a widow and she had three jobs to keep down and the kids had formed a tight unit over which the oldest sister ruled supreme. My mam had been subdued and bullied and, for several years of her childhood, rather ill in bed – though what with, no one had ever been able to say, exactly. Her mother would mutter darkly, something about her being 'bad with her nerves' – but that was about it. At thirteen Mam had been virtually paralysed and confined to her bed. That was when she had done most of her own reading. For her, reading was solitary and silent. For her, it was never a joyous, conversational, eventful thing as it is in my own earliest memories. To Mam it was lonely consolation for being stuck indoors as a young girl, while everyone else was running about out of doors.

It wasn't until much, much later that anyone knew what was really wrong with Mam. And no one ever really found out why more wasn't done or said about her illness back when she was thirteen. 'It was a different age back then.' I heard it said by various grown-ups. 'People didn't really talk about illness or anything that was wrong with them. Not like they do nowadays. People were ashamed of such things. You kept all the secrets in the family.'

Actually, this sounds rather like my Big Nanna talking. Maybe I heard this from her. She was a great one for keeping all the secret stuff tamped down and not dragging it out for anyone to see. Perhaps her own dreadful sense of shame about sickness went back to her own childhood, when diptheria went through her small community in the darkest wilds of Norfolk in the 1930s. She told me how she'd been placed in isolation for a certain amount of time, and all her clothes and toys and books were taken from her and burned outside in the garden by her father, so as not to spread the germs. She told me about sitting alone in her bedroom, hearing the crackle of flames, smelling the smoke. Knowing that all her belongings were gone for good.

'And that's why I grew up understanding the value of everything,' she told me. 'Not like most people these days. It's all easy-come, easy-go nowadays. People are too careless. And bally kids get given too much.'

Following her illness, my Big Nanna was given a new book the following Christmas. 'I kept ever such good care of it. I'd bring it out at night. I don't think I hardly ever read it. I just smelled the newness of the pages. It was like an Annual, one of them big story books with beautiful pictures and very tiny printing. I tried to make up my own stories to go with the pictures, because I was never a patient reader as a girl.' And she would snitch a duster and a dab of furniture polish from the kitchen cupboard in order to buff up the fake leather of the book cover. She treasured her book and when she saw, so many years later, just how many Ladybird books my Mam had bought for me, she was scandalized. By then I was onto the Noddy books by Enid Blyton, too, and my collection was flourishing. 'You're spoiling him rotten! Look! A little bairn like this and he's even got a whole bookcase of his own, nearly full already..! It's ridiculous! He won't value them at all!'

I loved that bookcase. It came from one of my auntie's bedrooms, I think. She was updating her bedroom and making it more mod and psychedelic, painting swirls on the walls and getting some new furniture. All her childhood stuff was being slung out and I inherited a little bookcase with three shelves and two sliding glass panels on the top shelf, behind which my most precious books – the Ladybirds – could be displayed.

I watched one Sunday as Dad laid down newspaper on the bare boards of my bedroom and painted the bookcase glossy white. I could barely wait for the paint to dry. I was so desperate to get my books lined up there. He had to warn me off. He was impatient with my keenness and he'd go red in the face when he shouted at me. I stood there with my arms full of fairytales, biding my time.

I'd also inherited a miniature Lloyd Loom wicker armchair, just the right size for me. It was currently sea green and he was painting it white for me, too. I would spend hours in that chair - until I grew out of it within a year or two – teaching myself to read and idly picking away at the flaking layers of gloss.

I suppose Mam was glad of having someone to read to and spend her evenings with because she was actually scared of being in that house alone. Dad was often away on courses for the police. Adult life meant getting along on your own. So she loved it when I listened to stories, and started using words myself, and became a person to talk to.

I was a person who had his own private library from a very early age...

I have a theory that when people stockpile books what they're really collecting is time. Compressed time, focused time. Good times. Time they are bookmarking for the future. Time they would gladly spend if only they could find the time. Time they can store away like squirrels store nuts for winter. For lean days. Boring days. Rainy days. Or maybe feast or famine or flood.

And even if they never get round to reading everything, then it's still money well spent. Even the illusion of time stored up is a pleasurable thing to contemplate. It's a luxury. The sight of all those colourful spines on the shelf is more than just the promise of being transported elsewhere, into lives not your own. It's the promise that you can accomplish this anytime, and there will always be time enough to do so. It's a metaphor for endless time. The titles lined up on those shelves represent all the time that can and hopefully will be yours to live in. It will be time you can lavish upon yourself. Selfish time. Shelfish time.

Books are things we find when we're very young, and days are endless and they will always represent immortality.

That's the secret joy of them.

When to Work

You must remember that there are no hard and fast rules. You will find the way of working that is right for you. You can't go comparing yourself to anyone else. You can't emulate them and you can't envy them. That way madness lies. If so-and-so writes more than you, writes faster than you, better than you, and sells more than you – then bully for so-and-so. Things are going right for them. You just have to look after yourself, and try to find a way to work that works for you.

Some writers waste too much time worriting over what other writers are up to. In workshops, very new writers sometimes get angsty over their classmates because they seem to be better, faster or more hard-working. It doesn't end there. Full-time professional writers, writers with books out, often spend their days angsting over agents and contracts, publicity, promotions, festivals and going out of print.

Face it: someone is always going to have it easier than you as a writer. Someone else is going to be having an easier, nicer, angst-free life. And your life is going to seem terrible. Your writing will seem rotten to you. And it will come too slowly. You'll find it pointless and thankless. You'll wonder why you bother. And some days you won't even bother.

That's how I've ended up feeling at times – futile, stymied and cross – when I've drifted into thinking about other people's writing rather than my own. It's easy to get miserable about your own stuff – just take a walk through some glitzy big chain bookshop. Be demoralised by the stacks of special offer three-for-the-price-of-two paperbacks! Look at the posters and lists of author events. Read down the bestseller lists… and be hopelessly dismayed by the canyons of novels. Who'd ever want to read yours? Who are you in amongst all this stuff? Why are you even bothering?

So keep out of bookshops for a while. Read the books that already litter your house in stacks: the ones you've been meaning to read.

Don't read the review pages of the Sunday papers. Especially if you're looking to see what kind of thing gets reviewed; what kind of thing sells these days. You can't second-guess the market. You can't second-guess the reviewers. I think it's best if you keep away from booky stuff and idle book-chat altogether.

If you get too involved in that rancorous stuff – ('Oh, just look at the rubbish they're putting out these days! Look at what sells! What chance do I stand?') – then you'll end up forgetting what it is you enjoyed about fiction in the first place.

Book-chat will start to replace real, proper thinking about fiction.

Have you noticed? A bunch of professional writers get together and what do they talk about? The business. Contracts, agents, publicity… all that malarkey. They aren't talking about Art and Life or anything high-flown. They keep those deep-down thoughts secret and private and they get on with them at home.

You've got to keep your real writing self safe and quiet. Don't upset yourself with ideas of failure or success or your moments of weakness in the face of how difficult writing can be.

You have to figure out the way that you need to work. For you, yourself. The way that only you can work.

Some writers work at their desks all day long. They keep virtual office hours, to make sure the work gets done. Earlier this year I heard a writer describe a typical ten hour writing day to an audience of very attentive student writers. Actually, they were more than attentive. They were agog. Ten hours! Six days a week! Such discipline and drive! The writer shrugged. 'It's just the way that works for me. There's work needs doing. I've got deadlines to meet.'

Ah. There's the thing. Some of us need encroaching deadlines in order to motivate us, just like we had at school. Some of us need to sail blithely past our deadlines with the work unfinished – just to get that sense of urgency, or of naughtiness, that will enable us to finish the job in hand. Some of us need the reassuring presence of an impatient editor / agent / teacher waiting for our work. We work happily to the sound of their fingers drumming on the desk.

Other writers would never be able to work with deadlines like that, or within the constraints of a ten hour, or six hour or four hour day at the desk. Their days are more sporadic and free-form, because that's the way that works for them. I used to be more like that. In Edinburgh, when I wasn't teaching, I would sit out in cafes and work when I felt like it. I ended up writing pages and pages of stuff that were seemingly unrelated to the novel I was meant to be writing. I typed and drafted through the night, or the mid-afternoon. Any time I fancied it. I didn't have many other constraints on my time.

It seemed like the best way of working, just then. It's also the slowest I've ever worked. With nothing else vying for my time and attention, the novel that I was writing then, in 1996, ended up sprawling all over the place. Later, when I was lecturing full time at UEA, I had huge demands on my time. The writing had to be shoe-horned into spare moments, weekends, holidays when all the assignment-marking was done. So then, because I had to, I worked in a much more disciplined fashion. I learned to complete a first draft novel-length manuscript in three months flat.

It suits me to write the full shape of a book out in three months: it seems just long enough. Any longer, and I seem to lose the rhythm of the story. The shape sprawls out of control and the book gets spoiled. I've noticed this.

So, for a few years it was my habit to wait till the long summer break – having spent a term or two thinking and making notes about the oncoming novel. Then, when summer starts up, and the students are leaving – that's when I launch into a new book.

In recent years – especially now that I'm teaching less and writing more - I've become even more regimented about the way I write. At the end of 2004 I started writing in public again. I went every morning to sit under the echoing dome of Manchester Central Library's reference section. I treated it like a day job, or the gym. I would arrive at ten in the morning, and find a place at one of the long tables. I would take out two exercise books. One was my warm-up pad, and I would write for a full half hour: anything that came off the top of my head. It was a sort of diary, detailing what was going on in Manchester for us that winter. I would also end up unearthing bits of memories too – things that would come in useful later. I'd check the clock, high up under the centre of the dome and, after exactly half an hour, and with no gap, I would switch straight over to my other book, and get back to my place in the novel. I was warmed up, supple, and raring to go. It was as if that novel was dictating itself to me. I wrote a two thousand word chapter every day I sat down in the library, and I went four times a week.

That seems like a decent enough weekly output to me.

On the whole I'd say that a thousand, or two thousand words a day is a fair amount to be churning out.

'Churning' is supposed to be a derogatory word, isn't it? Makes it sound like hack-work. But we *do* hack it out! That's how it feels. Hefty and strenuous. Hack hack hack. Chipping away in the middle of the forest. Clearing some space and yelling out TIIIMMMMBBBEEERRR when the day's work is done.

The summer of 2006 I was experimenting with early mornings. I would get up at six and go straight to my study. I'd plonk myself at the computer, sip water as I scrolled to the right place in my novel. And I would just start typing. I'd still have sleep in my eyes and I'd be all heavy-limbed. But it was warm and brilliantly blue outside and I'd still be dreaming, in a way – I would still have the bravado that my dreams usually have. When I dream I know that my stories can go anywhere and I'm content to see where they take me. I think I was waking up before my internal censor did, during those summer mornings.

That's what worked for me that summer. Now it's another autumn again, and I'm writing this book – and having to find a new way to work, all over again.

But at least I've got a project. At least there's something to anchor me in my days. I've got the whole problem of sorting out this book to wrestle with. I've got to get it to do the things I want it to do. I have to cope with the surprises it's throwing at me daily. I'm building up the pages, week in week out – just the way I like to.

I've realised I'm not really happy unless I've got a book on the go. I don't always enjoy the process of writing. Sometimes it's murder. But I like having written in a day. I like there being new pages in the world: pages that weren't there yesterday.

Not everyone's the same, though. Remember that. You have to find out the way that works for you. How, when, where, how much. Experiment and play around. Don't go comparing yourself with other people, and don't go feeling guilty if you're not doing what you think you should. Find your proper rhythm. Find your particular way.

How.

Trying writing in longhand first, in felt tip; in pencil; on file cards; in a nice new notebook. Try writing straight onto a Word document and conquering all that delicious white space. Try writing all the dialogue first, and structuring scenes like a film script – then go back and fill in the details. Try out a way of working you've never tried before.

When.

Dawn. Midnight. Mid afternoon. Have a think about when you haven't worked, and give it a whirl. Get up when you can't sleep. Write surreptitiously during a meeting at work.

Where.

A department store; a sauna; a park bench; your cellar.

How much.

Sit down where you're comfy, with a great idea and just keep going. How far can you push it? How much can you do before exhausting yourself completely? Michael Moorcock talks about writing fifteen thousand words a day, during his zesty Seventies heyday. He could write a Sword and Sorcery romance in a week. Pull an all-nighter or two, just to see where it gets you. Can you keep up the momentum? Is it like being Keith Richards?

On the other hand, try doing a few lines a day. Like John Lennon leaving the same sheet of paper in his typewriter, and coming up with a just a few words of 'I am the Walrus' every day, on his way past. Write very, very short instalments of your story: perfectly well-honed and crystalline fragments. Inch it along very gradually.

Overall: spend a week or two, trying out lots of different combinations of ways of working. If you already have habits and routines – and even if you think of yourself as dead set in your ways – spend some time doing the complete opposite of what you already do.

See if you can surprise yourself into writing something completely unexpected.

Who is it for?

I had a great student a few years ago who asked really very good questions. She was on the MA in Creative Writing at MMU and had reached the part of the course after the workshops had finished, when it was all about having one-to-one tutorials and working mostly on her own, completing her novel.

And all the big questions were coming up. Now that she was alone with her novel, she was really starting to think about it.

When you're in a workshop it's easy to spend your time thinking about the smaller things. Whether the imagery works. Whether the descriptions are good. Whether the dialogue rings true. Whether your point of view is consistent. The things I like to call the micro-level stuff.

But when you're left alone with your novel – if you're really working hard… you start thinking about the bigger picture. You start wondering about what your novel actually *is* and what it's *for* and what it is actually saying about the world.

My student Chris was great for this stuff.

For one particular workshop she arrived with a new chapter – but also two big questions about her entire novel.

Two questions that could be summarized like this:

Who is my novel addressed to?

And, what should its structure be?

She produced them with a self-deprecating flourish. She knew it was a tall order – figuring these out in an hour-long tutorial. And maybe they were just rhetorical questions anyway? Maybe they didn't need an actual answer?

But… the more I thought about it… the more I thought they did need answering.

And I thought they could be the basis for a workshop, or at least a set of exercises…

You can apply this exercise to a novel or a short story. You can apply these questions to something you have finished a draft of, or something you're in the middle of, or even something you're still preparing to write.

It's all about asking questions of your story.

Here are some questions…

What form does your story take?

Is it a confessional letter?

Is it accusatory?

An apology?

An explanation?

Is it somebody's testimony?

I think I'm trying to make you think about what your story might actually, materially be in the real world of your story. If, say, your story and its world were true – what form would your pages actually take?

A series of letters? From one person or more? Would they respond to each other?

Could it be a diary? Over how long? How many months or years?

A series of notebooks?

Or is your novel just taking place inside someone's head?

Is it their thoughts, tumbling through the mind? Does nothing ever get written down?

And what if your novel isn't actually in a character's voice? Is the story told by a free-floating narrator? Are they omniscient? Do they stick to just one or two characters or are they more promiscuous?

So – there are a few options.

What do you think? What do you want your story to actually be, in the world you are creating?

It's good to make a few decisions about this, pretty early on. It helps in so many ways, to keep this stuff in control.

Have a think about which is the best way of telling for you and this particular story you have in mind.

A diary written by one person is great – but is it a character who will be privy to all the information? Will the gaps in their knowledge be telling and intriguing – or just frustrating?

Would a completely omniscient narrator be able to find out too much – and would this run the risk of destroying all the mystery and atmosphere?

Would a story in the form of all the scribbled post-it notes stuck to a fridge be a good idea? Or would the seeming randomness be too distracting? Could you make a clear-enough through line to guide the reader through?

I love that term – 'through line'. It's a very simple term for something that is literally straightforward. It describes the guide rail that runs through the middle of your story. It's the basic thing that draws us from beginning, through the middle, and up to the end. It's the logical, sensible, reasonable order of events. It has to be present somewhere in your story – but there are all sorts of things you can do to it. Hide it, camouflage it, chop it up and redistribute it. But your through line has to be present somehow. We need to be able to follow the sense of your story. Even if the events are chaotically jumbled – in a story involving flashbacks, time-travel, clones, alternate histories, doppelgangers and killer sheep – we still need to be able to follow a reliable point of view. The emotional journey of our main character, say.

If we understand that, then we can journey through even the craziest of tales.

Okay. Next:

Spend some time thinking about this business of the 'materiality' of your story.

Is it actually written down in the world of your book?

Perhaps it's a book within the book?

In my favourite-ever novel, Armistead Maupin's 'Maybe the Moon' the heroine writes her journal through a series of differently sized and shaped notebooks – and all are presented verbatim within the covers of the novel were are reading, with letters in other hands as an appendix to finish the story off. This is a great example of a book that displays its own materiality.

My second favourite novel is Anne Tyler's 'Saint Maybe'. This doesn't do anything self-conscious about its presentation. It reads like straightforward domestic drama, like all of her books do. But hers are stories told by a confiding, conversational voice. An unseen narrator who knows everything, and who can go anywhere in the story. She can skip over years and take us straight to the significant moments in the life of this ramshackle family. It isn't hard to imagine these chapters being, say, long, conversational letters being written by a mostly unseen neighbour or relation, confiding in a friend far away. This is rather like how Jane Austen works, too. We feel we are being drawn into a confidence when we read both these women, and they are taking their time and writing a good, long gossipy, witty series of letters.

Let's think about the story we are writing as a series of actual, physical documents.

We need to think about questions like this:

Who is compiling this bundle of documents?

Does the writer know? Does the reader need to know?

Why are they compiling this evidence?

What do they want to prove by doing it?

Big, big questions. Questions that are making us really probe at the reasons as to why this novel or story needs to exist. What is it saying? And why?

Now, if we go back to the questions asked by my student Chris – we can see how these answers to question one really helps with her second question.

What should my structure be?

Because that structure would surely be implicit in the answers you've decided on? As with the Maupin book – he decided that his lead character was going to have a series of journals that would be placed together at the end of the story, together with follow-up letters from characters who will finish her story for her. His structure was set from there on. The journals would be stepping stones through the final months of her life.

I think that structure is a hard thing to get right. People fret over things like structure.

But don't worry.

I think structure should suggest itself.

I think if you fully understand the nature of your material and the way your story is going, then the shape of your story will be trying to make itself apparent.

The structure has to grow out of the material – and not be imposed upon it.

That's why some of those 'How to Write a Hollywood Movie' or 'How to Write a Bestselling Novel' books are often bullshit. They try to make everything into a recipe for success. There's no such thing as a perfect, one-size-fits-all structure. It needs to grow out of the needs of your own, unique story.

Here's an exercise.

You're in the middle of a story, right?

Put it on pause. Stop the action in the middle.

Let one of the characters look around and take stock.

Maybe it's a character who's narrating. One whose voice you already know well.

Or maybe it's a character whose view-point you haven't shown yet, and don't really intend to?

Doesn't matter. This is just an exercise. An experiment.

Choose an interesting character from your story.

They are going to write a letter.

You are going to write the letter that this character writes to you, as author.

Let them tell you how they think you're doing so far.

What do they think of your story so far?

Remember, you're their only hope. You've chosen to tell the world the story that they are caught up in. They will want you to do it justice. They might want you to take their side more…

They can tell you what you mustn't leave out. And also, what they think you out to cut out or exaggerate…

Let your character surprise you with the things they have to say.

Woman's Own

It's important to remember that, if you keep your eyes and ears open, everything is material.

It's Thursday in a quite stressful week. Thor's Day: and the men are thundering about in the attic space overhead, dragging out the last of the rubble (reluctantly) and laying down the last of the boards and putting up our new fold-down steps. Soon we'll have clean space to store boxes of books. Bernard Socks is trapped in the bedroom for his own good while all this is going on. Clouds of dust come puffing out with all the noise from upstairs.

One of the younger guys has a sooty face and football top and he tells me how horribly hot it is up there in the attic. He looks quite cross about it. Outside, as I'm leaving for a walk, I pause to ask him, 'Why don't you have one of those filter masks?'

He shrugs. 'Shit boss.'

'I think Jeremy has one he could lend you. I know how horrible breathing all that soot can be.'

'Nah, it doesn't matter.'

I went off on my much-needed walk, escaping from the house. Somehow Manchester was both muggy and cool at the same time. We should be on holiday, really. Our summer trips were always at the very start of August, which is when we figure our anniversary lies, somewhere nebulously around that time.

Various things are in the way of our travelling this year: not least money and the house lying in ruins.

I've written the first draft of a story that needs to be done. That's my week's work. Now I'm getting away from my laptop and spending time out in the world.

I've walked to Platt Fields Park, up the quiet Curry Mile, past the Whitworth Gallery – closed for refurbishment – and now I'm in Gemini Café, opposite the old Eye Hospital. Having a grilled Halloumi sub. Remember? You came here in 2004, when it was a bit more down-at-heel, and more of a greasy-spoon kind of place? Right at the very start of the autumn university term, just as you were getting used to having a new job at Manchester Metropolitan University. It felt so weird to be cut loose of all the demands of the previous job, and to be in the middle of a city, rather than a campus. And to be half-time, too! You felt strangely liberated and semi-detached, though you were nervous, too – having a coffee here before going up to the department to sit in your new office at the very top of that futuristic building. That was ten years ago: having a sausage barm in here, wondering if this might be a regular spot for lunch in your new job (it wasn't. There was never time to fetch anything more than a scrap of something in a plastic bag from the horrid bistro downstairs.)

Walking through Whitworth Park I was thinking about first being in this part of Manchester twenty-four years ago, having a day-trip with Steve and Laura in 1990. Laura had graduated and had got herself a job here, and she was looking for a room in a shared house.

I remember walking under the bridge by Blackwells Bookshop and coming as far south as here. Looking at university accommodation notice boards. Thinking how I had no money whatsoever, and how I'd never have the courage like Laura had, simply to move to a new city and get a job. She was about seven foot tall, dressed in Goth black, with flaming red hair down her back.

I was also thinking about what it meant to have a creative life: to live a Bohemian kind of life. I felt very free and scared at the age of twenty, I think: I had no idea what the future held and I was visiting this new place. Even though I was only staying for an afternoon, I still felt daunted. I was toying with the sensation of starting somewhere new, just to see how it felt. Then, in 2004 it really was my new place, to both live and write and teach. And now, ten years later again, it's a place I walk about in quite happily, escaping from home and gathering my thoughts, writing in my notebook.

You get used to new conditions and new periods in your life. I like to have days when I set off and walk around in my surroundings and try to see them afresh. I like to let the ideas and memories and impressions fall upon me. I like to see where they take me.

I walk to Central Library, which has been all done out inside. It took three years. Now the old pale stone dome looks like Star Trek: the Next Generation inside. I'm not sure of the wisdom of what they've done. Fewer books and more computers. Everything a bit more futuristic. That's how everything goes, isn't it? I'm just hoping there are still places to sit and read peacefully. To muse and stew over things. In 2004 I sat here every single morning in the reference library, writing two thousand words every time, and every single chair was occupied. The place was full of people working on something or other: even if it was simply the project of filling up their day.

Today I sit upstairs on a sofa beside bound volumes of journals. I spend some time reading the Paris Review and the Saturday Review. Soon enough I leave the literary stuff behind, because I'm intrigued by the fact they have bound copies of 'Woman's Own' magazine. This was the kind of thing my

Mam and Big Nanna used to read when I was a kid. As far as I remember it was all knitting patterns, gossip, recipes and heart-warming true-life stories.

I'm reading the volume that combines all the issues from autumn and winter 1979. What a revelation it all is. It's not as cosy a magazine as I seem to remember. It's filled with stern experts who are on hand to tell you exactly how to do just about anything. You simply must put two teaspoons of vinegar into a curry with your curry powder. You must be aware that KY jelly is not a contraceptive and a certain brand is less sticky than others and will enable intercourse at any age. There are Agony Aunts on hand to answer your questions about being homosexual, or snoring, or being embarrassed by your elderly father who fondles himself in front of the TV every evening. ('If no one else in your family minds – why should you?')

Other experts, elsewhere in the magazine, throw out doubts about the wisdom of psychologists for children. Glamorous novelist Jackie Collins tells you how to organize your life, home and family while still knocking out racy bestsellers, and why it isn't smutty what she writes. Also, there's the heart-breaking story – and you spend some time reading and taking notes about this article – about the man who is forced to give his daughter back to her mother following a custody battle.

"Being separated from Donna has, of course, been a tremendous psychological blow for me. I have to admit, I've even contemplated kidnapping her to get her back – but, on the advice of good friends, I have driven that thought from my mind."

Late 1979 seems like a place of certainties, with its Agony Aunts who round on their letter writers with, 'You should examine your own hidden feelings about this, and stop complaining about others! Are you avoiding thinking about your own happiness, by any chance..?' Even the recipes have absolute faith that all the necessary ingredients will be found, quite easily and inexpensively, at your local shop. Frozen food tastes just as nice as fresh produce. Mohair jumpers will look stylish whatever the season. High society is extremely glamorous and members of the Royal Family are attractively gracious in both manner and appearance. All these things are unchanging and true in 1979.

I went back to the Paris Review and flicked through some interviews, including one with a painter in 1975 who lived in a cage with a fox and who drew quite startling nudes. But nothing leapt off the page as usefully, I must say, as those few snippets from Woman's Own.

Writing in Pencil

I've had a few days alone in the house while Jeremy is with his mum in Perth. It's just me and Fester Cat here. I'm enjoying these days at the kitchen table, writing pages and pages in pencil. To break up the stretches of writing I go and clean up another corner of the house. Doing a bit of housework, dusting and tidying and organizing, or lugging baskets of washing about, feels like another way of making sense of the world, just as I'm working to make sense of the worlds I'm playing with on paper.

I'm exploring the planet Mars of my novel and finding out what it's like. Ten days in and I'm already off Piste with my synopsis and I'm feeling all the better for that: I don't want it being too linear. Interesting new tangents need to suggest themselves, and I need to follow them.

While Mars is my morning project my afternoons are spent writing new stories for Brenda and Effie and so, in the afternoons I'm back in Whitby. The familiarity of the place in my head and the kinds of adventures they have make me feel confident: in the afternoons I'm on familiar ground.

After all the rain this afternoon the sun came out and so I walked to Sainsburys. All their Back-to-School stationery was on half-price offer, so I snaffled all kinds of notebooks and pencils and sticky labels.

Writing everything in pencil means that I get to chance my neck more, line by line. Nothing seems set in stone. And also, the physical writing won't really survive in the actual books. Once it's used up it will rub and fade away over the years, like sketches slowly disappearing. I like that feeling of impermanence. Like the first drafts are just ghosts that will float away.

Writing longhand recently has meant that writing is a physical activity. I've had ten days with sore fingers and shoulder muscles that actually, gently, ache.

I'm home, making Assam tea with a spoonful of honey. For some reason I'm thinking about the 1978 cartoon movie version of 'Lord of the Rings' by Ralph Bashki. We went to Darlington's huge Odeon cinema to see it. Then I bought the Fotonovel in Fine Fare the following week. When I was nine that Fotonovel was one of my favourite books. When I saw a copy of the actual Lord of the Rings by Tolkien I was horrified by the size of it and the density of the tiny text – the pages thin as school toilet paper and all that claggy, arcane language. To me, the Fotonovel seemed wonderfully succinct and preferable...

Maybe today I'm nostalgic for easy-to-read Fotonovels as a gut-level response to the media hoo-ha about the Booker shortlist, which has just been published. Last week I was reading books that took themselves far too seriously. Right now I'm thinking – just bring back Fotonovels with about six words per page and hundreds of colourful pictures. I'd be quite happy.

Really, what I need to read, right now, is something fun, light and funny. But something with awesome hidden depths.

Actually, that sounds good for any time.

An editor recently said that he likes the way I mark the changing of the seasons in my life. I have a real sense of time and where we are in the year. I think it's true that I'm very influenced by the seasons and the changes. I think it's a recent return for me, to the person I was when I was a kid. Even as far back as Woodham Burn Infants and Juniors, when we'd have the Ladybird books for nature study: 'What to Look for…' in summer, winter, autumn and spring. We'd have poems about squirrels and leaves and we'd be avid for the changes in the weather and our surroundings.

Everything that happened to me between leaving school at eighteen and eventually leaving my most recent teaching post in 2011 seemed to pull me away from the sense of the seasons passing. The artificiality of university semesters and terms moved me away from appreciating the way that years turn.

When do we live closer to the seasons? For me it's when we are rooted in the place we live and we have a garden. As I write this we've lived in this house over seven years. My tiny study looks out on the horse chestnut trees which line our street and it's mid-September, so there's a smattering of yellow and brown amongst the extravagant green. Conkers have smashed on the pavements and they're gleaming amongst the mush.

It's my favourite time of year – one of them, anyway. It's so blue out there at nine a.m and the light is slanting over the terraced rooftops and everything looks cheery, even in the wet. It's been pouring since the early hours and the paths and roads look like licorice. It's sunny, though, and I'm glad because for me today involves going out with my books and pencils and writing away from my desk.

It's going to be luxurious to write in public, after two weeks sitting diligently, every day at my desk. I've found the rhythm of the two projects I'm working on – Mars and Brenda – morning and afternoon. I'm deep in the thick of both separate stories. I've been good and sat still and sharpened pencils in a kind of daze. I've filled up writing books till they're completely chockablock with handwriting: presents from Gillian in Glasgow, and other presents from Jeremy that have waited to be filled up. All the fanciest blank notebooks I've had waiting for me, I've used up in these long days of writing by hand. I've made the days seem luxurious, and that has helped me along.

I think for five years I've been addicted to writing straight onto the computer. It's ever since I bought my first laptop. That's what caused it. The laptop was so convenient and easy. I'd dream something up and FLASH – it would appear on the screen in that hard, dark efficient type. It was magical. In those days I'd get up at seven and go straight to my desk and I would plough straight into my novel-in-progress. I would reel pages off.

That sounds good… but although I was writing lots of my novel, I wasn't looking after myself. I look back and see that I was neglecting my writing self. I'd stopped doing my writing practice. I didn't warm up properly. I didn't write my journal. It was as if I was afraid to waste any of my time looking after myself. Is that what it was?

And did it do me any actual harm? Did it harm the writing – making it less fiery or alive? Maybe not. But I do know that I succeeded in making writing feel like work, and hard work at that. And I carried on treating it like that in the years that followed – novel after novel. I was wrestling with them and manhandling them, and all my writing time was turned over to simply racking up the pages. I never gave myself any time to wonder or surmise or play. I had my deadlines and I had quotas and I had to meet them. Each year I had to write about two hundred thousand words for publication – as well as teaching at the university. That was how it had to be.

Of course, you can't go on doing it at that rate forever.

Now, a few years on and there's no day-job. There's no constant teaching. But I still fill all my days with every project that I can. I'm freelance, so of course every project has to buy its time, and bring some money in.

I've always dreamed that one day I'd have a huge success and I'd be able to give my mam a massive amount of money. I'd keep her in luxury. I'd buy her a house. I'd change my family's life forever and make things easy for them. This year there's been a kind of rift between us and it seems that I can acknowledge to myself that one of the things always driving me on has been this dream of making some cash to make things right for them. It's a terrible thing to drive after. It makes you push the work and yourself too hard. It makes you feel a hopeless fool and a failure, too. You've tried to make everything okay. But it's never enough.

Later, and I'm in the community café of the church on Levenshulme High Street. At the counter there's an oldish woman in a white anorak telling Crusty Peter all about getting her visa for flying to India. She only decided on it last week.

Peter – a hippy with blonde dreadlocks - is dishing out her lasagna, and he's impressed. 'Is it just for the general tourist stuff you're going? I think it's amazing of you to just decide you're going and then fix it up…'

'It's for the spiritual enlightenment I'm going,' she tells him. Then they start discussing the Western world's general lack of spirituality.

'We're completely out of balance,' says Crusty Peter. 'With the way the world operates. It's completely shifted… and to turn that back is so hard.' He's very softly-spoken. 'Yeah, yeah, completely… it's become kind of negative history now… Unacceptable these days… Have you been to the People's History Museum in town? It's all Greenham Common and the Miners' Strike and it's like a barrage of information, really… so you come out not knowing anything at all…'

This sends me off in a reverie for a while.

The thought of 'not knowing anything at all' makes me think back to my first term at university, back in 1988. Windswept autumn days on campus and hurrying into that huge lecture hall.

All those great big questions: What is language? What is narrative? Does any of it really exist? Can we trust any author's intentions? Is there any such thing as an author anyway? Would books be written anyway if authors didn't exist? Where does the world start and the text finish?

Now at the counter there's a discussion going on about faith. Another café volunteer has joined in and is talking about the hoo-ha years ago when she, as a Protestant, started dating a Catholic boy. She says her grown-up son can hardly believe there was such a fuss back then. 'It can cause a lot of bother, can faith.'

And Crusty Peter talks about how Christians would probably never even recognize Christ if he came back to Earth today. He was a rebel then and he would be a rebel now as well.

This is how I do my writing practice. Just as I always have.

I sit somewhere comfy like this and I just absorb the scene around me. I write down the conversations that grab my attention and, with another bit of my mind, I'm still thinking about those questions from the English lectures all those years ago. The idea of books being symptoms of societal malaise and how they're mostly interesting for giving away secrets their authors never even intended…

'There's always been murders in the world,' says the boy with blond dreadlocks and now I look at him, he might look a bit like Jesus would today. In his pinny, dishing up multi-coloured salads and organic lasagna. 'Maybe the world's always been a horrible place. Maybe now it's just global media and the way everything gets instantly reviewed – that makes it seem worse. Maybe none of it's really changed at all.'

The woman in the white anorak peers over her jam jar glasses at him. She's drinking her tea at the counter to carry on their conversation. She cradles her cup and saucer and holds her shopping bag in the crook of her arm. A queue is building up behind her. 'Do you think?' she frowns, skeptically. 'I think the world is getting much worser.'

The Stone Roses are playing on the radio, like a glorious flashback to 1990. It's as if, here in Manchester, you can tune your radio straight into the jangly guitar riffs of the past: all cocky and splashy and psychedelic.

Now Crusty Pete is describing how he lives in a squat and the police woke everyone up this morning, threatening to chuck them all out. 'Just because you're white and live in the west, it doesn't mean you're rich anymore.'

'I know!' says the woman in the white anorak. 'I'm going to India and they'll all think I'm rich. But I'm not. I'm on benefits, same as anyone. And no one was ever rich round here, were they? Doesn't matter what colour you are.'

I've let my cappuccino go cold as I scribble in pencil in my notebook from Sainsburys special offer stationery. I'm listening to Crusty Peter's tales of this morning's eviction and how the police turned up and there was a terrible scene.

I blush fiercely when I write. It's exertion rather than embarrassment, I think. Though I'd be ashamed if they realized I was writing down everything I heard...

Maybe they'll just assume I'm daft, and in a world of my own.

I guess that's as true as anything.

Author's Biography.

Paul Magrs was born in 1969 in Jarrow, in the North East of England. He went to Woodham Comprehensive School in Newton Aycliffe and the University of Lancaster, where he got a First in English Literature, a Distinction in Creative Writing and a PhD on the novels of Angela Carter.

He has published over thirty-five books. He has written novels for grown-ups, including 'Marked for Life' and 'Never the Bride', and for younger readers, including 'Strange Boy' and 'Lost on Mars.' He wrote a memoir – 'The Story of Fester Cat' in 2013 from the point of view of his recently-deceased cat, and a sequel, 'Welcome Home, Bernard Socks.' He's also made a number of literary contributions to the Doctor Who universe. He has written in every genre from Literary Fiction to Science Fiction, Magic Realism to the Gothic. Lethe Press in the US has recently republished his first four novels.

He was a Senior Lecturer in Creative Writing at the University of Anglia for seven years, and then for another seven at Manchester Metropolitan University. With Julia Bell he is the co-editor of The Creative Writing Coursebook, published by Macmillan. He has taught Creative Writing in an academic context, but also at literary festivals, in schools, on residential courses for the Arvon Foundation and others, and also for libraries. He runs a private manuscript critiquing service called The Fiction Doctor.

He has been teaching writing ever since 1992 and is still learning new things every time he teaches or sits down to write.

He lives in south Manchester with his partner, Jeremy Hoad, and their cat, Bernard Socks.

Lightning Source UK Ltd.
Milton Keynes UK
UKHW021125141220
375064UK00007B/244